W9-BNW-850

EDUCATIONAL LEADERSHIP

Critical Studies in Education and Culture Series

Critical Pedagogy and Cultural Power
David Livingstone and Contributors

Education and the American Dream: Conservatives, Liberals, and Radicals Debate the Future of Education
Harvey Holtz and Associates

Education and the Welfare State: A Crisis in Capitalism and Democracy
H. Svi Shapiro

Education under Seige: The Conservative, Liberal, and Radical Debate over Schooling
Stanley Aronowitz and Henry A. Giroux

Literacy: Reading the Word and the World
Paulo Freire and Donaldo Macedo

The Moral and Spiritual Crisis in Education: A Curriculum for Justice and Compassion
David Purpel

The Politics of Education: Culture, Power, and Liberation
Paulo Freire

Popular Culture, Schooling, and the Language of Everyday Life
Henry A. Giroux and Roger I. Simon

Teachers as Intellectuals: Toward a Critical Pedagogy of Learning
Henry A. Giroux

Women Teaching for Change: Gender, Class, and Power
Kathleen Weiler

Between Capitalism and Democracy: Educational Policy and the Crisis of the Welfare State
H. Svi Shapiro

Critical Psychology and Pedagogy: Interpretation of the Personal World
Edmund Sullivan

Pedagogy and the Struggle for Voice
Catherine E. Walsh

Learning Work: A Critical Pedagogy of Work Education
Roger I. Simon, Don Dippo, and Arlene Schenke

EDUCATIONAL LEADERSHIP

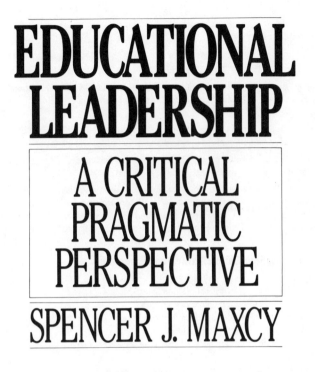

A CRITICAL PRAGMATIC PERSPECTIVE

SPENCER J. MAXCY

CRITICAL STUDIES
IN EDUCATION AND
CULTURE SERIES
Edited by Henry A. Giroux
and Paulo Freire

LIBRARY

BERGIN & GARVEY
New York • Westport, Connecticut • London

Copyright Acknowledgments

The author and publisher gratefully acknowledge permission to print material based on and to reprint extracts from the following:

Spencer J. Maxcy, "The Democratic 'Myth' and a Rational Concept of Education," *Educational Philosophy and Theory* 17, no. 1 (May 1985), pp. 22–37.

Spencer J. Maxcy, "Leadership, Administration and the Educational Policy Operation," *Philosophy of Education 1984*, edited by Emily Robertson (Normal, Ill.: Philosophy of Education Society, 1984), pp. 329–38.

Spencer J. Maxcy and Stephen J. Caldas, "Moral Imagination and the Philosophy of School Leadership," *Journal of Educational Administration*, forthcoming.

Spencer J. Maxcy, "Postmodernity and the Future of Teacher Education," *Proceedings of the Southwestern Philosophy of Education Society* 39 (1989), pp. 139–51.

Spencer J. Maxcy and Joseph Claudet, "Practical Judgment, Empowerment and Leadership in Educational Administration," *The Review Journal of Philosophy and Social Science*, forthcoming. Used by permission of Joseph Claudet and *The Review Journal of Philosophy and Social Science*.

Library of Congress Cataloging-in-Publication Data

Maxcy, Spencer J.
    Educational leadership : a critical pragmatic perspective /
Spencer J. Maxcy ; Foreword by Henry A. Giroux.
        p.   cm.—(Critical studies in education & culture)
    Includes bibliographical references and index.
    ISBN 0–89789–258–5 (alk. paper).—ISBN 0–89789–259–3 (pbk. :
alk. paper)
    1. School management and organization—United States.
2. Leadership. I. Title. II. Series.
LB2805.M295   1991
371.2'00973—dc20   91–4637

British Library Cataloguing in Publication Data is available.

Copyright © 1991 by Spencer J. Maxcy

All rights reserved. No portion of this book may be
reproduced, by any process or technique, without the
express written consent of the publisher.

Library of Congress Catalog Card Number: 91–4637
ISBN: 0–89789–258–5 (hb.)
ISBN: 0–89789–259–3 (pb.)

First published in 1991

Bergin & Garvey, One Madison Avenue, New York, NY 10010
An imprint of Greenwood Publishing Group, Inc.

Printed in the United States of America

∞™

The paper used in this book complies with the
Permanent Paper Standard issued by the National
Information Standards Organization (Z39.48–1984).

10 9 8 7 6 5 4 3 2 1

LB
2805
.M295
1991

For Doreen, Colleen, and Spence
(Penelope, Ann, and Ralph)

Contents

Series Introduction: Toward a Discourse of Leadership and Radical Democracy

The enormity and seriousness of the political and social problems that face the United States as it moves into the twenty-first century are, in part, exemplified in the debates that have been waged around the issue of leadership and the crisis of schooling. At stake in these debates is not simply the issue of educational reform, but the nature of democracy itself. The crisis and fragile nature of American democracy cannot be addressed in bloated calls to force students to say the pledge of allegiance or in such patriotic fervor as developed in the aftermath of the Gulf War. Instead, the growing threat to democracy, in this case linked to citizenship understood as a form of self-management constituted in all major economic, social, and cultural spheres of society, can be seen in the growing crisis of authority that has beset both the sphere of education and the larger society. The crisis of authority is evident in the refusal of the American government over the last fifteen years to address the most basic issues of meaning and purpose which link public education to the development of critical citizens capable of exercising the capacities, knowledge, and skills necessary to become human agents in a democratic society. In this sense, the crisis of authority is both a political and ethical issue. Politically, the issue of educational reform has been dominated at the federal and local levels of government by a discourse that abstracts schools from some of society's most pressing problems. Issues concerning child poverty, unemployment, illiteracy, health care, and the drug culture have been removed from the discourse of educational reform. Instead of addressing how these issues impact upon schools, how they undermine how children learn, the current educational reform movement has focused on issues such as testing and choice. In the first instance, testing has become the code word for training educational leaders in the langauge of management, measurement, and efficiency. Testing has also become the new ideological weapon in developing standardized curricula that ignore cultural diversity, in defining knowledge narrowly in terms of discrete skills and decontextualized bodies of information, and in ruthlessly expunging the language of ethics from the broader purpose of teaching and schooling. The issue of what knowledge is taught, under what conditions, for what purpose, and by whom has become less important than developing precise measuring instruments for tracking students and, increasingly, to disempower and deskill teachers.

In addition to the current emphasis on testing, the notion of choice has become a fundamental element in the new educational reform movement of the Reagan/Bush era. In this context, choice is organized and developed according the logic and imperatives of the marketplace. Ignoring the primacy of the social, choice appeals to the logic of competitiveness, individualism, and achievement. While these attributes might sound plausible as fundamental elements in the logic of educational reform, they are, in fact, used by neo-conservatives to develop a notion of educational leadership that undermines the responsibility of public service, to rupture the relationship between schools and the community, and to divert educators from improving education in all schools.

Ethically, the crisis of authority is also evident in the refusal of the new educational reform movement to develop a critical moral discourse. More specifically, missing from the current neo-conservative emphasis on educational reform is a discourse that can illuminate what administrators, teachers, and other cultural workers actually do in terms of the underlying principles and values that structure the stories, visions, and experiences that inform school and classroom practices. Accountability in this discourse offers few insights into how schools should prepare students to push against the oppressive boundaries of gender, class, race, and age domination. Nor does such a language provide the conditons for students to interrogate how questions and matters concerning the curriculum are really struggles concerning issues of self-identity, culture, power, and history. In effect, the crisis of authority is grounded in a refusal to address how particular forms of authority are secured and legitimized at the expense of cultural democracy, critical citizenship, and basic human rights. Refusing to interrogate the values that not only frame how authority is constructed but also define leadership as a political and pedagogical practice, neo-conservative educational reformers end up subordinating the discourse of ethics to the rules of management and efficiency. Accordingly, leadership in the age of Bush does not focus on how to educate prospective administrators and teachers to address the problems facing public schools in the United States as a crisis of citizenship and ethics. Instead, the current infatuation with "leadership" by the Bush Administration presupposes that the solutions to the problems of American schooling lie in the related spheres of management and economics rather than in the realms of values and politics.

The meaning of leadership has been narrowly defined by neo-conservatives as a practice that emulates the style and ideology of leading corporate executives *and* legitimates training students for the work world as the primary objective of schooling. Hence, Secretary of Education Lamar Alexander selects David Kearns, former chief executive officer of the Xerox Corporation as the nominee for deputy secretary of education. Similarly, a central thrust for the current reform movement has been to forge a new alliance between the corporate sector and schools. In this case, the business of leadership becomes the leadership of business as industry increasingly is called upon to intervene in local schools to provide teachers, advisors, curriculum materials, and other fundamental support and policy-oriented services. This view of educational leadership is quite paradoxical. Not only does this approach to educational reform ignore the discourses of community, solidarity, and the public good, it also draws upon a sector of society that has given the American public the savings and loan scandals, the age of corporate buyouts, and the proliferation of "junk" bonds, and has made leadership synonymous with greed and avarice. To be sure, it is precisely the business community that prides itself on abstracting leadership from ethical responsibility, subordinating basic human needs to the rules of the marketplace, and legitimizing commodification as the highest virtue of American society.

This is not meant to suggest that questions of leadership and schooling should avoid engaging issues concerning work, economics, and the marketplace; on the contrary, students need to learn the necessary skills and knowledge to qualify for decent employment, but they also need to be literate in the discourse of economic and social justice. More important, the purpose and meaning of schooling should not be defined through a notion of leadership that simply sees schools as an adjunct of the corporation; on the contrary, the real challenge of leadership is to broaden its definition beyond the narrow parameters of these concerns to more vital imperatives of democracy, citizenship, and social justice. (This issue is dealt with in detail in Giroux, 1988.) In this perspective, leadership takes up the issues of power, culture, and identity within an ethical discourse that points to those practices between the self and others that oblige one "to make an ethical decision, to say: here I stand . . . here and now I face an other who demands of me an ethical response" (Kearney, 1988, p. 361). Within this discourse, leadership poses the issue of responsibility as a social relationship in which difference and otherness articulate with practices that offer resistance to forms of domination and oppression. This points to the need for a discourse of leadership that prompts a discriminating response to others, one that makes students, for example, attentive both to their own implication in particular forms of human suffering and to the oppression of others whose voices demand both recognition and support. Leadership in this view means being able to imagine otherwise, which "entails, at the socio-political level, an 'acting otherwise'" (Kearney, 1988, p. 457). This suggests a need for educators to redefine the language of leadership in ways that commit administrators, teachers, and students to a discerning conception of democratic community in which the relationship between the self and the other is constituted in practices sustained by historical memories, actualities, and further possibilities of a just and humane society.

I have drawn in very general terms some of the major issues surrounding the issue of leadership and authority facing public education in the United States. Spencer Maxcy's book, *Educational Leadership*, not only greatly expands on this debate, it also reconstitutes the very ground on which it is waged. In doing so, Maxcy provides a devastating critique of existing models of educational leadership and an original reformulation of the meaning, potential, and practice of educational leadership informed by notions of self and social empowerment.

In opposition to the emerging neo-conservative view which defines leadership against democracy as part of a broader politics of equity, justice, and representation, Maxcy draws upon the traditions of critical pragmatism in order to reconceptualize the interface between institutional structures, human agency, and leadership as a form of cultural politics. Deeply concerned that the discourse of leadership within the field of education has been undertheorized and underconceptualized, Maxcy is not content to frame his analysis of leadership in traditional disciplinary boundaries. Hence, his work draws on a wide range of philosophical and theoretical traditions and is developed in a critical discourse that refigures the fundamental meaning of leadership along with the questions and practices that generally characterize it as a field of inquiry.

Central to Maxcy's project is the development of a notion of leadership as both a vision and practice inside rather than outside of history, semiotics, culture, and ethics. Maxcy's wants to expand the possibilities of leadership by addressing its relationship to authority and ethics, politics and power, and ideology and culture. In this perspective, leadership presupposes the ability of educators to engage in the practice of representation and in the representation of such practices. In the first instance, Maxcy argues that educators need to be self-conscious about how they construe conditions that portray specific visions of what it means to be a political, moral, and aesthetic agent. In the second instance, he develops the insight that educators need to be made aware of the consequences of their actions in terms of their effects on students, parents, the community, and the larger society. Leadership for Maxcy is a form of political and ethical address that is self-conscious and attentive to the ways in which it extends and deepens the quality of democratic life. It is to Maxcy's credit that he sees leadership not only as a crisis of authority but, more fundamentally, as a part of a wider crisis of democracy and ethics. For him, leadership as critical pragmatism means organizing schools in ways that enable students to make judgments about how society is constructed historically and socially, to understand how existing social relations are organized around racism, sexism, and other forms of oppression, and to struggle for critical public cultures that both challenge and transform those configurations of power that characterize the existing system of education and the larger social structure.

This is an important book for everyone interested in the notion of leadership as an emancipatory practice. Working at the interface of a number of critical traditions, Maxcy offers educators a new langauge as a way of rethinking and reformulating leadership in terms of new problems, objects, relations, values, and possibilities. Maxcy's book offers the opportunity for educators not only to address the limitations in the current debate around educational leadership but also to reconstruct their own identities within a discourse that deepens and expands the possibilities for human agency and social justice.

Henry A. Giroux

REFERENCES

Giroux, Henry A. *Schooling and the Struggle for Public Life*. Minneapolis: University of Minnesota Press, 1988.

Kearney, Richard. *The Wake of Imagination*. Minneapolis: University of Minnesota Press, 1988.

Acknowledgments

This book has been a long time in preparation, and during that time I have drawn heavily upon the support of family, friends, colleagues, and critics. I am indebted to my family, in particular my father, Spencer T. Maxcy, mother, Marian Maxcy, and brother, Paul Maxcy, for providing encouragement—and at times resources—to support this project. Thanks to my wife, Doreen, for all professional and personal sacrifices she has made to insure the completion of this work.

Friends, such as Dick Hansen, Bob Buciak, Ron Ladwig, George New-kome, and Domo Flores provided long hours of conversations in which I came to work out the picture of leadership displayed here. To colleagues Bill Stanley, Bob Slater, Sam Britt, Bill Pinar, Steve Bensman, Bill Doll, Jacques Daignault, Gary Crow, and Tony Whitson; and to many of my graduate students, such as Joe Claudet, Steve Caldas, Cheryl Boutte, Sue Roy, Cheryl Edwards, John Konopak, and Wen-Song Hu—thank you.

The present work is richer owing to the opportunities to interact with scholars at other institutions throughout the world. A sabbatical leave granted by LSU in 1980 and lively walks with John Wilson along the streets of Oxford provoked my shift to the scholarly examination of educational administration. An invitation from Robin Barrow in 1983 to speak before the Philosophy of Education Society of Great Britain fueled my interest in the concept of leadership. Jim Garrison's invitation to play a role at the Philosophy of Education Society sessions aided my resolve. Long smoozings with colleagues in the Southwest Philosophy of Education Association, including, among many others, John Pullium, Chuck Fazzaro, Jim Bowman, Jim Van Patten, and Teryl Anderson, provided critical reflection on the role of leaders in schools. A sojourn in Arlington, Texas, and trips to Oregon to talk with Bill Cowart and his staff and faculty at Oregon State University and Western Oregon gave focus to my project. Above all, I have benefited from engaging in dialogues and written correspondence with scholars such as Christopher Lasch, R. S. Peters, Bill Foster, Cleo Cherryholmes, Bob Donmoyer, Phil Smith, and many others.

I am grateful for the help given me in the preparation of this book by my graduate assistant Sue Weishar and to Cyn D. Reynaud for her Cajun kindness. Finally, thanks to my editors at Bergin & Garvey, Sophie Craze, Henry Giroux, and Nina Neimark.

Chapter 3 is based upon a paper presented before the American Educational Research Association annual meeting in Chicago, April 1985, and draws upon ideas advanced in my article "The Democratic 'Myth' and a Rational Concept of Education," published in *Educational Philosophy and Theory*, 17, no. 1 (May 1985).

Chapter 4 is based upon a paper published in *Philosophy of Education 1984* (Proceedings of the Annual Conference of the Philosophy of Education Society).

Chapter 5 is an expanded version of a paper authored with Donna Harrison and presented before the American Educational Research Association, Southeastern Regional Meeting, Baton Rouge, March 1986.

Chapter 6 is a revised and expanded version of a paper, authored with Stephen J. Caldas, an early version of which was presented before the American Educational Research Association, in New Orleans, April 1988, and a second version of which is to be published in the *Journal of Educational Administration*.

Chapter 7 is based upon a paper published in the *Proceedings of the Thirty-Ninth Annual Meeting of the Southwestern Philosophy of Education Society*, 1989.

Chapter 8 is based upon a paper, co-authored with Joe Claudet, presented before the American Educational Research Association, San Francisco, March 1988, and an article co-authored with Joe Claudet, "Practical Judgment, Empowerment and Leadership in Educational Administration," in *The Review Journal of Philosophy and Social Science* (forthcoming).

EDUCATIONAL LEADERSHIP

1

Introduction: The Quest for Leadership

The crisis facing American public education, it is said, is one of leadership: a lack of effective leaders who will redirect teachers and children back toward the basics, the essentials and foundations of American life. Current social conditions reveal a splintering of interests, each calling for attention, with no consensus as to who shall lead or what direction must be taken. This modern collapse in leadership, coupled with a fracturing pluralism of followers, has parents, teachers, and administrators in a quandary. Traditionally, Americans have searched for "the man on horseback," but who today is able to take charge and lead the nation's schools and teachers into the future? No modern counterpart of a Horace Mann or John Dewey has stepped forward to take command.

Furthermore, Americans are beset by a pervasive relativism that finds no alternative any more valid or warranted than any other. Allan Bloom (1987) and Richard J. Bernstein (1983) lament the fact that Americans have fallen into this stage of abject relativism. Whereas Bloom finds comfort in the uncovering of culture-driven absolute ideals, Bernstein encourages us to look beyond such objectivism to a new world of emerging communities of discourse and debate. A normative view of educational leadership, then, would be seen in light of a mind-set that is caught between a search for heroes and the latitudinarian attitude toward values that finds everything having an equal claim to the public attention—a mind-set that conflicts with the view that leadership is an organizing idea that grows from democratic consensus.

The present crisis in leadership is characterized by John Goodlad, writing in *A Place Called School*:

During the decade of the 1970s—a decade dismally devoid of educational ideas—I became increasingly depressed over the noneducational agendas of educational leaders. Preoccupied with crises, they were forced to delegate or push aside central matters of curriculum development and school improvement. Worse, some school board members and superintendents forgot what is essential to the mission. Some appeared to enjoy jousting with heads of unions and special interest groups, even as they complained about it. (Goodlad, 1984, pp. 353–354)

What Goodlad, and others, have discovered is that contemporary school "leaders" have shifted their priorities from leadership to issues of collective bargaining, desegregation, dropouts, enrollments, test scores, and so forth—while neglecting the broader questions of who we are and what we stand for as a nation. Gone is the interest in improving the quality of educational life for its citizens-to-be, and in its place we find *management*. In large measure this shift from inspired leadership to managerial expertise was fomented by universities, colleges, and professors of educational administration, but it was supported against a backdrop of business-related philosophies that called for a shift in attention away from humanistic and personal values to the good of the company. School leadership programs became a vehicle for imposing good business sense on the schools.

LEADERSHIP STUDIES

Historically, researchers have tended to view leadership in terms of three theoretical constellations: leadership as traits of character; leadership as behavior; and leadership as a function of culture/climate.

Leadership Traits

One way of treating "leadership" is to focus upon the psychological traits of the leader. Leaders are taken to have "initiating structure," and to have certain aspects of character that make them into leaders of others. Strength, dedication, determination, organizational ability, vision, moral fortitude, and so on, have all been pointed to as enabling leaders to do their jobs. Psychologists have dedicated research time to highlighting these variables and in confirming the notion that leaders may be more born than made.

We shall have more to say about leadership as personal traits later; however, it is important to keep in mind that leadership as traits has served well the educational administration department that was in the business of preparing school administrators for leadership roles. Where the traits of successful leaders have been identified, it is argued these traits may be taught to others. A wide range of self-help books in business and industrial management have pointed to this possibility of teaching anyone the skills to lead.

Unfortunately, such research has generated conflicting claims as to what may be the necessary and sufficient traits needed to lead effectively. Since there is no agreement relative to such matters, some writers are willing to write it off to a matter of *leadership style*. Hence, how a leader leads is, in the last analysis, a matter of his/her style of leadership.

Leadership as Behavior

One of the most popular characterizations of leadership has been that of *behavior* or *style*. In future chapters we will discuss this theory of leadership in more detail; however, at this point it is necessary to depart somewhat from earlier characterizations of leadership as behavior by pointing to the distinction between "behavior" and "action": the event in nature versus the human act guided by matters of value. Whereas positivistic thought held that knowledge of human society was tied to a reduction of human action to behavior, the contribution of recent hermeneutic and phenomenological research has stressed the interest in *meanings*. Leadership, viewed in this way, is the concern for understanding and the additional requirement that human values pervade leadership-initiated actions and responses. In addition, taking a clue from George Herbert Mead, it is important for us to seek to understand meanings such leadership acts have for the actors. Placing ourselves in their position (taking the role of the other) results in a mining of the meanings leadership may have in any particular act (Hindress, 1977, pp. 24–25).

Theoretical sciences today must meet a larger need if their work is to be relevant to the problems educators face in the day-to-day world of schooling. Traditional philosophic approaches have focused on a limited number of concepts (e.g., "education," "learning," and "subject matter") at the expense of social and cultural conditions that set the scene for our beliefs. Barrow (1983) has taken a broad stroke at conventional philosophy by arguing that some of the traditional concepts that the British have dwelled upon (e.g., "learning") are not worth philosophers' attention. Learning for Robin Barrow is not sufficiently problematic to warrant analysis!

This study of leadership departs from earlier efforts. We will be looking at leadership in the context of schooling, but shall draw upon other areas of social life for insight into its meanings. The conception of leadership ranges quite broadly and the many meanings of this notion are found wedded to business, athletics, military science, and politics. Moreover, there has been a fusion of the meanings of leadership in these allied domains with the variegated notion of leading in educational settings. Talk of leadership in education can be enhanced through an exploration of the literatures of other areas of life.

Leadership is not reduced to behavior, in the narrow Skinnerian sense of that term. Rather, we shall look to leadership transactions as part of the discourses/practices of leading. This is to say that leadership is thought/speech/performance, with no primacy of any one of these facets. The error made by behaviorism is to attempt to explain away the mental and archival dimensions of leadership. The present text is interested in seeing the fusion of the polarities of thought/action and the subsequent *understanding* of these dimensions.

Leadership and School Climate

What is the school climate? Current controversy in educational administration pivots around the school climate, or the context wherein school leadership takes place. The insightful work of Karl Weick (1976) pointed to the fact that schools are "loosely coupled" organizations. This is to say that schoolteachers and pupils are less driven by rules and regulations than by norms and standards of belief about the school culture. The remarkable fact is, according to Weick, that school personnel are less connected with the managerial system than with the norms of fellow teachers and students. The impact on school leadership dissolves into a concern for the cultural climate and contexts wherein teachers and pupils do their work (Weick, pp. 1–19).

The effort to tag leadership to some organizational variables has persisted in the research on education. Few inquirers are content to let stand the fact that this search has been barren. Recently, "school effectiveness" studies have sought to trace the effective school to some mix of principal and school setting, with less than spectacular results (Levine and Lezotte, 1990, pp. 21–22). Administrative researchers, however, reluctantly admit that such inquiries have failed to show that school climates generate school effectiveness over teacher variables or student variables, or combinations of these. This is to say that the principal, as CEO of the school culture, appears not to have that much impact on whether the school is "effective" or not (Grady, Wayson, and Zirkel, 1989; Levine and Lezotte, 1990).

Sergiovanni and Moore (1989) tell us: "Principals and other school administrators get uncomfortable when one starts to talk about shared leadership, leadership density, and similar ideas" (p. 221). Somehow, leadership must mean that schools are organizations that must be *led from above* or they will not succeed. Thus, Thomas Sergiovanni capitulates to the fear that "though teachers can be expected (and should be empowered) to respond to professional norms and accepted standards of best practice, accountability in education must be institutionalized at the level of school and district." And although Sergiovanni sees some sharing of power, he does not foresee peer-run schools in the future (p. 221).

The present project looks to the fuller explication of leadership relative to culture and teacher empowerment, and hence vows to move the conversation along.

A CRITICAL STUDY OF EDUCATIONAL LEADERSHIP

While there may have been a noticeable lack of leadership in the nation's public schools over the past two decades, it is not clear that contemporary leadership proposals are theoretically well-funded enough to produce the kind of leadership we need to redirect schooling in this country. In the pages that follow, we shall examine the crisis in leadership in the United States, calls for new educational leadership, and suggestions for the recasting of the leadership idea for the future. It shall be argued that what is required is a new philosophy by which to test leadership ideas in present educational crisis situations. We shall explore alternative theories of leading and their impacts upon the character of American education and life. We shall look at normative proposals for leading. In part, our analysis calls for looking seriously at what schools and social life are like today. It will be argued that our educational institutions and educational leadership must make a better fit within the societal problematics we see operative.

Any philosophy of leadership must rest upon the physical and social environment in which it developed. An empirical understanding of the sociocultural conditions from which it emerges is essential to the clear perception of how leadership has functioned in the United States. There are certain characteristic features of the present circumstances in American culture that warrant a rethinking of leadership theory and practice.

Individualism and the Lost Community

America is characterized by an intense individualism. Christopher Lasch, in *The Minimal Self* (1984), writes of a new "personhood" that sets in bold relief our concerns relative to leadership. This new personhood is found arising out of social changes:

the substitution of observation and measurement for authoritative, "judgmental" types of social sanctions; the transformation of politics into administration; the replacement of skilled labor by machinery; the redefinition of education as "manpower selection," designed not so much to instill work skills as to classify workers and to assign them either to the small class of administrators, technicians, and managers who make decisions or to the larger class of minimally skilled workers who merely carry out instructions—have gradually transformed a productive system based on handicraft production and regional exchange into a complex, interlocking network of technologies based on mass production, mass consumption, mass communications, mass culture: on the assimilation of all activities, even those formerly assigned to private life, to the demands of the marketplace. (pp. 51–52)

It is likely that the drive for personal power and the individualist penchant of U.S. citizens is about to undermine one of our most cherished institutions: democratic community. With the search for lost community on hold (John Dewey wrote extensively about the need for community in the face of technological and industrial changes), we are seeing an atomized and fractured population desperately grasping for direction from leaders as we face an uncertain future. In response to the loneliness and alienation that springs from individualism comes the search for the meaning of leadership. Compelled to deal with institutional problems, and unwilling to join with others in communal action, Americans look for the strong leader, the charismatic leader, the expert leader, or any one of a variety of leader types to provide the vision and methods to deal with issues of importance, solutions to which seem to evade our grasp. "Let the other guy do it" feelings are linked with the cult of the manager or the expert to produce a programmed search for leadership conceived of as technical expertise. Leaders are not to be democratically determined, but rather selected owing to their specialized knowledge, we are told. And, because expert knowledge can bring with it power and position, it is no wonder that universities have taken to "training" leaders for the vacancies in our schools created by this vacuum.

Given this cultural condition, it is not surprising that school administration currently is beset by the "leadership panacea". As a one-shot solution to educational problems, the expert leader is seen as both an insurance that programs in educational administration may be sustained and enhanced and also as a means of control of the chaotic situation into which our public schools have fallen.

As the press for school reform increases, the theoretical as well as the practical dimensions of leadership receives greater attention. How may the schools be improved? What are the roles of the principal and teacher in leading the school? How can the legislature, the school board, the superintendent, and the community provide leadership for school change? In what ways can leadership make education a more systematic and scientific study? All of these questions have been raised in recent years as leadership has moved onto center stage in the school reform process.

Finally, following Henry Giroux (1986), it is important to see that while the struggle to resurrect community, especially with respect to schools, is crucial, we need also to know how educators, parents, and students should organize themselves within community, which kinds of communities are to be supported and which denied, and what forms of human interests are worth fighting for in community (p. 26). The alternative vision of democratic community we shall explore here provides enabling criteria for reconceptualizing educational leadership; a critical and emancipatory conception of leadership as it becomes a practical part of the rediscovered community needs to address these issues.

Authority

Despite the large number of empirical studies conducted on leadership, there is still an enormous conceptual confusion regarding the meanings and bearings of the term. Certainly, the shift from seeing leadership as entirely a function of bureaucratic school management and administration to the idea of leadership as democratic and participatory direction over future conditions is an enormous leap at this time. Most of the barriers to reconceptualizing the meaning of leadership seem to be driven by a larger idea network—an ideology of mandarinism—that distorts democratic and communal control over leading. Knowledge-driven models of inquiry such as those most popularly assumed within the paradigm of structuralist administrative theory have so clouded our view of how practical judgments are made in day-to-day institutional life, we seem unable to conceive of leadership as anything other than rational/technical expert authority.

The fundamental difficulty with rank-and-file conceptions of authority found in educational circles is that they build upon, and in turn legitimate, narrowly controlling techniques that seek to maintain the inequities in school leadership while disabling critical alternatives to such doctrinaire views. Traditionalists support this conserving function of authority by demonstrating in their research that leadership entails the voluntary conferring of rights by followers to the leader. Authority, Sergiovanni and Moore (1989) point out, is the means whereby compliance is obtained, "even if it is given grudgingly" (p. 213). Authority converts persons into subordinates rather than followers, with performance becoming marginal and satisfactory, but never extraordinary, according to John W. Gardner (Sergiovanni and Moore, p. 213).

I shall argue that the person functioning as an authority or in authority thus need not demonstrate leadership. Rather, leadership seems to imply some bond between leader and followers that does not hinge entirely on either expertise or compliance (Pfeffer, 1978, p. 14). Moreover, humans who compel followership owing to their role or position (dictator, martinet, etc.) are criticized for the absence of regard for individual human rights of choice.

Hence leadership seems to involve a kind of interchange or dialectic between leaders and followers that bears deeper scrutiny.

An emancipatory view of authority based upon a critical and pragmatic perspective is required (Giroux, 1986). That the school administrator needed to move away from the purely technical expert conception of leadership by fusing the educational and the social relations phases of work was pointed out by John Dewey (1935). He wrote: "His leadership will be that of intellectual stimulation and direction, through give-and-take with others, not that of an aloof official imposing, authoritatively, educational ends and methods" (p. 10). Giroux (1986) helps us to see that conservative, liberal, and radical views of authority have under-represented the potential found in authority to emancipate and reconstruct our schools and society.

One of the first tasks in clearing up the language of leading must be to distinguish "leadership" from "authority." Kenneth Benne (1970) created the notion of "anthropogogical authority" to counter the essentialist and conservative notion of Weberian authority as power over others. If education as a conserving of tradition through cultural transmission is replaced by education as dedicated to a futuristic process of personal and cultural renewal, what will be the role of authority, Benne asks. Because we are interdependent and because we also seek to influence, authority has some importance to us as a subject. Benne writes:

Authority is always a function of concrete human situations however large or complex the situation may be. It operates in situations in which a person or group, fulfilling some purpose, project, or need requires guidance or direction from a source outside himself or itself. The need demarcates a field of conduct or belief in which help is required. The individual or group grants obedience to another person or group (or to a rule, a set of rules, a way of coping, or a method) which claims effectiveness in mediating the field of conduct or belief as a condition of receiving assistance. Any such operating social relationship—a triadic relation between subject(s), bearer(s), and field(s)—is an authority relationship. (Benne, 1970, pp. 392–393)

The person bearing authority receives willing obedience from the subject of his/her authority as he/she attempts to mediate the field of conduct or belief in which the subjects are in need of advice, leadership, guidance, or direction (Benne, 1970, p. 393). Authority emerges early in the child's socialization through schooling.

It is also important to distinguish "authority" from "power." The latter is not rational, whereas authority is, for Benne. Someone in the authority relationship claims *competence* and could be called upon potentially to give reasons why he/she is an expert in this or that field, Benne asserts. Efforts by social scientists to reduce authority to power are "rhetoric" and a desire to "bless and justify all established power relations" Benne asserts. Benne goes on to identify three types of authority: authority as expertise, authority as rules, and "anthropogical authority" (Benne, 1970, p. 399). The expert authority is one who has knowledge, skill, or practical competence in a domain; the rule authority is one who is invested with control by virtue of the rules, regulations, or norms; while an anthropogical authority is a teaching authority who seeks to both mother and wean the young relative to the wider life in a community. The educator is seen as an example of this anthropogical authority.

However, there must be a concerted effort to develop in children and youth the kind of understanding of authority relations that aid in their growth both personally and communally. Several barriers present themselves to a fully worked out anthropogically-induced future: (1) the kind of community that is needed in the future is not known; (2) there are conflicts over what is desirable. All of this leads Benne to assert that what is needed in schools is a means for recognizing conflict and using it to maximize the benefits for the future generations. A reconception of valid teaching authority relations is tied to the reconstruction of the schools themselves, Benne concludes.

Power and Control

Concomitant with the growing atomistic individualism and loss of democratic community is the desire to regain control over issues and events that have critical, if not survival, aspects to them. Drugs, AIDS, poverty, family dissolution and parental disinterest, lack of intellectual and job skills, the increasingly global competition for superiority—all impinge upon the school in a variety of ways. School boards, superintendents, principals, and teachers sense a need to redirect their schools and classrooms against a surge of directionless events. Fearful of being caught up in "epidemic-proportion" social problems, educators are turning to "leaders" to provide visions, plans, and programs for social change.

The precise ways in which leadership interfaces with the desire to reconstruct the United States is problematic. It is unclear how successful leaders may be in controlling social situations through educational reform. Part of the control issue is that of decentralization. As one effort to democratize leadership by moving decision-making power to smaller educational units (individual schools and teachers), decentralization as a movement in educational reform focuses upon structural change as the means of educational improvement. Leadership thus becomes a crucial tare in the balancing of demands upon schools for more "effective" performance versus the necessity to involve larger numbers in the reform movement itself. Leadership is to be "spread around" in the hope that excellence in educational product will result.

What Benne's work has done is surgically remove the authority concept from that of the concept of power. Importantly, Giroux (1986) demonstrates that Benne's liberal conception of authority is incomplete. Benne's conception of authority "exhibits an inadequate understanding of how power is asymmetrically distributed within and between different communities" (p. 26).

This power dimension of the contemporary socioculture is often linked with leadership in unthinking ways. The term "power" has acquired a variety of meanings in ordinary language; nevertheless, certain shared or family characteristics that linguistic philosophers have employed to mark its use remain. It is generally assumed that there is some *locus* of power and that this usually takes the form of an agent or agencies which dispense it. Moreover, it is thought that power is *distributed* or allocated to agents (individuals, groups, societies, nations, etc.). And finally, power is regarded as both unacceptable as it functions to dominate and make submissive human action, while being applauded as a "show of force" when exercised by leaders.

A reconceptualization of power must be explored. The meaning of power shifts in several ways: Power may be seen descriptively as a relational concept in the sense that it serves to characterize activities between agents and events.

Michel Foucault introduces the power concept into his post-structuralist analysis of human culture by rejecting its traditional legal/political meaning. Viewed historically, the transformation of power in society has been a function of its machine-like nature. Leaders and followers are caught up in the mechanized and ideological forms of life that propel them into futures not of their own making. For Foucault, "truth" is always *relational*, in the sense that, what is true is dependent upon historical, cultural, and power factors (McLaren, 1989, p. 182). Foucault writes: "Power is everywhere: not because it embraces everything, but because it comes from everywhere. . . . One should probably be a nominalist in this matter: power is not an institution, nor a structure, nor a possession. It is the name we give to a complex strategic situation in a particular society" (Sheridan, 1980, p. 184).

From Foucault's perspective, power is not something that can be acquired, seized, or shared; it is a relational concept known through its consequences. Viewed in this way, power is the subtle mechanism; while leadership is the external and observable role manipulation effort. Power is something that happens to us over which we have no real control, while authority is something we exert upon others. Power relations are found embedded in other kinds of relations (sexual, pedagogical, familial, religious, etc.). The divisions and breaks, the inequalities and imbalances, are found within these relations. There is no cause for power, only points at which it manifests itself—although, fundamentally, power is directed at the search for knowledge.

There is resistance to power which is as decentered as is power itself (Sheridan, ch. 2).

McLaren (1989), following Foucault, warns that "teachers need to recognize that *power relations correspond to forms of school knowledge that distort understanding and produce what is commonly accepted as 'truth'*" (p. 182). Calling for the development of "critical educators," McLaren argues that knowledge should be analyzed as to whether it is oppressive and exploiting, and not on the basis of whether it is "true" or "false." "Empowerment" means for Peter McLaren helping students understand and engage in the world, as well as enabling them to exercise the courage needed to change the social order where necessary (McLaren, p. 182). Following Foucault, McLaren believes that truth is relational and not an absolute. Critical educators are to use *praxis* and *phronesis* in such ways that they are working at "eliminating pain, oppression, and inequality, and promoting justice and freedom" (McLaren, p. 182). Thus, leadership is able to either quell or resist the micro-mechanisms of power in the lives of people. Where teachers as leaders surface at the concealed points at which power influences life and choice, they can empower students to gain control and direction over their lives.

The literature of business and industrial management is replete with references to the need for power in leadership. Business theory is supported by psychological theory, which has dominated the generation of leadership concepts over the decades. As examples of popular renditions of leadership qua business savvy, Warren Bennis and Burt Nanus in *Leaders: The Strategies for Taking Charge* (1985) present an example of a self-help text for business people facing managerial powerlessness. Bennis and Nanus argue that the leadership concept is in utter confusion: what is needed is to see that "there is something missing from all the 'new age' formulations—one issue which has been systematically neglected without exception: *Power, the basic energy to initiate and sustain action translating intention into reality*, the quality without which leaders cannot lead" (p. 15).

Bertrand Russell argued that "the fundamental concept in social science is power, in the same sense in which energy is the fundamental concept in physics" (Bennis and Nanus, p. 15). The power concept is distrusted but necessary, according to Bennis and Nanus. We seek to avoid conflict arising from the use of power, but in so doing we inherit a fragile universe. The solution is to be found in defining leadership as the wise use of power, the capacity to translate intention into reality and sustain it, Bennis and Nanus argue (p. 17). Bennis and Nanus couple this power with *vision*. "Vision is the commodity of leaders, and power is their currency" (p. 18). Thus, leadership is seen as taking charge and exercising power over others to compel them to do what the leader wishes done.

While Bennis and Nanus see the shift to the powerful visionary leader as part of the new "paradigm shift" in business management, a counterparadigm has emerged among select schools. Calls for the "empowerment" of teachers have been sweeping the country. "School-by-committee" is being tested in a number of school districts across the country. Essentially, these experiments are working from the classroom up in an effort to reform teacher effectiveness and hence student learning. Teachers formed into governing councils control the schools. Efforts to empower teachers in Rochester, New York, and Dade County, Florida, began in the mid-1980s and saw the implementation of "lead teachers," salary raises, and greater voice in the operations of schools. Advocates point to the factor of accountability and professionalism that this new empowerment move seems to create. Critics point to the threat of unionization and collective bargaining that such empowerment poses (Garcia, 1989, pp. 1A, 24A). However, the shift in leadership from managerial control to collective collegial decision making highlights a new conception of leadership.

Henry Giroux's work has appropriated innovations in social theory and research for a deeper textured understanding of schooling in America. Giroux has shown how empowerment of all individuals, regardless of race, class, faith, or gender, has been aborted by the privileged. Building a "critical pedagogy" aimed at empowering educators and pupils through language, Giroux's early work sits comfortably with that of Paulo Freire, William Pinar, Michael Apple, and Jean Anyon (McLaren, 1988, p. 6). More recently, Giroux has shifted to an involvement with the issue of agency and student resistance. In the 1980s he was more concerned with the role students play in culture and the power ideology exerts upon their lives. In *Education Under Siege* (1985), Stanley Aronowitz and Giroux set forth the notion of schooling and "democratic public spheres." Schools, as public networks, were seen as means to develop democratic principles/practices, through debate, dialogue, and opinion exchange. Aronowitz and Giroux set forth a democratic conception dedicated to social justice, equality, and diversity. Schools play a role in creating local democracy and work toward connection with other democratic public spheres. Educators need to develop a critical public language and to begin to function as intellectuals if this vision of schools as mini-democracies is to work and American society is to be reconstructed (McLaren, 1988, pp. 11–12).

Aronowitz, Giroux, and McLaren are not alone in suggesting that educators need to develop a powerful language of "resistance" to the prevailing truths of educational management. The concept of resistance has been taken by Michel Foucault and others as central to the problem of power and ideology. Both McLaren and Giroux subscribe to a notion of teacher as transformative intellectual leader, an idea made the centerpiece of the social reconstructionism of the 1930s. Here leadership is to take the form of critical social practice rather than expert authority. McLaren writes of this new leader/teacher:

Quite clearly, the teacher as transformative intellectual must be committed to the following: to teaching as an emancipatory practice; to the creation of schools as democratic public spheres; to the restoration of community of shared progressive values; and to the fostering of a common public discourse linked to the democratic imperatives of equality and social justice. (McLaren, 1988, p. 13)

Hence, a mere verbal analysis of leadership is not sufficient, and our critical pragmatic study must move beyond mere formal analysis. Language and life are joined. In the present study, we shall be interested in tracing the impacts of notions of leading upon the practical affairs of schools. In what ways do alternative concepts of leadership qua power and empowerment result in differing ways of teaching, administering, and counseling children and youth? The kindergarten study discussed in Chapter 5 traces the influence of views of leadership held by teachers upon their five– and six-year-old charges. We shall discover that leadership meanings are impregnated in us at a very early age. While we may believe that leaders are made, not born, in fact we treat leadership as an inherited human trait in the education of children and youth. Thus, the fuller techniques employed in this study are pragmatic as we see ideas as instruments for the control and direction of people and events.

Given these reconstructed notions of power, it is important to see leadership in relation to the professionalization of teaching/administration in new ways. It may be argued here that power in the senses indicated here is related to leading and that it is tied to the transactional nature of leadership discourse/practice. Professionalization implies power be lodged in the hands of teachers such that they may possess leadership in policy and decision making affecting learning in schools. To overlook this triadic relationship between power, profession, and leadership is to hamstring educators and prevent them from freely exercising their craft.

METHODS OF STUDY

The older methods of studying leadership have been empirical, positivist, and structuralist, but more must be said about how leadership may be made understandable for today's educators, parents, and students. What is needed is a systematic critical and philosophical view that makes sense of the often competing programmatic uses of the leadership idea in the arena of educational practice.

While social scientists have wrestled with the task of locating leadership in some concrete and observable behaviors, human traits, or contexts, philosophers rarely investigated the practical impact of such conceptual difficulties inherent in the language of leadership research and policy. Analytic philosophers of education in the 1960s and 1970s typically dealt rather narrowly with concepts like "teaching," "learning," and "indoctrination," as these have fallen under the general category of "education." It was seen as irrelevant to the project of philosophy to draw upon the methods of ordinary language analysis in unpacking "leadership," "empowerment," or allied notions. In part this reticence has been a historic legacy of R.S. Peters and others in Britain who had stressed the necessity of doing conceptual analysis with those notions centrally of concern in education. The tendency was to view *philosophy of education* as necessarily involved in the institutional desire of promoting learning in the uninitiated. Barrow (1981b) points out that the traditional (Peters) approach to philosophy of education has had a number of drawbacks. For our purposes, it is important to understand that just as "education" does not necessarily entail the passing on of worthwhile activities to others, philosophy of eduation is not necessarily restricted to the analysis of the concept of education and its band of related notions. This is not to say that linguistic analysis may not be fruitful for our clarification of the leadership concept. The present work will draw upon just those tools of ordinary language analysis in releasing the complex meanings of leadership as it relates to education (p. 26).

Newer philosophic approaches to the understanding of the issues that face us in education and culture have emerged, some prompted by European philosophers such as Friedrich Nietzsche, Jacques Derrida, Hans-Georg Gadamer, Michel Foucault, and Gilles Deleuze, and others suggested by American thinkers such as Richard Rorty, Richard Bernstein, and Cleo Cherryholmes. Hermeneutics, deconstructionism, critical theory, pragmatism, and other strategies for uncovering the meanings of characters and events in our time have come on the scene.

As part of the solution to the present leadership crisis, there is a call for an illumination of the ideological and normative (in the sense of recommendational) conceptualization of leadership as it relates to knowledge, authority, and power. Seeing leadership in terms of an ethical and informed practical knowledge (*phronesis*) rather than the currently accepted technical knowhow (*techné*) augers for newer notions of "professionalism" in education. Authors such as William P. Foster (1986), Cherryholmes (1988), Bates (1990), Landon Beyer (1988), Beyer, Joel Feinberg, Jo Anne Pagano and James A. (Tony) Whitson (1989), and Robert Scholes (1985) point to the "mystifying ideology" that holds that techné, or technical expertise, grounds exclusively our educational efforts.

By ignoring the non-technical and non-rational elements upon which leadership must be based, submerging the moral/ethical dimensions of educational policy, and removing the artistic interest as an expression of leading, mainstream educational administration research, as it treats educational leadership studies, has turned method and inquiry against liberation and empowerment. To overcome this tendency, the present study will be relying upon a variety of philosophic moves derived from philosophic schools such as hermeneutics, critical theory, deconstructionism, and pragmatism.

Broadly construed at times as "post-structuralist," or "postmodern," the present effort shall use a mode of thinking that is speculative but eschews any privileged language/writing form (Norris, 1987, p. 211). To deconstruct "leadership" is to elide any "transcendental signified" or meta-narrative warrant for the notion. This is to say that leadership is nothing more than what a subtle deep-textured understanding of leadership/texts provides. Conventional authors of popular leadership books mislead us if we take them to be transmitting an intended meaning of leadership: There is a deeply layered set of meanings attached to the notion of leadership that must be uncovered. Foucault and Derrida, for example, provide us with liberating meanings of concepts such as "power" and "empowerment" that have been hidden in the so-called "normal discourse" of leadership.

The pragmatists and neo-pragmatists, such as Rorty, Bernstein, and Cherryholmes, find traditional philosophic analysis of such notions as power and authority to be just another voice in the effort to understand. "Critical pragmatism" serves to blend the features of the postmodern critique into a fruitful new taking of the culture (Norris, 1987, pp. 159–60). Rorty rejects metaphysical "essences" as explanatory of philosophical objects. Here leadership would be seen as "true" or "accurate" to the extent that people, as William James argued, found the notion "good in the way of belief" (Rorty, 1982, p. 162). By looking at action rather than contemplation, practice rather than theory, pragmatism forces us to trace our meanings of leadership in the concrete ways of doing in the schools.

The present effort will draw upon certain "moves" from analytic, pragmatic and neo-pragmatic, hermeneutic, deconstructionist, and critical theory philosophers in an effort to reveal the conceptual and practical difficulties of leadership and education.

THE AIM OF THIS BOOK

The present study finds efforts to invoke leadership in education as the palliative to the current malaise surrounding the goals and directions of schools in the United States in need of analysis and deeper understanding. Whatever else has been going on, numerous studies and reports, such as the Holmes Group's report *Tomorrow's Teachers* (1986) and the Carnegie Forum's *A Nation Prepared: Teachers for the 21st Century* (Task Force,

1986), point to the need for rethinking the lines of American educational leadership as it is set against the backdrop of reform. The relationship between administration, management, and leadership; moral vision and leadership; policy and leading; leadership and the preparation of administrators; and leadership and teacher empowerment shall be explored here. It is argued that the leadership construct must be delineated if the work of improving schooling in America is to go forward with any fruitfulness.

This study is one focused upon "leadership" but departs from some of those notions commonly examined in educational philosophy. We shall be looking at educational leadership in the context of schooling, but our analysis will reach beyond the schoolhouse door, just as the concept itself reaches into the domains of business, athletics, politics, and so forth. The concept of "leadership" ranges broadly and the multiple meanings of this notion tend to overlap and intertwine in the educational domain. This infusion of the various notions of leadership into educational talk can be illustrated through a search of the literature in the social sciences (political science, sociology, psychology, and anthropology) as well as a review of the writings in educational research (educational administration, instructional methods, curriculum, guidance, and counseling, etc.) where leadership comes into play. A mere verbal analysis is not enough however. We shall also be interested in looking at the various cylinders of experience in which leadership plays upon our institutional lives. Thus, we are interested in the discourses of leaderships plus the practices of leaders.

METHODS USED IN THIS BOOK

Although the philosophic school of thought called "pragmatism" has many versions (William James called it a new name for some old ways of thinking), there are features of this approach that may be highlighted here relative to our project of investigating leadership in education. Unfortunately, pragmatism has received some bad press. Often equated with opportunism and simple efficacy, the more "vulgar pragmatism," as Cherryholmes terms it (1988), tends to argue that whatever works is therefore good. This vulgar pragmatism is both misleading and destructive. Instead of the vulgar version of pragmatism, I will draw upon a "critical pragmatism" drawn from the methodological work of John Dewey, William James, John L. Childs, Kenneth Benne, R. Bruce Raup, and other early pragmatists joined with the contemporary neo-pragmatism of writers like Richard Rorty, Cleo Cherryholmes, and Richard J. Bernstein. A kind of fused critical pragmatism may be deployed on the issue of leadership in American culture today. This strategy will be used to treat the distorted views of education and social life to provide a helpful guide in unraveling the leadership question in education.

The present study attempts to draw upon the "moves" in this pragmatic tradition to make sense of leadership in the context of American education. What are the characterizing features of this critical pragmatism?

Emphasis on the Experimental/Scientific

The experimental/scientific dimension of pragmatism focuses upon the need of people not just to think, but rather to think *reflectively* in an attempt to develop more reasoned ways of accomplishing their collective end (Hullfish and Smith, 1961, p. 19). Leadership is a social concept, in the sense that for there to be a "leader" there must be at least one follower. Humans use reflective thinking to negotiate their way through a problem-fraught world. Ideas are tools in experimental use. Logic has never been a transcendental a priori to science and inquiry, but rather a consequent of an ordinary kind resulting from experiment.

Meaning Based on Sensory Perception

The pragmatic view, following W. O. Quine (1976), argues that our knowledge of linguistic meanings rests in sensory evidence and is not derived from the analysis of logical or conceptual relations among language terms solely. This is to say that we come to know the meaning of X when we engage in rigorous analysis not of pure conceptual essences, but rather by means of the analysis of fuller arguments and theories (Walker and Evers, 1984, p. 26). For the pragmatist Quine, philosophic criticism approaches and is continuous with science, if not being a part of science itself (Magee, 1979, p. 170).

Now this view differs from that of Rorty (1979), who holds that pragmatism has no business passing itself off as a science or mirror of nature. At best, pragmatism for Rorty is an "edifying" activity, closer to art and literature than the hard sciences. In the following pages I shall adopt Rorty's vision of the task of philosophy as we look more closely at leadership from an aesthetic perspective.

Democracy as a Way of Life

Dewey conceived of democracy as a sociopolitical way of life. This is to argue that democracy names a means of social arrangement as well as a set of values enabling human beings to reach the fullest meaning of life. In his book *Democracy and Education* (1916), Dewey demonstrated the tight interrelationship between democracy as a social idea and education. Democracy maximizes human freedom in which persons are released to inquire. This release is essential for education to take place. On the other hand,

education is a means for teaching about the value of democracy and perpetuating it as a set of conditions enabling freedom to continue. The importance of democracy is vital to any discussion of leadership, given this view.

R. W. Sleeper (1986) notes a significant feature of pragmatism that must
be stressed here. Pragmatism is essentially *meliorist* in nature. While Heidegger and Wittgenstein shared some of Dewey's concern to move philosophy
away from the dead weight of tradition, neither was particularly interested
in applying philosophy to the social problems of their day. Dewey, however,
was concerned to show the ways in which philosophy could aid in the
resolution of social issues.

Results

Critical pragmatists look to fruits, ends, results. This study is interested in
the concrete results of notions of leadership in school acts. The assumption
that ideas may change our behavior, institutions, and ways of life is not held
by all philosophers. Ideas undergo change over time, and these changed
notions deeply change our behavior.

The Concept of No Absolutes

There are no external verities, no absolutes to rest upon. Critical pragmatists have abandoned the search for "foundations" of knowledge and
value. Even the search for "moral principles" has produced conflicting
results. For Rorty, the fundamental role of language as informing some
correspondence theory of truth is wrongheaded.

The Cartesian View of the World

Bernstein (1983) traces our current plight to Descartes and what he terms
the "Cartesian Anxiety," or the setting up of a foundational point of view to
solve the historical philosophic problems of the ancients. The result is a whole
array of dualisms (such as, mind-body). We have inherited Descartes's world
view (principally in the scientific community and the educational research
enclave). However, a generation of post-empiricist philosophers and historians of science have successfully criticized the Cartesian solutions and
method (e.g., Thomas Kuhn, Imre Lakatos, Paul Feyerabend).

Opposition to Metaphysics

Critical pragmatism eschews metaphysics. Unchanging revelation, cos-
mological interpretations, or other supernatural sources of knowledge and

value are rejected on the one hand. On the other hand, instrumentalism is suspicious of personalism and egoistic efforts to explain phenomena from simply human-centered theorizing. Mysticism and myth, fear and superstition, lie at the fringes of the central project of placing experience in meaningful frames of reference. The instrumentalist vision is essentially a naturalistic one (Sleeper, 1986, p. 202).

Skepticism

The approach used in this text is pragmatic, but critically so. William James wrote of this skeptical dimension of pragmatism:

All philosophic reflection is essentially skeptical at the start. To common sense, and in fact to all living thought, matters actually thought of are held to *be* absolutely and objectively as we think them. Every representation becomes relative, flickering, insecure, only when reduced, only in light of *further* consideration which we may confront it with. This may be called its *reductive*. Now the reductive of most of our confident beliefs is that they are *our* beliefs; that we are turbid media; and that a form of being may exist uncontaminated by the touch of the fallacious knowing subject. The motive of most philosophies has been to find a position from which one could *exorcise* the reductive, and remain securely in possession of a secure belief. (Barzun, 1983, pp. 20–21)

James identifies a central problem facing social philosophy as a method: How may we deal with the relativism of competing beliefs, theories, conceptual schemes, and so forth, without acceding to a dogmatic high ground, some privileged position from which to view the passing show? On the other side, how many individuals remain open and ready to admit new and alternative systematic perspectives while retaining some commitment to reason and rationality? Historically, philosophy has viewed relativism as the enemy of reason. However, democratic openness and the passion for equality in social life have released minds to the possibility of alternatives, pluralities, and difference in rationality itself.

CONCLUSIONS

In the pages that follow, we shall explore the notions of leadership operative in American schools from this more open-textured point of view. The explanatory method used here is more on the order of an aesthetic pragmatism that is both artful and practice-oriented, critical as well as explanatory. The arguments set forth in this book will build to the conclusion that what is needed in contemporary debates about school reform is the critically imaginative vision that sees leadership as a community effort to redesign schools for the maximization of the interests of that community. I shall employ the aesthetic feature of pragmatism to develop a "criticism of criticism" of the leadership construct in the chapters to follow.

Thus, the problematic aspects of school and social life may be approached with a reflective and critical attitude we shall term "critical pragmatism," allowing us to focus on competing views of leadership. A sharply critical pragmatic accounting of the current crises in American social life is required to fuel understanding of contemporary reproductive practice, resistance to such practice, and practical solutions for the future. The fundamental assumption has it that social philosophy, while perhaps possibly failing to resolve social debates, offers hope in the fact that it shall shed some light on them, and thus help us back and warrant change.

In the pages that follow, I shall make an effort to show the manner in which a new emancipated vision of leadership may interface with the crucial sociocultural issues facing the educator today. Issues of discipline, drugs, AIDS, and so on are all open to the methods of this reconceptualized aesthetic leadership. Where human intelligence becomes melioristic agentry for the continuous reconstruction of experience, problem-fraught as life may be, it becomes possible to reorder experience to maximize human good.

In all of the approaches discussed here, there is a call for reconceptualizing the way we view human institutions in general and social leadership in particular. The school is not simply an organizational complex, with a structure and function, peopled by workers exercising some status or role. We are seeing exciting new notions of how to view education in society as living "texts." Attached to this reconceptualization is a new interest in the ends toward which institutions and the people within them are pledged. By reconstituting human freedom through new linguistic community and a new pragmatism, in the face of technology and totalitarianism, we find theorists prompting a non-foundational continuous conversation, with concomitant edification. The horizons of education and leadership may be seen as expanding as a result of these new ways of seeing.

As Bernstein points out (1983), these post-philosophy thinkers converge upon certain basic tenets: a new vision of people living and working in a non-objectivist, non-relativist world of local communities dedicated to praxis and phronesis. A world in which the process values of dialogue, conversation, phronesis, practical discourse, and judgment are linked to the universal values of solidarity, participation, unity, and mutual recognition (Bernstein, pt. IV). Importantly, this position is in sharp contrast to "back to the basics" conservatives, such as Allan Bloom (1987), who reject openness in favor of universal natural human rights; relativism in favor of objectivism based on classical texts; and minority, racial, ethnic, or gender interests in favor of self-righteousness.

A new pragmatism results when a sense of crisis comes to inform our choosing process, when we come to see that the values and beliefs that have formed our standards for judgment are themselves under suspicion. Pragmatism at this juncture becomes self-reflective and instrumental relative to the prospects and future of human institutions and events. Critical pedagogic inquiry, I wish to maintain, is at a turning point in its career, one in which it must move away from its traditional assumptions or self-description. Conditions force this. There are a number of theorists who provide a new justification for philosophy as it helps in understanding the changes in socioculture in the future. It is vital, it is argued here, to review what contemporary theorists propose and to distill the likely impacts for a social philosophy of educational leadership at this point in history. In light of competing notions of leadership there is a need for us to rethink the way we view the concept as it operates within institutions like the school. Part of the rationale for the present text is to provide a means by which new theories of leadership in education may emerge that will aid in the improvement of educational settings.

2

Research on Leadership in Education

When we look at the research studies on leadership in general, the numbers are astonishing. Work on educational leadership is also extensive, but not quite so unwieldy. The early work on leadership was primarily along political lines. The key writing in this perspective may be traced to Max Weber (1947). Research by others has followed this political or a psychological approach (Bass, 1981; Burns, 1978; Gouldner, 1950; Misumi, 1985; Sashkin and Fulmer, 1987).

Research on educational leadership was dictated by versions of "positivism." Today these methodological assumptions are in upheaval. The critical stance toward social scientists and their work began to shake the foundations of inquiry during the last three decades. Led by John Dewey, Sir Karl Popper, Thomas Kuhn, Imre Lakatos, and Paul Feyerabend, the rationality of science has come under question. In the 1980s new directions in research methodology seriously undermined the older positivistic models for the conduct of research in the social sciences and education (Phillips, 1987, pp. 1–19; Stove, 1982, pt. 1). Called "qualitative research" or "naturalistic inquiry," these new directions challenge the notion that a single brand of "rationality" or logic drives the search for knowledge and understanding. Justification for such strategies now rests upon assumptions identified as central to hermeneutics, critical theory, and neopragmatism.

In this chapter, we shall look at the historic character of research on leadership, discuss the social philosophic implications of early research postures regarding leading and following, and propose a new support for a "merger" of views that will move inquiry into leadership along new vectors.

THE HISTORY OF LEADERSHIP RESEARCH

Leadership has been the object of much scrutiny by social scientists, with very little consensus on what it actually refers to in social life. Despite the volumes of research studies and reports, leadership is a notion that defies a singular definition. Why is this so? And what makes leadership such a confusing notion in education?

The absence of a commonly held definition of leadership has tended to frustrate researchers and yield a lack of consensus in findings. Yet, in everyday affairs, people seem to believe that leadership, whatever it may mean to academics, matters. Some of the definitions of "leadership" are:

Leadership is power based predominantly on personal characteristics, usually normative in nature. (Etzioni, 1961, p. 116)

Leadership in organizations involves the exercise of authority and the making of decisions. (Dubin, 1968, p. 385)

The leader is the individual in the group given the task of directing and coordinating task-relevant group activities. (Fiedler, 1967, p. 8)

Leadership is the initiation of a new structure or procedure for accomplishing an organization's goals and objectives or for changing an organization's goals and objectives. (Lipham, 1964, p. 122)

Leadership may be considered as the process (act) of influencing the activities of an organized group in its efforts toward goal setting and goal achievement. (Stoghill, 1950, p. 3)

Leadership is a process of influence between the leader and those who are followers. (Hollander, 1978, p. 1)

Leadership . . . is the behavior of an individual when he is directing the activities of a group toward a shared goal. (Hemphill and Coons, 1957, p. 7)

"Leadership" is defined as the process of influencing the activities of an organized group toward goal achievement. (Rauch and Behling, 1984, p. 46)

The foregoing definitions reflect the penchant of researchers to postulate causal models of leadership, vectoring force, and control over groups. They are tied closely to organizational theories and require for their legitimacy power and managerial skill. Yet despite the effort to convey precise and controlled conceptual territory, less is known about the nurture and care of "leadership" today than ever before. Leadership research, especially within organizations, is a field in free fall. Experts are no longer convinced that leading is subject to the methods traditionally used in social science inquiry.

THE CONCEPT OF LEADERSHIP

When we look at the use of the leadership concept (actually there are many *conceptions* of leading in operation today), we see certain characteristics, or clusters of ordinary usage. Grammar can be divided into *phonetics* or the study of the relationship between sound and representation; *semantics* or the understanding of the relationship between meaning and its deep structure; and *syntactics* or the study of logical context of meanings. Louis Pondy (1978) argues that we should expand the way we think about leadership and what we think of as leading. Leadership fails to fall neatly into forms of social situational influences or behaviors and style. We have neglected the deep structures of leadership in favor of quick answers. What is needed is to move beyond defining leadership in terms of small groups and strategies for accomplishing work. Researchers have been forced to look at face-to-face varieties of leading because these lent themselves to scientific research instrumentalities. What is needed in the future is to look at *indirect leadership* and the technology that makes this happen (Pondy, 1978).

Pondy (1978) suggests that one influence upon our behavior that is difficult to define is the manner in which we share language. By looking to language as an effort to set out meaning, Pondy finds communication by leaders to be tightly connected to language use. A leader's subtle use of language may be an important factor in his/her effectiveness. Leaders are often rated on how well they get followers to do something: essential to this activity is the shared understanding of what is meant. Thus, linguistic expressions provide meanings that can be shared, changed, and amplified.

The term leadership itself has several levels of meaning. First, the word constitutes its meaning, in the sense that it has at least an instantaneous autonomy and control over the nature of variations of its use. Second, a leader's understanding of the subtleties of meaning are important to his/her effectiveness. Individual words have different meanings, and words in general differ in function. Third, we ought to think of leadership, like language, as a collection of *games* with some similarities, but no common single characteristics (Pondy, 1978, pp. 85–99).

Following up on Pondy's recommendations, a philosophical analysis of leadership reveals some interesting insights. First, very often the word leadership operates to name some particular empirical property: it is seen as equal to a set of traits, style, or enabling conditions or setting. The psychological variables, moreover, are found shared by leaders in different occupations or jobs. The team captain, corporate head, elected official, or military commander—to be regarded as a leader—must possess the correct trait(s), behaviors, style, and so forth. Such traits as "organized" or "initiating" come to stand for what we mean by leading activities, for example. Thus, the effort was to locate "real world" representations of leadership, to trace its concrete causal connections with workplace change, and to somehow capitalize on these insights in the training of new leaders for more effective businesses and industries.

It was not difficult for educational thinkers to adopt these research models and strategies in their treatment of educational leaders. As a result, school principals, superintendents, supervisors, and others in positions of responsibility were examined by researchers for evidence of these traits of the leaders. Thus, "leadership" was taken to be such a generic term that it was accepted that leaders in all areas of human life (and some animal life) share in common characteristics.

A second feature of leadership as a guiding notion in management is that it is essentially a *normative* concept. Leadership is quickly tied to aims and goals. Leaders take institutions, enterprises, teams, businesses, and armies, along some path toward an identified endstate. Leaders help increase production, raise scores, or secure hills against enemies. They are achievers, either themselves or via their confederates and followers. Some have argued that leaders get others to commit to goals and goal attainment, while followers achieve for the leader. The fact that leaders do not stand still or let things ride, but focus upon objectives and seek to push for accomplishment all ties in with the normative dimension of the concept of leadership.

In quite another sense of the term normative, leadership carries with it a heavy value load. Leaders set upon attainment of objectives that are prized or valued—visions. They are not only in pursuit of oughts and recommendational matters but take them to be uncritically accepted by others. Thus leading, it is assumed, entails trying to achieve ends that are prima facie deemed worthwhile by others (the school board, PTA, Democratic party, Madlyn Hunter, etc.). As John Dewey (1927) put it: "*Leadership*: The investiture of certain individuals with a public character, and responsibility for the common consequences for all participants in the group" (pp. 18–19). The public nature of leadership and its responsibility component are clearly laid out by Dewey here.

Moreover, there is often no critical judgment allowed regarding these values. "The dress code is set by the superintendent and the school board: implement it in your school." As a middle manager responsible to those above him/her, the "leader" must carry out policy, must achieve the prized value of a rule-governed student body (if only relative to dress).

Certainly, such an enterprise as educating is not free from rules and regulations. It is in this sense that we may see leadership as normative in a rule-governed sort of way. For example, the leader of a university may be deeply involved in ethical or moral questions (whether the athletic department should be investigated for unethical recruiting of team players, or whether human beings should be involved in research projects where their welfare is not paramount). Leaders must take into consideration the prevailing moral order of a society, its mores, even though they may choose to violate that order in private (e.g., Jimmy Swaggert or Jim Jones). Leaders are intimately tied to the "oughts" and "desires" of social groups, and where they deal with policy they are engaged in a normative enterprise that seeks to operationalize the mores of the group in certain perceived ways. "We want our school to represent strong agrarian values, the virtue of farm life."

A third characteristic of leadership in research studies, both today and yesterday, is the strong link to moral virtue found in leadership discourse and practice. Talk about leading is often accompanied by strong notions of *virtue*. David Tyack and Elisabeth Hansot (1982b) point out that educational administrators operating as leaders have been seen as "managers of virtue." By this they have in mind that the moral dimension of educational leadership is displayed not only in the ways in which principals and superintendents got the job done, but also how they lent moral certitude to the enterprise of education. Educational leadership was not just delivery of some service to the public, but rather a moral patina was added to administrators' pronouncements and policies. Today, scholars in educational administration are attempting to revive this eighteenth- and nineteenth-century notion of the educational administrator exercising a moral role (see W. Greenfield, 1987a and b; Blumberg and W. Greenfield, 1980) in school leadership. However, it is not often clear either where this moral view comes from (fundamentalist religion, Machiavellian politics, or the McGuffey Readers) or what gives educational administrators a moral edge rather than teachers or counselors.

Fourth, the problem of educational leadership is part of social inquiry. It is related to questions affecting groups of people, children in particular, not a few isolated individuals. More than this, leadership is tied to questions of freedom and authority, culture and society, and rights and responsibilities *in the school setting*. Leadership in its educational phase may look similar to political leadership, for example, but it is different owing to the involvement of unprotected children and uninitiated youth and the nurturing arrangements found operative in schools. Hence, the social philosophy of educational approach and parameters helps us to focus on some of the uniquenesses identified with educational leaders and the context of the school.

Quite another way of looking at leadership characteristics is to ask what educators take to be leadership concerns. This is to say that we must ask what people in leadership positions (they may not in fact be doing a very effective job leading, but nonetheless) deem to be their role expectations. In some measure, the answer to this question may be found in the types of educational and training programs educators sign up for that promise leadership skill-enhancement. A rather typical display of advertisements in educational periodicals mentions short courses and conferences in leadership training for educators at all levels. There is a large industry dedicated to making people into leaders. Packaging courses and tapes treating related topics in the leadership bag (e.g., staff development, cost-effectiveness, negotiating, etc.) show the tricks of the trade to be learnt by the novice.

The most significant contribution to the literature on leadership must be located in the work of Max Weber (1947). The study of formal organizations was spurred on in the United States by the translation of Weber's writings on bureaucracy after 1945. Although the German sociologist had died in 1920, his work did not become available to Americans until after World War II. Weber's theories fit with the emergence of the new professional managerial class. From the 1940s until the mid-1970s, the study of bureaucracy became the centerpiece of inquiry in administration. By the 1960s educational administration was caught up in this general concern about questions of bureaucracy (Campbell et al., 1987, pp. 63–64).

Weber discovered that human social organization could be characterized by three kinds of authority: *charismatic leadership*, *traditional domination*, and *legal domination*. The charismatic leader was one who commanded respect and obedience from followers and was sustained by their respect. Traditional domination was a form of leadership resting upon inherited position. But a newer form of leadership which he termed "legal domination" had emerged in the modern age and rested for its legitimacy upon the right of law. It was the legal form of leadership that had produced bureaucracies (Campbell et al., pp. 64–65).

For Weber, legal domination was more rational than the other forms of leadership because it rested upon training and competence. He was certain that bureaucracies arose out of the changes in the factory and business world. Increased specialization, the division of labor, and the growth of large corporations required a changed mode of management: bureaucratic leadership was the answer. More disciplined and orderly, bureaucracies led by trained managers introduced rules and regulations, divided up tasks by qualified workers. Hierarchical management, super-ordination and sub-ordination, written memos, chain-of-command, and other hallmarks of modern bureaucracy were identified by Weber (Campbell et al., pp. 65–66).

Beneath it all, Weber saw the bureaucratic leader as separate from the "Great Man" and "The Prince." Bureaucratic leadership was the means of saving democracy, Weber felt, through the reduction of differences among social classes and the rejection of autocracy and absolutism. The virtue of the new bureaucratic leadership lay not in its efficiency, for the layers of workers performing routine tasks compounded the complexity of decision-making, but rather in its impartiality (Campbell et al., pp. 66–67).

The downside of bureaucratic leadership was evident to Weber: Impersonalization and emphasis upon rules could stifle creativity and individual freedom. Rules could constrain individual efforts to change the system. Also, bureaucracies controlled information, and by keeping knowledge and intentions to themselves, the bureaucratic leaders, although preserving professionalism, would contribute to the exclusion of outside criticism and hence monitoring of operations. The expert leader, moreover, could keep elected officials and policy makers ignorant. Democracy might well suffer (Campbell et al., p. 67).

Robert Michels, like Weber, was vitally concerned about leadership in human societies. In a debate with Marx's ghost, he argued that Marx's socialist vision was unfounded owing to the fact that it rested upon certain forces or tendencies in society: (1) the nature of human nature; (2) the nature of the political struggle; and (3) the nature of organizations (Zeitlin, 1968, pp. 220–221).

For Michels, man seeks to transmit his material possessions as well as his power to his heir or kin. This motive is either an instinctual drive or originates in the economic order (in our case capitalism); Michels never resolved this issue (Zeitlin, p. 220). Nevertheless, his writings on human nature and leadership were significant for theoreticians.

It was, for Michels, man's inherent nature to crave power and, once having gotten it, to perpetuate it. From this view it followed that democracy as a form of social organization inevitably led to oligarchy. Drawing upon the psychological study of crowds, Michels asserted that the people were incapable of governing themselves. Crowds, especially large ones, are subject to irrationality and suggestion. Looking at political parties, Michels found that as the scale of an organization grew, it left the principles of democracy and equality behind and along with them the "Chief." A division of labor became necessary, with certain complicated tasks and duties now requiring ability, training, and knowledge. Specialization bred expertise. What resulted was a class of professional politicians. These experts come to resemble leaders as they withdraw from the masses and concentrate power. This aspirant group of leader-experts separate from the rank and file of the organization.

The leader-experts, although originally delegated to serve the interests of the organization, now develop interests of their own (some of which are often opposed to the interests of the group). Thus, democracy implies organization, and organization leads to oligarchy: as a result every organization becomes divided between a minority of leaders and a majority of followers (Zeitlin, pp. 222–223). Every organization exhibits these bureaucratic tendencies. Hence, "experience" and "expertise" become the main slogans of leaders to insulate their indispensability. This feeling of indispensability works as a tool of the leader. Faced with a challenge, the leader threatens to resign. This apparently democratic gesture masks his desire to force submission to his will. The followers, on the other hand, are too busy and too incompetent to challenge the leadership.

The followership of an organization has a need for leadership and is quite content to let someone else attend to its affairs. This fact supports the aristocratic and bureaucratic character of the organization (Zeitlin, p. 224). Michels found the German people prone to follow the leader uncritically. The masses were both incompetent and indifferent and tended to defer to leaders who were older and experienced (Zeitlin, p. 226). Hence, leaders promulgate the dissolution of democratic governance into oligarchy.

This "iron law" of oligarchy stood as a constant reminder to those who were to embrace a notion of democratic organization that their leaders would betray them in the end. Whether Michels meant to be so pessimistic is questionable; nevertheless, sociologists and political scientists have retained his skepticism regarding democratic leadership as it pertains to education and particularly to teachers. It may be argued that teachers are incompetent and inexperienced in governance and therefore ought to defer to the authorities (principals and superintendents). Teachers neither have the time nor the training to govern educational organizations. Increasingly educational administrators and college professors of educational administration have taken the view that a wide gulf separates teachers from administrations. Without proper training, educators cannot know the intricacies nor possess the knowledge to govern school organizations effectively. We may witness the oligarchy of administration (principal and assistants) gaining increasing power as teachers lose interest in the process of administering. Certainly, Michels gives us reason to pause in our call for "empowerment of teachers."

A closer look at the clustering of research studies in leadership finds leadership studied from the following vantage points.

Leadership Traits

Stimulated by Weber's work, leadership research began as a serious enterprise in the United States in the late 1940s and early 1950s. The dominant model that informed researchers at this time assumed that leadership could be identified in terms of *personality traits* (Bryman, 1986, p. 35). The traits or abilities of leaders were identified and grouped under such categories as physical characteristics, social background, intelligence and ability, personality, task-related characteristics, and social characteristics (Bass, 1981, pp. 375–376). The results of trait research were mixed. Researchers became disillusioned. First, researchers could not agree on what "trait" signified and in which category an ability ought to reside. Traits listed under "task-related" and "social characteristics" were often placed under "personality" and vice versa. Second, the research seemed to favor technical and administrative skills. It was questioned whether these were "traits" in the usual meaning of the word. Some traits were more a matter of leadership "style." And finally, the list of traits became long and complex (Bryman, pp. 21–25). Moreover, since much of the research was motivated by a search for screening devices for new leaders, one could ask from a critical theory perspective whether the rational/technical motivation was not paramount. The search for some set of universal traits or abilities failed.

The shift away from leadership trait research was the consequence of a methodological issue. A large number of research studies on leadership were based on who became leaders in leaderless contexts such as small work-groups (such as classrooms). These findings, critics argued, could not be extrapolated to real life situations. When more and more research was sponsored by business and industry, researchers felt compelled to identify characteristics in the workplace that marked successful managers (Bryman, pp. 22–23). Abraham Korman (1968) found that this search for effective managerial style in organizations was fruitless. The traits were expanded to include technical and administrative skills. Moreover, although the search for traits and styles occupied researchers from the 1940s until the 1970s, little was found to highlight the problem of understanding leadership (Bryman, p. 23). The mixed results of leadership trait research and leadership style in the late 1940s through the 1970s make stable comparisons among trait and style variables most difficult, but beyond this such studies have yielded little that illuminates the problem of leadership in general and educational leadership in particular. Scholars reveal that leadership and management cannot be the same: effectiveness as a leader is not the same thing as managerial success (Bryman, p. 34).

Leadership Behavior and the Search for Style

Ralph Stogdill's work in 1948 appears to have been pivotal in turning researchers away from traits to the examination of leadership *behaviors* and then on to an explanation of leadership *styles*. A second factor that influenced the shift to behavioral research was a growing interest among psychologists in what leaders actually did when they led. Kurt Lewin's "Iowa Childhood Studies," begun in 1938, sought to create different climates and test them relative to leadership. Three styles of leadership were subsequently identified: authoritarian, democratic, and laissez faire. Lewin and his graduate students found that in an autocratic environment the children appeared discontented, aggressive, and without initiative; in a laissez-faire climate children lacked direction, failed to finish tasks, and appeared frustrated; while in the democratically led groups the children appeared productive and socially satisfied, demonstrated more originality and independence, and were less hostile (Campbell et al., 1987, p. 49).

A third influence grew out of the "human relations movement." This approach to research in leadership and administration was made up of two interwoven bodies of ideas. The first was democratic administration, begun after 1900 and inspired by the work of John Dewey. The second began after 1945 and was characterized by the melding of the earlier democratizing views with the behavioral science and industrial studies pioneered by the work of Elton Mayo and Kurt Lewin (Campbell, p. 43).

After 1900, American society had become more sensitive to the problems of workers' rights. The rise of labor unions and the use of the strike forced attention to the conditions under which workers labored. The problem of business became the problem of "human relations."

The first writer to provide a major social philosophy of administration was Mary Parker Follett. Leadership was seen as a relational notion, a "circular response" within organizations between leaders and followers. She wrote: "we should think not only of what the leader does to the group, but also of what the group does to the leader" (Metcalf and Urwick, 1942, p. 248). Leadership was aimed at a functional unity and not arbitrary authority. She argued that leadership was to be dedicated to organizing experience.

The concept of "power," for Follett, was changing.

Power is now beginning to be thought of by some as the combined capacities of the group. We get power through effective relations. This meant that some people are beginning to conceive of the leader, not as the man in the group who is able to assert his individual will and get others to follow him, but as the one who knows how to relate these different wills so that they will have a driving force. He must know how to create a group power rather than to express personal power. He must make the team. (Metcalf and Urwick, p. 248)

For Follett, morale and communications were important. Businesses and factories needed to restructure their power relationships and decentralize authority. Decision making, slowed down and enlarged, was to be moved to those involved in the situation (Campbell, pp. 45–46). Follett proposed a "multiple leadership" in which the full power of the group would emerge through the organization of related experience. Finally, she argued for the teaching of leadership, for different situations demanding different kinds of knowledge and hence shifting leaders (Metcalf and Urwick, p. 277).

Elton Mayo's Hawthorne studies of a General Electric Company's plant in Chicago conducted in the 1920s looked at supervisor/leaders and what they did that yielded superior performance among workers. The study concluded that the quality and type of interaction within the workplace significantly affected morale and productivity. The researchers discovered that positive or negative changes made to the workplace were not as important as the factor of leadership expressing a care and interest in labor. The upshot was that if management did not see the nature of the human factor as related to group productivity, the company would fail to get the utmost out of the workers (Bryman, pp. 36–37).

Another influential program that contributed to the data on leadership was the Ohio State Leadership studies and the *Leader Behavior Description Questionnaire*. The LBDQ, as it came to be known, produced 130 questions which were then clustered via factor analysis. The analysis produced some interesting findings. Leaders who scored high in "consideration" (or are considerate toward subordinates) and "initiating structure" (or maintained standards of performance, made their attitudes clear to workers, and assigned particular tasks to crew) tended to be more successful. Variations in the LBDQ have emerged over time; however, they have reinforced the earlier assumptions of the researchers. Interestingly, the research results have not been identical when different versions of the LBDQ have been used. Nor have situational variables been looked at carefully. Style researchers seem to hold that leadership style in some sense is a causal variable in group performance, job satisfaction, and so forth. Another difficulty with the Ohio State studies was their focus on the leader/group relationship, with variations in the group often overlooked. Informal leadership is overlooked and most of the LBDQ data was generated from groups where the leader was in a role or position of managerial authority. Also, the data is drawn from subordinate accounts of leaders and not peers or others. Observation was a very real problem. Finally, critics point out that questionnaires have limited use in detecting complex behaviors such as leadership (Bryman, pp. 47–60).

More recently, Gary Yukl (1981) has begun listing leader behavior categories that seem to make leaders effective in specific situations. By becoming more specific as to which leading behaviors seem to cut across situations, this research harkens back to earlier searches for specifiable leadership traits. Somehow the combination of leader behavioral characteristics is to reveal what leading really is in contexts (Bryman, pp. 121–122).

Despite this recent work and many years of use of the LBDQ and its variants, traits and behaviors research has yielded inconsistencies, prompting researchers to look at some other factor to account for leadership besides consideration and initiating structure (Bryman, p. 83). The situation has become more interesting of late.

Leadership and Situations

The third approach to the study of leadership focused on the settings in which leading took place. Researchers grew frustrated with the failure of trait and behavioral approaches and switched to the notion that leadership was always context specific. The situational approach has as its goal the identification of particular characteristics of the setting which seem to impact on leader behavior. Researchers attempted to isolate specific situation variables determining leadership. Some of these variables have been: structural properties of the organization (size, hierarchical structure, formalization); organizational climate (openness, participativeness, group atmosphere); role characteristics (position power, type and difficulty of task, procedural rules); and subordinate characteristics (knowledge and experience, tolerance for ambiguity, responsibility, and power) (Hoy and Miskel, 1982, p. 223). Before long researchers sought to link personality traits with setting. Called the "contingency model" of leadership, the work of Fred Fiedler (1967) can be seen as the earliest systematic effort to locate style within differing organizational settings. By looking at leaders in the military, sports, and industry, Fiedler and his followers sought through situational variables to discover what made leaders effective (Bryman, pp. 126–127). By developing a scale (LPC), researchers attempted to discover variables tied to the "least preferred co-worker" and from these findings to locate what leadership would be. Critics of this research approach emerged in the 1970s and 1980s and the validity of the model was questioned. Leaders were found to be both high and low on the LPC scale. Fiedler was prompted to recommend that rather than training leaders for situations, business and industry should match the leader to the situation (Bryman, pp. 132–136).

Other research models that stressed situation were: House's Path-Goal Theory of Leadership; Hersey and Blanchard's Situational Leadership Theory; and the Vroom-Yetton Contingency Model. Each of these theoretical configurations has its conceptual and empirical problems. Studies underwritten by these models have mixed results. Alan Bryman, following P. M. Podsakoff et al. (1984), reports that researchers may question how far the effects of leaders' behavior are situationally contingent (Bryman, pp. 126–159).

NEWER DIRECTIONS IN LEADERSHIP RESEARCH

Significantly, of late leadership has tended to be defined in terms of the organization and mirrors the large-scale interest in business organization research (Hunt et al., 1987). Focus on "school climate" and its relationship to principals' leadership has gained in popularity. Researchers provide statistical support for the view that the behavior of the school leader, as perceived by the teachers, is related to school "productivity" as well as teacher morale. Looking closely at the kinds of climate conditions necessary to enhance leadership has resulted in a number of theories of organizational effectiveness: the open/closed (Halpin and Croft, 1963); robust/non-robust (Willower and Licata, 1975); input/output (Bidwell, 1972); needs/press (Silver, 1983); and coherent/non-coherent (Wynne, 1980).

Nevertheless, business-type organizations are only one kind of social collectivity. Researcher efforts to identify the controlling variables have led to the listing of hundreds of variables and their combinations. In attempts to locate the forces impinging on leadership, scholars seem only to reveal the amorphous character of the concept, with little practical relevance to the people involved in organizations (Mintzberg, 1973; 1982). Leadership in its informal dimensions, manifesting non-organizational features, has largely gone untreated. Additionally, work needs to be done on the relationship between leadership and the language we use in describing it (Pondy, 1978). Conceptual difficulties seem to undermine the large number of research theories that have sought to dominate the literature of organizational thinking. When we turn to leadership in educational matters, the problems encountered in leadership research vis-a-vis business and industry organizations become magnified.

Wayne Hoy and Cecil Miskel (1982), when looking at leadership in education, conclude that all three orientations (traits, behaviors, and setting) play a role in understanding educational leadership. They write, "the concept of leadership remains elusive because it depends not only on the position, behavior, and personal characteristics of the leader but also on the character of the situation" (p. 221). The argument appears to be that if the research findings of social scientists are contradictory or confusing, adopt them all.

More helpful is the sociologist Robert K. Merton's insight: "Leadership does not, indeed cannot, result merely from the individual traits or leaders; it must also involve attributes of the transactions between those who lead and those who follow. . . . Leadership is, then, some sort of social transaction" (Merton, 1969, p. 2615).

Despite the compelling reasonableness of the transactional definition of leadership, when we look at options presenting themselves for the researcher on school-based leadership today, there has been a renewal of interest in three approaches.

Charismatic Leadership Revived

To a large extent, modern research into educational administration rests upon a resurrected interest in charismatic leadership. The spate of self-help management books for school administrators reflects the assumption that leadership is to be acquired through an investment in personal assertiveness, "vision," and imposition of "mission statements" on the rank-and-file.

Authors such as William D. Greenfield (1987a and b) have called for leaders with "moral imagination" to become school principals. There is a fundamental assumption here that the impersonal and positivistic dimensions of leadership research findings can be tempered by substituting a more empathic and sensitive leader who pays attention to the realm of values as well as facts. However, beneath the patina of "value leadership" lies the accepted structure of Weberian bureaucracy in which everyone knows his/her place, power flows from above, and organizational goals are paramount. The difference for the new charismatics is found in the fact that the school principal/leader is more than a technical expert; he/she is also to be seen as an authority on values. And since values are amorphous and incapable of scientific determination, "moral" leadership is largely a matter of conviction (Greenfield, 1987a).

It is important to note that as more recent research in educational administration has focused on challenging the Weberian triadic concept of leadership, the distasteful aspects of bureaucracy have come under attack. "Management by Objectives," or the reduction of leadership to minute goal-setting, has resulted from the behaviorists extending this bureaucratic model to all levels of the organization.

Most leadership research studies are based on a relatively modest number of cases, and hence generalizing for the purpose of reforming the teaching/training of leaders or reorganizing institutions is shaky. Warren Bennis and Burt Nanus (1985), for example, base their normative "strategies" for becoming a leader on interviews and observations of a total of sixty CEOs in the $400,000 income bracket. Of these sixty, most were interviewed for no more than four hours on the topic of leadership, and only in five cases did the researchers spend five days with the leader, and in only two cases they "lived with the leader." The small sample led the authors to footnote the fact that only six were black and six were female in their leadership study.

The small-sample problem has not hindered researchers from making the most powerful recommendations for change in the preparation of leaders for organizations. We are led to believe that any of us can become a leader if we buy the researchers' books and follow their plans. Five minutes a day and three or four steps are all that need be followed to transform a follower into a leader, this popular approach asserts.

Much of the recent literature on the topic of educational leadership derives in one way or another from James McGregor Burns's book *Leadership* (1978). Burns's genius was in the invention of the concepts of *"transactional leadership"* and *"transformative leadership."* Burns attempted to characterize the typical activities of leadership—for example, listening, building coalitions, altering agendas, creating teams, reinforcing, and at times exercising power. These bureaucratic activities are mostly mundane transactions for Burns. Something more is needed if an institution is to get over the rough spots.

The "transformative leader" goes beyond the bureaucratic actions of the transactional leader. He/she builds upon followers' need for meaning and institutional purpose. The need for a transforming leader is not continuous, but unless such a leader takes charge at the pivotal points in an institution's history, the future of that institution is at risk. Burns felt that the transformative leader was a manipulator of values—someone who could shape the path toward the future. Burns assumes a transcendental set of values that this leader can plug into more readily than his bureaucratic counterpart. Burns wrote: "Leadership over human beings is exercised when persons with certain motives and purposes mobilize, in competition or conflict with others, institutional, political, psychological and other resources so as to arouse, engage and satisfy the motives of followers" (Burns, 1978, p. 18). He goes on to say that transforming leadership

occurs when one or more persons *engage* with others in such a way that leaders and followers raise one another to higher levels of motivation and morality. Their purposes, which might have started out separate but related, in the case of transactional leadership, become fused. Power bases are linked not as counterweights but as mutual support for common purpose. Various names are used for such leadership: elevating, mobilizing, inspiring, exalting, uplifting, exhorting, evangelizing. The relationship can be moralist, of course. But transforming leadership ultimately becomes *moral* in that it raises the level of human conduct and ethical aspiration of both the leader and the led, and thus has a transforming effect on both. . . . Transforming leadership is dynamic leadership in the sense that leaders throw themselves into relationship with followers who feel "elevated" by it and often become more active themselves, thereby creating new cadres of leaders. (Burns, p. 20)

The value leader notion was an important one for restructuring businesses and corporations. In 1957 Philip Selznick published *Leadership and Administration*, in which he argued that the leader "*is primarily an expert in the promotion and protection of values.*" The challenge to the leader was that of transforming men and groups from neutral and technical units into participants with a stamp of sensitivity and commitment. Followers were to be *educated* by the leader into doing things as persons rather than technicians. The social machinery of the institution had to be reexamined as largely a reflection of individual and group needs. The aim was to rework the institution into an organism that embodies values (Peters and Waterman, 1982, p. 85).

Selznick's contributions marked some of the first research on excellent corporations, but there is a deeper tale to be told. Selznick took Weber and stood him on his head: No longer did the bureaucratic institution dictate rules to unfeeling technocrats. Now the personal and private desires and needs of the petty bureaucrats could be used as leverage by the leader to overturn the institution. Burns would add the luster with his notion of transformative leadership, but the message was the same: Something was desperately wrong with institutions and a new kind of leader qua educator was needed. For Weber, rational bureaucracy was the model of the age of modernity; but the price was heavy, with its implications for knowledge control and impersonality. Selznick and Burns sought to build upon the bureaucratic features of modern social organizations by cauterizing the amoral and impersonal features of such institutions via transformative and value leadership.

It is more significant to examine the popular literature on leadership, for it is these works and not obscure research reports that are being read by administrators in search of solutions to the problems facing the schools. Popular books, textbooks, and, last, research papers and scholarly articles seem to impact upon the school manager. Significantly, it is the fundamental assumption that leadership can be learned and that such books teach that stands out in current school crisis situations. In a way, these are self-help books preaching a means for improving one's control over others. It is perhaps significant that such control be seen as "value transformative," for there is a basic humanistic element in educational administration that is not destroyed easily.

Tom Peters's book *Thriving on Chaos* (1988) offers further challenge to Weber's compelling conception of bureaucracy. Peters writes:

Management, as it has been professionalized and systematized, has developed many axioms over the past century. But in the last twenty years, the stable conditions (large-scale mass production) that led to the slow emergence of these universals have blown apart. So now the chief job of the leader, at all levels, is to oversee the dismantling of dysfunctional old truths and to prepare people and organizations to deal with—to love, to develop affection for—change per se, as innovations are proposed, tested, rejected, modified and adopted. (Peters, p. 388)

Peters's solution is found in three "leadership tools": (1) developing an inspired vision; (2) managing by example; and (3) practicing visible management. Leadership must also seek to empower people through listening to them, deferring to frontline people, delegating authority, and by "bashing bureaucracy." Leading must involve a love of change (Peters, pp. 388–389).

Peters argues that when faced with radically changing times, leaders must learn to flex and give by empowering followers and developing a humanistic attitude toward workers. The rapid rate of change is the sole rationale for adopting this new form of leadership. However, the results (from Peters' investigation of case studies such as IBM, Federal Express, and other Fortune 500 companies) are startling. Decentralized and follower-empowered leadership has boosted sales and holdings. The impersonal rational bureaucrat leader a la Weber is no longer "in."

Studies in "Machiavellian Leadership"

With all of its publicity, "Machiavellian leadership" studies have not met with success in the educational sector. Primarily this is owing to the fact that educators (and we include administrators in this group because they are largely drawn from the teaching ranks) see their work as humane in the sense that students are vulnerable and trusting. They have to be dealt with ethically and fairly. Political leadership is more susceptible to Machiavellianism, and the business sector is more likely to adopt self-centered philosophies of wealth and power (see, for example, Robert J. Ringer's *Looking Out for Number One*, 1977).

Amos Drory and Uri M. Gluskinos (1980) looked at Machiavellianism as a leadership construct. Machiavellianism assumes a mistrust in humans, an absence of morality, being opportunistic, and lacking interpersonal relationship skills (p. 81). A scale was developed and an experiment run on university students. Leaders scoring high on the scale tended to give more orders, were more responsive to the demands of the situation, and were less sensitive to group members' feelings. Interestingly, variations in Machiavellianism had no impact on group productivity (Bryman, 1986, p. 25). Thus, the Machiavellianization of leaders was abandoned in mainstream social science.

Nevertheless, there is some danger that, if not in overt form, a subtle Machiavellianism may be played out in some educational settings.

Democratic Leadership and the New Human Relations

Despite the criticism by the far right that humanism is *the* underlying tone in American schools, humanistic leadership did not achieve much success after World War II. Termed the "human relations" model of administration, the educational progressives pushed the notion that educational leadership ought to be a matter of leaders and followers sharing in leadership. Neither charismatic nor impositional, leadership was seen as an interactive process rather than a bureaucratic role.

"Democratic administration," as we have seen, impacted upon educational administration, emerged in the United States as early as 1900 (influenced by the writings of John Dewey), gained significant popularity after 1945, and was later simply called "human relations" (Campbell et al., 1987, p. 43). Despite the initial wide popularity of the human relations model of educational leadership, the model lost appeal in the 1950s.

There has been until recently a distrust of "democratic" as attached to the notion of educational leadership. Emil J. Haller and Kenneth A. Strike (1986) assert:

You may have noticed that we failed to use the terms *democratic* and *autocratic* in our discussion of leadership. The failure is deliberate. We do not believe that describing an administrator in those terms is particularly enlightening, nor that "democratic leadership" (whatever that might be) is necessarily superior to "autocratic leadership" (whatever that might be). (p. 50)

Since schools are not political democracies, but hierarchical organizations with a steep gradient of authority and power lodged in school boards and elected officials rather than teachers and students, Haller and Strike believe administrators must rely upon those above and not the people they rule for their power. Also, the quality of administrative decisions is judged upon reason. The kind of style, democratic or autocratic, matters not at all (pp. 50–51).

A newer interest of critical pedagogical research (e.g., Freire, Giroux, McLaren, and Foster) argues that this dissection of democracy and life is artificial and repressive. The fundamental assumptions underlying modern bureaucracy are immune from attack unless the entire project is seen in the light of its failure in twentieth-century life to provide freedom and equality to the underclass.

Power and authority are co-related with leadership. Recent literature tells of inspired school principals with visions and moral intuition who face inspired teachers with curricular and teaching expertise motivated by student learning. Which party must give in during confrontation? There is precious little the leadership construct says about this basic division of interests, yet without a clear notion of how far to impose one's rule, the principal-leader is on a collision course and teachers will abandon ship. Excellence seems highly correlated to empowerment here and not charisma or domination or rational bureaucratic rule.

As Sergiovanni and Moore (1989) put it: "The culture of management in general, and educational administration in particular, sometimes makes it awkward to speak of transformative leadership in moral terms" (p. 324). However, unless the profession of educational administration rests upon a moral basis, there is little hope that the technological control over others will lead to improved school practices. The key is to understand the competing moral claims that seek to underwrite the leadership in education.

Hence, we see that research has been broadly impacted by trends in the social and behavioral sciences. This interest can further be demonstrated by observing a number of channels of research that have been tied significantly to the educational leadership idea. The following issues have received a good deal of press.

Effective Schools and Leadership

In what ways does leadership impact upon the quality of schooling? The effective schools literature has wrestled with the role of the principal relative to teaching and learning (Austin, 1979; Blumberg and Greenfield, 1980; Bossert, 1979; Clark, Lotto, and Astuto, 1984; Cohen, 1982; Edmonds, 1982; Hoy and Ferguson, 1985; Lipham, 1981; Morris et al., 1984). Not surprisingly, there is little consensus on the importance of administrators, viewed as leaders, and teaching effectiveness. Despite the large number of effective schools surveys and research reports, experts cannot say for certain whether effective schools are a consequence of administrator or teacher variables. The result has been that educational administration organizations, such as the UCEA, have backed off from recommending leadership training for administrators. Marilyn Grady, William Wayson, and Perry Zirkel (1989), writing in a UCEA publication, conclude: "On balance, research evidence weighs as much against as for the notion that great principals make great schools. . . . In view of the seeming contradictions in research relating to the leadership factor, an examination of the terms 'effective schools' and 'effective principals' is in order" (p. 16).

Instructional Leadership

Another dimension of the leadership puzzle is that of "instructional leadership." Simply put, instructional leading is what principals say and do relative to "promoting growth in student learning" (De Bevoise, 1984, p. 15). Generally, these ideas and actions are aimed at school goals, involving supervision and evaluation of teachers, providing resources needed for learning to occur, coordinating staff development, and creating collegial relations with and among teachers (De Bevoise, p. 15). The effective principal literature often includes material on instructional leadership. Arthur Blumberg and William D. Greenfield (1980) in their study of eight school principals argued that leadership was a function of the *character* of the principal. Based on interviews, the Blumberg and Greenfield study relied upon principals' own self-descriptions to provide a consensual list of qualities possessed by leaders in schools. The setting did not matter so much as the notion that the individual principal was able to adapt to and manipulate different environments (De Bevoise, p. 16). Other studies support the Blumberg and Greenfield research, De Bevoise reports.

Viewed from a critical and pragmatic perspective, it is interesting to see "character" masking as the old leadership traits position. Leader/principals are supposed to be innovative, powerful, analytic, "take-charge" types. Whatever the setting, the instructional leader will test the limits of the organization to accomplish his/her ends. Beneath this leadership conception is a Machiavellian self-interest. Manipulative and self-centered, the instructional leader molds organizations to his/her own liking. There is little regard for followers or for institutional culture and history. There is an interesting use of the term "character" here. Blumberg and Greenfield seem to adopt one kind of character (highly manipulative) and moral traits such as treating others fairly, allowing for freedom of expression and action in subordinates.

Humanistic Leadership

One popular solution to the lacunae of leadership in modern schools has been the call for replacing the bureaucratic leader with the humanistic leader. This is based upon the prevailing assumption that leaders in educational settings, because they deal with young and impressionable children, should be more "humanistic" in their leading activities. Additionally, moves are made to identify humanistic educators and place them in leadership roles. Whether one looks at personality traits, situations, or behaviors, leadership, it is assumed, can be taught to neophyte administrators, teachers, and guidance counselors. The argument is that too few people have looked at the rich heritage humanism offers for the development of educational leadership.

While conservative critics may argue that "humanistic leadership" is just another version of "secular humanism"—that making leaders into humanists is just another means of removing religious values from America's classrooms—leadership of a humanistic sort goes back historically to the humanist period in Europe in the fifteenth century. In the United States the argument for humanistic leadership held sway in the late 1960s and in the 1970s until humanism lost its popularity and the conservative attack on secular humanism reached its height.

Efforts to define humanistic leadership often center on some of the characteristics or traits of classical humanism. Humanistic leaders are supposed to avoid rigid structures and processes, they are more people-centered, and tend not to be task-oriented. Humanists historically stressed human freedom over control; they favored scientific procedures over religious revelation or moral intuition; and they tended to be democratic, using group processes to arrive at policy. The ultimate goal of humanistic leadership is typically human happiness through group consensus.

Attacks upon secular humanism as *the* faith underlying the public school philosophy in the United States confuse a sloganized use of humanism with the historic meanings attached to the word. By labeling every evil identified in the schools as secular humanism, the conservative religious critics sought to erect a straw man that could be knocked down easily. The moral majority invented "scientific creationism" as a counterpoint to secular humanism, thus stealing the legitimacy of science for their biblical interpretations. In effect there was an exchange of legitimacy in which science came to mean faith, and faith came to mean myth.

Since it was illegal to teach a religious faith in schools, the critics were able to point to secular humanism as an illegality, while attempting to smuggle their own faith in under the guise of science. The effort failed in the courts, with Louisiana proving the last stronghold of the effort.

However, far right campaigns to undermine humanism in education failed. The historic meanings of the term were preserved by special interests such as liberal political leaders, humanities teachers, and librarians. Dictionaries, encyclopedias, history texts, and other sources could be shown to depict "humanist" as someone who studied the "humanities."

CRITICAL PRAGMATIC RESEARCH ON EDUCATIONAL LEADERSHIP

During certain periods in the history of education, talk of leadership and allied notions of power or authority have come to dominate educational rhetoric. For example, during the "Nationalist" period in education (the nineteenth century), we find a variety of passionate calls for education and educators to take on leadership roles in making the nations of Europe and the Americas fulfill their destinies in the forefront of civilized states. France, England, and the United States experienced a wave of nationalistic schemes for educational reform. The public school system in the United States was a direct consequence of reformers' interest in using schooling as a means of insuring political stability in the face of fragmenting forces such as labor unions, immigrant groups, and so forth. The idea of a centralized school system had been thought of before by such reformers as John Amos Comenius (1592–1670), but it took figures such as Napoleon and Horace Mann to actually implement it.

Thus, centralized leadership and control equaled excellence for educational theorists in the past. Historians David Tyack and Elisabeth Hansot, writing in "Hard Times, Hard Choices: The Case for Coherence in Public School Leadership" (1982a), argue that a public philosophy of education as Thomas Jefferson, Horace Mann, or John Dewey may have understood it had become fragmented in the 1960s and 1970s by splinter group politics. As a result, people for the most part were "unconscious about the forms and direction that leadership in education should take—or even whether leadership is possible" (p. 511). Writing of leadership in 1982, Tyack and Hansot found education in the United States to be a "closed system" of governance by educational experts, who reluctantly faced pluralistic interest groups' demands on the schools. Traditional leaders were dispossessed. Social scientists, with their claim of expertise, had fueled blacks, Hispanics, the handicapped, Native Americans, and others in their efforts to demand dignity and equal opportunity.

Tyack and Hansot wrote in 1982, "One result of these changes—many of them long overdue attempts to achieve social justice for excluded groups— has been fragmentation and discord in the governance of education. Leaders have lost the power to command securely either as aristocrats of character or as experts" (p. 513). With the competing claims of interest groups and the infighting found in the education profession, along with the confusing and sometimes conflicting demands of the "new paperwork empire," "people have sometimes wondered if *anyone* was in charge, if *anyone* spoke with authority and wisdom about public education" (p. 513).

By the end of the 1980s this was no longer true. Americans had come to expect their educational administrators to be leaders and to push schools toward excellence. Competing interest groups no longer competed. In fact, interest group methods that had achieved such success in the 1960s and 1970s had come to fail. In the law courts, the once mighty expertise of social scientists degenerated into petty arguments between advocates of "studies." Efforts that had appeared to be in the best interests of minorities (for example, busing) now appeared to promote even greater segregation and resentment. Behind this barrage of criticism of social science and its methods in the 1980s was the retreat of educational leadership under the guise of respectability. Now school leaders were to be seen neither as men of virtue nor as experts versed in the law, but as strong men armed with the authority of the baseball bat.

Tyack and Hansot called for a new breed of educational leader in 1982, skilled in interpreting the diverse claims of interest groups, a kind of negotiator or interpreter of what the public of publics really wants for its children. Instead the image of the school leader today is someone who is professionally trained in the finer points of deception, authority, and control. Today's educational leader is not cast in the role of moral savior, nor as a social scientist, but rather as a legal officer.

The proposal calling for educator-leaders to redirect the schools is not new. The radical "progressive" educational thinker George Counts argued that teachers be placed in the forefront of change in America during the Depression years. In his speech before the Progressive Education Association (PEA) in February of 1932, he argued that the child-centered approach to education (linked with John Dewey and William H. Kilpatrick) was too narrow a view for progressive education to take. What was needed, he reasoned, was a vital program of social reform with the school teachers in the lead. Later, in a book entitled *The Social Foundations of Education* (1934), he wrote that "the educator should conceive his task in terms of broadest statesmanship" (p. 5). As society had become more complex, the school had assumed the role of a mediating institution with the future. The educator-leader, in the position to shape school policy, was to take his place in the front ranks of society (p. 5). The teacher was to pass on the best knowledge available leading to the transformation of the social order. As leader, the teacher was to indoctrinate the children for this new, improved social order.

John Dewey was not free from the sweeping social reformist rhetoric that marked the 1930s. In one of only a few pieces written specifically about educational administration, Dewey in 1935 said:

His leadership will be that of intellectual stimulation and direction, through give-and-take with others, not that of an aloof official imposing, authoritatively, educational ends and methods. He will be on the lookout for ways to give others intellectual and moral responsibilities, not just for ways of setting tasks for them. . . . He will realize that public education is essentially education of the public; directly, through teachers and students in the school; indirectly, through communicating to others his own ideals and standards, inspiring others with enthusiasm of himself and his staff for the function of intelligence and character in the transformation of society. (Dewey, p. 10)

Thus, from time to time, especially when society finds its goals ill-defined or unrealistic, the schools and educators come under criticism. Historically, the common response has been to call for greater or renewed leadership. A leader is seen as "the man on horseback," inspiring followers to turn defeat into victory and to lift up the downtrodden. The source of such leadership, for Counts and Dewey, was found in the uninitiated teacher and school administrator. Before talk of leadership style or traits, intellectuals in education and social science were willing to let the leadership mystique occur naturally, but with reinforcement. They found leadership to be a normal part of participatory democracy. Leadership arose, for Dewey and Counts, from the circumstances of the social and economic conditions in the United States in the Depression decades of the twentieth century.

More recently leadership, as it has become attached to educational administration, has emerged in the Marxist–socialist literature of the Frankfort School as a solution to the problem of bureaucracy. Leadership has come under critical scrutiny here. William P. Foster, in his article "Administration and the Crisis in Legitimacy: A Review of Habermasian Thought" (1980), attempts to apply the ideas of the philosopher Jürgen Habermas to the plight of educational administration. Drawing upon Habermas, Foster sees educational administration facing a crisis in legitimacy. People no longer have confidence in educational administrators' ability to run the schools; while educational administration has adopted a "positivistic" attitude toward its work in which administrators speak of value-free processes of decisionmaking. By placing emphasis upon how the problems are to be solved rather than the solutions, modern school administrators have become blinded to ethical values (pp. 496–498).

Foster sees Habermas providing an alternative to the positivist stance of current administrative thinking. He is significant in two ways: by linking the present crisis in administration to modern administrative (positivistic) theory in a well-formed argument; and by attempts to develop a "critical theory" with empirically verifiable norms (Foster, p. 499). Drawing upon historical knowledge, Habermas concludes that there are certain key crises modern governments face (rationality, legitimation, and motivation) that are brought on by their assumptions.

First, the crisis in rationality is the consequence of the belief that the ends of administration are not subject to debate, but only the means are to be rationally analyzed. This viewpoint is fairly common, Habermas asserts. Where administration promises to deliver (in the case of education) equal opportunity, reading, writing, and math skills, and then fails, a crisis in legitimacy emerges. And where the technical structure fails to maintain the system, a crisis in motivation follows. A sense of powerlessness pervades the schools today, and it may be argued that this feeling is the result of the crisis in legitimation.

As Foster points out, where the school cannot deliver the goods, the public (and teachers themselves) begins to question the educational system. One result has been the further effort to objectify its own status and to adapt other institutions to the needs of the school system (e.g. preschool, intervention programs, behavior modification, etc.). Thus, the thrust is toward *technical* control, and the myth of management is transferred to teachers and the learning process. Teacher evaluations, testing, and so forth are used to keep the locus of power in the central educational establishment (Foster, p. 501).

The crisis of legitimation continues while the so-called science of administration is unable to completely rationalize itself. The crisis in the schools is related to the larger societal crisis. But the crisis in legitimacy is insufficient to fully decipher the conceptual problems surrounding the use of the conceptions of leadership in education. It is certainly important to realize that administrators pledged to leadership may commit certain errors in analysis and implementation of policy, but the fuller matter of conceptual crisis needs investigation. This book is aimed at doing precisely this.

Foster identified three research thrusts in leadership. "Leadership seems to be related with, or interpreted in terms of, such other dimensions as politics, power, management and supervision and, in these terms, is considered largely a concept of either *political science* or of *social psychology* " (Foster, 1982, p. 3).

Foster goes on to identify a third thrust in leadership study he refers to as a *"sociological orientation"* (Foster, 1982, p. 3). It is this third perspective that seems critical to our understanding of leadership in education, where schooling is seen as a sociocultural process.

As Foster points out, the majority of leadership research studies tend to focus on leadership as either (a) a skill involving the direction of groups, or

(b) a process of personal interactions taking place within a distributive or political framework. Both of these approaches are incomplete and inadequate when seen in the context of modern society owing to the fact that this position (1) rationalizes leadership as a technical act, and (2) idealizes social relations without the benefit of social critique (Foster, 1982, p. 5).

Foster's reconstructed notion of leadership finds the concept to be contextual in the sense that leadership is found in interactions within a community and understood only in terms of the participant members of that group. The definition of leadership is thus situational and "perhaps culture-specific" (Foster, 1982, p. 18). Foster posits three tiers or levels upon which leadership may be studied.

Macro = leadership activities in context of social development, change, and relationships
Meso = leadership in the context of groups and organizations
Micro = leadership seen as individual in which (psycho) biographies of identified and accepted leaders may be studied (Foster, 1982)

Research may be conducted along three lines: (1) What is the nature of leadership in historical, evolutionary, and cross-cultural settings? (2) What are the psycho-biographical dimensions of persons who as leaders engage in decisions leading to social change? (3) Is leadership to be seen as a form of symbolic communication? Is there a manipulation and distortion of this communication? Foster provides us with a Marxist, cultural relativist view of leadership study in which the notion of leadership is seen as contributing to class dominance. Foster sees leadership as ideological. Leadership legitimates the organizational stratification system. What results is a managerial ideology that finds one class subordinate to another. Leadership in schooling has been historically a means to the end of creating an organizational dominance by one elite class (Foster, 1982).

When we apply a critical pragmatic standard to the research on educational leadership it is clear that what is absent is a concern for the normative dimension of leadership. School leadership studies narrowly concentrate on a list of variables, seeking statistical relationships among them, while neglecting the overarching issues that leadership presents. Educational administration theory, dominated by positivistic methods, has promoted this turn away from social philosophic concerns such as ends and values.

Controlled by the "managerial model," educational administrators have lost sight of the need to rethink what they are about. As John Goodlad has indicated (1984), educational leaders have been overly concerned with legal and political matters. We would add that there is a need to discover the ways in which leadership has intervened in the more normal or "natural" ways in which people seek to get things done in a work context. At least part of what the critical pragmatic investigation has revealed (Scholes, 1985; Cherryholmes, 1988) is that school board members, principals, teachers, and students engage in the writing and reading of a "text." The degree to which we see the text as multi-authored is the degree to which we are able to discover the richer ways in which people and organizations solve their problems.

The historic period in educational administration theorizing that seems most rich pragmatically is that of the first half of this century when a more humanistic and participatory mode of educational leadership was advocated. Here the desire was to develop a critical leadership, shared in democratic contexts, with the aim of both enhancing the solution to problems and the skills of the followers as problem solvers. We would like to advocate that research into leadership operations would benefit from this kind of stance today.

From this discussion of the research on leadership it is clear that there has been no long-standing consensus as to what the leadership concept means. Most studies of leadership have centered on very few subjects and have dealt with small settings from business or industry. School-based research draws heavily upon this mainstream inquiry on leadership.

In part the lack of agreement upon what leadership means has been a function of the objectives researchers have had in mind when doing their studies. Leadership, as we have seen, was taken to name some internal set of traits a person possessed despite the situation; or leadership was a set of observed behaviors; or finally, leadership was seen as a function of the situation or setting. During the first part of this century, work was done on viewing leadership as a shared value intimately tied to the democratic context. We believe that this latter view has been largely overlooked in the research literature today.

If we are to make sense of "leadership" for education, we must turn to other sources for aid. It is proposed that leadership must be seen in its wider social and philosophical dimension if adequate use of the notion may be deployed for education.

When we talk of leadership today, it is often in a variety of senses and with a great deal of confusion. Politicians are said to be leaders, manufacturers strive for leadership, military officers seek to manifest leadership, and even educational administrators and teachers are told to acquire leadership qualities to do their jobs better and more efficiently. But, what is "leadership" and how does it fit the tasks of the educator? What is to be argued here is the fact that the variety of conceptions of leadership in vogue today, with their lack of rigor and precision, seriously hamper educational administration by setting up false hopes and unrealistic expectations. Detrimental consequences may result from efforts to graft leadership onto educational administration, supervision, guidance, or teaching. A secondary task is to alert readers to the importance of "critical pragmatism" in the work of educational policy. Where we can gain a clearer vision of the concrete consequences of our conceptualizations, we are the better for it in controlling our life quality.

It is not unusual for educators who are ambitious and wish to improve to model themselves upon the business person. But it is important in viewing the various meanings of leadership and the contexts in which they operate not to make the mistake of simple translation from one setting to another.

We find that educational administrators, in particular, are under extreme pressures to turn their institutions into "excellent schools." The excellence movement reminds us of the Lake Wobegon children (all "above average"). School administrators are "under the gun" to make their units above average. As a result, the competition is so keen that the losers (and there must be some given the statistics) are fearful and sensitive to criticism. It is no wonder, given the pressures of competition, that if "leadership" is a variable that will bring about the desired ends (excellence) then leadership must be had.

School administrators stay on the job for shorter periods now than at other times in our history. Part of the reason for this is that the pressures are too extreme. Perhaps it is too much to ask of them that they manage schools and be leaders as well. Clearly there is something seriously wrong with American education today, but we are using up our human resources (school administrators) at a rapid rate. The added burden of striving to be a leader is more than some educators can stand.

CONCLUSIONS

In summary, in spite of the large body of research on leadership, the definition of the term and the dimensions of the concept are largely unmined. The present study is interested in the ways in which "leadership" has been conceptualized in the literature and world of education. The common talk of leadership and related notions of guidance, bellwethering, directing, command, chieftainship, superintendence, stewardship, headship, and so forth are crucial to our understanding of the conceptual geography and force of ideas regarding leading in the schools today.

We have seen that talk of leadership is conceptually flabby and under-developed. The term "leadership" is used in so many and varied ways that rigor is seriously restricted. It is difficult, for example, to equate admonitions that teachers ought to become educational leaders of the new social order with calls for educational managers and economists to become "instructional leaders." There are stark differences in the context and the responsibilities attached to leading in these two instances. Yet educational thinkers seem untroubled by such gross contradictions.

Michels's pessimistic view of leadership in democratic organizations augers ill for reformers today unless attention is focused upon competing models. Irving Zeitlin (1968) points to the idea of the leader as "conductor" of an orchestra (organization) (p. 227). The symphony will always require a leader in this sense and we may rightly speak of "good" or "bad" conductors based upon the music generated by the group. If we grant the technical necessity of a conductor, we may dispense with the idea that conductors are oligarchs or that followers are disinterested. Rather, the notion of orchestration seems to provide a rich metaphor for education.

We would assume, based upon the large number of research studies of leadership, that more should be known of this concept. This is clearly not the case. Despite the huge literature, no clear-cut generalizations regarding leadership seem to hold. Programs designed to train administrators qua leaders are seriously underconceptualized from the beginning. It is argued in this book that educational leadership requires more philosophical work if it is to function effectively for educational administration. The lack of proper theoretical grounding of the leadership concept has had the result of allowing muddled and contradictory research on leadership to become the norm rather than the exception. We can only blame the philosophers for this.

Another assumption underwriting the present effort is that leadership in education has become so mechanical and axiomatic, with experts advocating the acquisition of leadership "skills," "attitudes," and procedures, that the purposes of education have become blurred and indistinct. As a result, a thrust in the direction of "humane leadership," or "empowerment leadership" (stressing the redirection of dictation of power, focusing upon feelings over facts, and in other ways reframing the leadership concept), is evident today. In the face of calls for greater efficiency and excellence, school administrators, teachers, and parents are being called upon to form "partnerships" in which goals may be accomplished without the formal structures that have marked education in the past. The "Adopt a School" movement may be seen as an effort to move business and industry closer to educational institutional borders (and in some cases cross them) so as to improve academic outcomes in terms of test scores and love of work. These two movements are built upon the simple assumption that leadership is in a state of flux. There is no longer a belief that a "strong man" will take over the reins of the school and redirect it. Present day conditions have forced us to rethink educational leadership.

Among the many possible normative meanings of leadership, we must consider the "philosopher-leader" and "artist-leader"—as these approaches contribute to the idea that leadership involves learning-leaders in school settings. If the research on leadership reveals anything it tells us that all leadership must involve teaching and learning (Senge, 1990). Thus, in educational settings in particular, leaders qua teachers, as creative and innovative thinkers, will be necessary if we are to make the kinds of significant reforms in education required today and in the future.

3

Administrative Leadership, Democracy, and the Qualities of Philosophic Mind

Any theory of leadership must be nested in some notion of a social and political way of life. Leadership is a particular problem for free democratic societies owing to the fact that, unlike totalitarian regimes in which citizens have no say as to who their leaders shall be, democracies require good leadership to grow from public selection processes. Our American republic was established giving citizens the right to choose their leaders, thus the nature of that leadership became focal. However, while a democracy allows us to pick our political leaders based upon criteria (campaign promises, political platforms, voting records, experience, moral character, and decision-making ability all play a role in these choices), this freedom to choose has not always resulted in the best kind of leadership. There is another factor that must be included in the leadership-social/cultural way of life for the equation to work: a critical method of intelligent thinking.

Democracy, as a social way of living, necessitates that leadership, for it to succeed, must grow out of the collective interests of the group and the means that are elected to achieve group ends. It matters not whether the group is a nation or a school, the interest of individuals in the collectivity will be served—eventually.

Traditionally, the view that schools in democracies must represent democratic values and methods has led to a related question: How much democracy is necessary and sufficient to provide the principled continuity of the system while allowing for the maximum democratic participation of human beings involved? The institution of the school provides a test case for this concern.

Two major theories exist: (1) Those I shall call the "democratic maximizers" (e.g., John Dewey, A. S. Neill, Paulo Freire, Henry Giroux, William McLaren) assert that most schools display insufficient amounts of democracy in practice. They point to the lack of parental say in school policy, the voicelessness of students, and the powerlessness of teachers. (2) A second group of thinkers, here referred to as "minimalists" (e.g., Gutmann (1987), Bloom, Wilson, and Barrow), on the other hand, argue that democracy cannot be extended fully into classrooms without risk. Imposition is required if the principles of democracy, as part of the larger societal values, are to be passed on to uninitiated students. Some minimalists point out that expertise nullifies the rights of the untrained in the decision-making processes. They offer as example the restriction of the mentally ill or criminal in such choice-making processes.

At least since the rise of the "common school" in the first half of the nineteenth century, the fundamental democratic principle of freedom of choice never extended down to our schools. Horace Mann and the early school reformers set up a bureaucratic administrative hierarchy which made certain that students did not choose their teachers, teachers had no say in selection of their principals, and principals had no voice in who would serve as superintendent. Parents were not to determine to which school their children would go. Despite efforts to reform it, the institution of the school to this day is not noted for its democratic character—at least not in the classic meaning of that term.

Where democracy does bear upon school operations is in the legislative dictates that are passed down to the educational leadership. Laws and subsequent policies are generated by legislatures and the educational administrator is in the position to interpret and enforce these mandates.

Contemporary calls for change reflect upon this minimalist versus maximalist controversy in schooling. Vouchers, site-based management, teacher empowerment, and other efforts all aim at maximizing the democratic dimension of schooling. Principal academies, certification and licensure, testing of teachers, and other credentialing efforts seek to restrict the voice of those out of power.

While both sides admit the importance of democracy in schools, the type and amount of internal democracy, and with it the kind of leadership that is important for a school, is open to debate. John Dewey believed that a school should be a miniature community, purged of the evils of its larger relative. The University of Chicago Laboratory School under Dewey's direction allowed for exceptionally large democratic participation. Dewey, as leader, treated the teachers as colleagues and met with them weekly to discuss curriculum and other matters. Teachers had a planning period each day during which they discussed teaching ideas with one another. Students, however, did not have the same control over curriculum or teaching, but they too engaged in community discussions regarding learning activities. Amy Gutmann (1987) tells us that the Chicago Laboratory School "was an embryonic democratic society because it elicited a commitment to learning and cultivated the prototypically democratic virtues among its students, not because it treated them as the political or intellectual equals of its teachers" (Gutmann, p. 93). Thus, schools that are most internally democratic seem to balance human participation with the disciplinary purposes of education. These schools leave some educational decisions—such as curriculum and the criteria for promotion—largely, but not exclusively, to the educational leaders (Gutmann, p. 93).

If the ideal school is not a mirror image of the ideal democratic state it is owing to the fact that the school must prepare children for the kind of citizenship that exists in that state. Children do not come to the school with such skills. Thus, minimalists, such as Gutmann, must argue paradoxically that schools may use non-democratic disciplinary means for inculcating democratic values.

Leadership emerges as a variable in this equation. And a critical and pragmatic theory of leadership is required that takes seriously the debate over the democratic nature of schooling. Moreover, leadership is fundamentally a problem of freedom, and freedom always entails consciousness of conditions and voice. Where people have no voice, they must accept leadership as imposed. Authoritarian regimes, dictatorships, and so forth are fundamentally comprised of power and force. Democracies must focus on questions of choice if they are to avoid repression and silence.

It follows that once choice has become central (as it is in democratic ways of life), the processes whereby choices become informed and rich become central. Jefferson argued that education was important because informed citizens made the best choosers. The maximization of democracy is thus warranted on the grounds that reasoned deliberation is enhanced by the skills and information derived from education. An educated electorate is seen as essential to the propagation of the democratic state. John Dewey was perhaps the most outspoken defendant of the importance of education for democracy. In his book *Democracy and Education* (1916), he pointed out that schools needed to be free and open institutions capable of reasoned discussion. Schools themselves had to be democratic if they were to teach children and youth to exercise democratic choice. On the other hand, political democracies were the very best social systems owing to the fact that they allowed for the fullest exercise of choice and judgment; options could be openly discussed in the schools given this floor of freedom.

Democracies were not viewed by philosophers as particularly conducive to philosophy as an enterprise. Plato's *Republic* finds democracy an inadequate form of social life for this and other reasons. Allan Bloom in *The*

Closing of the American Mind (1987) perhaps best represents this view of a minimal democracy in schooling when he argues that the good, the true, and the beautiful cannot be determined by casting ballots.

The third element in our democracy and leadership equation is reflective thinking. A critical method of thought is necessary if participants in schooling choices are to exercise good judgment; and this reflective process must be attuned to the practical changes ideas may make in human conditions. What is the nature of this type of intelligence? Can a critical practical thinking method be learned? How may this type of reason be taught to children? Can we expect of our citizens that they exercise critical thinking in making schooling choices? These and other questions arise from a consideration of the nature of the thought processes which should enable a maximized democracy internal to schools.

In this chapter, I wish to further develop our inspection of leadership by demonstrating a view of democracy as a way of living as it rests upon the greatest possible development of a critical and philosophic method. I utilize the term "philosophic" as a shorthand device for the type of critical thinking or rational process that supports the making of significant choices leading to practice. This kind of critical thought is important as a set of skills to be learned and exercised by citizens, and it is important as a means for interrogating the problem we are dealing with here.

Where we attempt to develop a critical, pragmatic philosophic view to interrogate the leadership issue in its democratic setting, we find a great ambiguity relative to what leadership means in a democracy, as well as face a lack of faith in the methods of philosophy to help resolve this panoply of choices. I shall lay out my argument against the backdrop of the important issue of how our school leaders shall best be prepared for their work.

Thus, when we ask the practical question—Should educational leaders be philosophic?—we have a difficult time making our way toward a reply. Nicholas Burbules (1989) argues that if philosophy is to have any relevance for the administering of schools, it must rest in the promise of philosophy aiding in the investigation of communicative relations that undergird education. These relationships he takes to be crucial in all organized life, "where maintaining lines of democratic authority requires the participatory consent of others" (p. 247). These communication processes are taken to be such activities as negotiating, listening, arguing, understanding, and correcting misconceptions. These actions are pedagogical in nature and by examining them from a philosophic perspective, it is possible "to reveal, for example, how the role of a school administrator is always essentially the role of a teacher and learner, and how the constraints of bureaucratic organization and power relations often interfere with the legitimate performance of that role" (Burbules, 1989, pp. 347–348).

I wish to argue that philosophy has a larger role to play. As part of a pragmatic and critical perspective on leadership, it requires that we seek a critical and reflective approach toward communicative processes in education, but also a critical eye toward the social relationships and undergirding power that support these processes. This is to say that a critical and pragmatic philosophic view of leadership will emerge only as we think critically about the theories in use, the social constructs of reality embraced within organizations, and the forms of knowledge legitimately allowed. Heretofore, notions of leading have subsumed either a rational/technical ideological perspective or a "commonsensism" based on practice alone.

The more theoretical matters revolve around what we take leadership and philosophic mind to be relative to other notions of management and expertise and how conceptions of democracy in education may bear on the entire issue of school administration. This nest of questions is not entirely new, yet it remains highly charged. Without a clear notion of what we mean by "leadership," "democracy," "educational administration," and "philosophic mind," it is difficult to confront rather practical issues such as how we shall educate school administrators. In this chapter, I shall look at some of these questions. The argument will be made that educational administrators should be philosophic, and that the political and cultural context in which the school operates should be seen as a maximally democratic one.

THE CLAIMS

There are a number of logically discrete claims that may be made relative to the preparation of educators in the schools for philosophic skill in leading. These viewpoints have been oversimplified for the purposes of emphasis.

According to the first point of view, "the school administrator should be prepared primarily for educational leadership and only secondarily to perform administrative tasks" (Smith, 1956, p. 83). Philip G. Smith goes on to say that the best way to do this is to teach the new administrator to be "philosophic minded." Without going into the details of Smith's argument, let us characterize this position as L + PM (for leadership plus philosophic mindedness).

The second point of view, which may be termed Sergiovanni #1 (for it was proposed a number of years ago and the author has since modified his position), claims that administrators have so much to do it is too much to ask of them that they lead the school as well as administer it. Therefore, this position argues, the primary task of educational administration programs in colleges and universities is to teach administrators-to-be specific tasks and skills. Since this approach focuses on skills and specific tasks, we may assume that the educational leader need not be trained in philosophy to accomplish them (Sergiovani, 1979). This viewpoint shall be called A – PM/L (for administration without philosophic mindedness or leadership).

A third viewpoint has it that "if heads [school administrators] are characterized by philosophic competence, we should be thankful for their leadership" (Barrow, 1981a). Following Plato, Barrow seems to be saying that how a school is organized (as an autocracy, a democracy, etc.) is not so important as the fact that the shots are called in a competent manner. It may be assumed here, for the sake of argument, that what this position holds is that school administrators should be (hopefully) philosophic in their work, and if they are, then they are capable of leadership. But how schools are organized does not really matter. This view we may characterize as PM + L – D (or philosophic mind plus leadership, minus democratic organization).

A fourth position is also authored by Sergiovanni. This view (we will call it Sergiovanni #2) holds that "leadership and administration are operationally so interrelated that, practically speaking, both behavior modes should be considered as necessary and important variations in administrative style" (Sergiovanni and Staratt, 1979, p. 7). This position is somehow interested in countering the notion that administration is "a less essential lower-status activity, while leadership is viewed as superior." Sergiovanni goes on to say that we find unrealistic expectations of administrators when leadership is prescribed. Sergiovanni writes: "The professional administrator is likely to view his or her role as that of one who finds out what consumers want from schools and who delivers educational services accordingly. The educational leader, by contrast, is very much concerned with the issues of purpose and direction." Sergiovanni here equates "antecedents" with what I wish to term "philosophic mind" (Sergiovanni, 1982). Neither alone is sufficient, for the educational administrator will need to provide both a vision of what ought to be and knowledge of the means to achieve these ideals (Sergiovanni and Staratt, 1979, pp. 4–21). Some balance is needed, therefore, between leadership and administration. This position may be characterized as Some A + Some L + Some PM (or some administration plus some leadership, plus some philosophic mindedness).

ADMINISTRATIVE LEADERSHIP AND DEMOCRACY

It is often assumed that educational administrators ought to be leaders. But, as we have seen, it is not entirely clear what criteria are to accompany this recommendation. On the one hand, leadership is characterized as a superordinate class of philosophic or intellectual insights, while on the other hand, leadership is taken to be synonymous with administration and tends to be reduced to the tasks of managing the school. These tasks are specifiable and lend themselves to repeat performance. Leadership given this latter view is nothing but the routine tasks of management. Moreover, it is assumed that anyone trained in these tasks or skills can be an administrative leader. According to John Wilson and Barbara Cowell (1983), "leaders ought to be chosen on the basis of their expertise, and on no other basis (although ultimately they should be accountable to all of us)" (Wilson and Cowell, p. 114). We should assume that "the fact that some people are just better at politics or indeed morality—flies very much in the face of the Protestant, post-Kantian culture in which we have (most of us) been raised" (Wilson and Cowell, p. 113). In place of arguing for an ideological view (e.g., democracy or totalitarianism) on the basis of its stylistic or regime status, they substitute arguing for philosophic mindedness arising out of the assumed notions that we (1) have pluralistic epistemological notions (some varying according to local conditions); and (2) that an elite of "better" governors ought to be placed in leadership roles (Wilson and Cowell, p. 114). In his article, "Politics and Expertise" (1971), Wilson argues that there can be "political experts," in the sense that "there are people better equipped than others to decide what is right, in the context of ends as well as means, for a society or a state" (p. 34). But such experts are not entitled to enforce their status as experts or their decisions on society. At most, Wilson argues, it would be wise for us to entrust such decisions to these experts. In seeking to justify this claim, it is assumed that we would all agree that lunatics and children ought not to be regarded as political experts, but it is easy for us to determine who in fact are political experts.

But is it all that easy? Simply ruling out people by virtue of their gross mental disabilities or age does not get us out of the woods. Rather, those who lay claim to political expertise are often difficult to evaluate in terms of their claim. This fact is further confused by the raw power, genetic inheritance, or social class that gives certain individuals a prior claim to the credentialing that places them in the corridors of political expertise. We are not far along the way in clearing up what we mean by "political expertise" through Wilson's simple sorting.

Wilson goes on to assert that there are some standard interests and needs that are common to human beings; that not everyone is aware of these; and that political experts have a greater understanding of what people need (as opposed to what they *want*). The conclusion is that the political expert can tell us what is in our own best interest (what it is that we need). Unfortunately, what happens in this kind of argument is that needs are equated to what it is that makes people happy—a utilitarian assumption that twentieth-century citizens of advanced technological states can no longer make. Clearly, there are things that we need, in the sense of should have, which will not make us happy (either in the short run or the long run). The notion that somehow political experts know what is best for us (meets our needs) flies in the face of rational good sense. For who knows better than the human being what he or she really wants, and what service does the institution such as the school, church, and family serve except to teach us how to sort out actual needs from simple desires and wants? It must be recognized too that human beings differ in their needs, and that political experts do not automatically possess psychological insight. Often the contrary case abides. Special education for the handicapped, for example, did not come into existence owing to political experts, but because a number of parents of handicapped children in the United States began applying pressure to the legislators to pass laws removing restrictions (Ravitch, 1983, pp. 307–311). This is to say that a political expert may simply fail to understand human needs where they exist. The political expert may understand them and still fail to implement policy to satisfy them, for purely selfish reasons (e.g., it would lose votes) (Wilson, 1971, pp. 34–37).

One of the difficulties with this particular view of the political expert qua leader (i.e., that leaders are experts, and they are selected for their knowledge of facts and processes) is that it sounds strangely like Plato's *Republic*. We are not far from the view that certain people, either because of heredity or particular gifts of circumstance, are just superior in leadership than others. The idea is that leadership is not so much a set of learned skills as it is a delegated honor bestowed upon the virtuous "philosopher kings." The *Republic* sets out alternative future states, with merits and demerits outlined in advance. What remains is the primary assumption that certain types of conceptual notions (i.e., a view of what "justice" is, for example) legitimatize the authority of the leader. We must then have leaders (men and women, and here Plato was clearly ahead of our own time) who possess the capacity to think rationally and make proper judgments based upon their insights into the "sovereignty of the Good." It is the type of person you are that determines the place (status) you take in society or the state. Leaders are not artisans— and never can be. Leadership revolves around the type of knowledge base that leading requires. Since knowledge is virtue, and one can learn to be virtuous if one has the "right stuff," there is no doubt that the leaders will govern wisely and justly.

It would be incorrect to assume that Wilson and Cowell simply wish to adopt Plato's suggestions, because they point out that "he too put his money on one specific regime" (Wilson and Cowell, p. 116). However, there is much in Wilson and Cowell that Plato would applaud. Certainly he strongly recommended that we exile the poets, because they portrayed the gods in anthropomorphic terms. This can be translated into Wilson and Cowell's suggestion that our leaders should be persons that we imitate. Plato too wished that children imitate good role models and not bad or evil ones. Hence, he called for clear moves of censorship of normative ideological values. In fact, Plato did not really wish to suggest the single utopian solution to all governmental functions; he provides only one kind of ideological scenario for us to contemplate, and it is not clear that he saw his Greece actually adopting any of his views.

If we peel back the conception of human nature in this account of leadership, it is clear that these leaders are special. Just as the reason why democracy and participation "are popular with certain types of people; briefly, it makes them feel powerful" (Wilson and Cowell, p. 114), so it is the case that the reason an a-ideological context is to be preferred is that it allows for the philosopher-king to rise to the position of leadership. Even the method of electing leaders is wrong for Wilson and Cowell (i.e., "No serious business or other organization would choose a leader by the sort of public methods which seems to apply for selecting presidents of the USA, or emperors in the later Roman Principate"). Since we need rule by *experts*, the capriciousness of democratic vote is to be jettisoned as too risky; democratic consensus yields demagogues rather than experts (Wilson and Cowell, p. 114).

What we may call "democracy" is only one term representing a much broader doctrine or ideology currently rampant in the West. The indictment has it that "democracy" does not mean anything very clear; and that it seems to be related to the notion of *power* (which translates to mean: (1) what one thinks important in life; and (2) what particular area or time of conflict or negotiation one is considering). It is assumed that we commonly take for granted the conventional notions as to what is important as the only possible ones, and that democracy refers to *styles* of doing things or regimes. If we buy this argument, then philosophy is rather useless if it focuses on such styles or regimes and how they ought to suit certain sorts of people, under certain conditions. These authors warn philosophers not to take for granted one substantive or specific set of values: to do so makes them "mere ideologists," they argue. This "democracy" refers simply to a style or regime. We are led to believe that it is nice if circumstances allow for democracy and autonomy, but these conditions do not justify democracy (Wilson and Cowell, p. 112).

What seems to be at stake is whether democracy possesses some agreed upon normative status. Wilson and Cowell state: "Many philosophers in fact more or less assume that there is general agreement about the merits of democracy, and hurry on to the question of its practicability" (p. 113). Taking issue with Patricia White's (1983) treatment of democracy, it is asserted that outside of an asylum, everyone can assume: (1) that people can master some body of knowledge; (2) that people are capable of reasoning about moral aspects of political problems; and (3) that people are capable to some extent of altruism. These three factors form the basis of White's assumed value of democracy, it is claimed (Wilson and Cowell, 1983, p. 113).

Thus, in the final analysis we must reject

the idea (to repeat) that there must be a *single regime* which mirrors or incorporates reason, as if political life had somehow throughout to reproduce the social conditions for a philosophical seminar. But (a) this conception of reason is too narrow; it is also (often) reasonable to defer to authority, give and take orders, accept expertise and so forth . . . (b) it is not even true of seminars; here too there are—so long as we are serious about meeting certain standards—authorities, leaders, experts, the wise, people to be listened to and imitated more than others. (Wilson and Cowell, p. 116)

It seems clearly wrong to argue (as have Wilson and Cowell, 1983) that democracy is a style of administration and that it does not much matter relative to education. Democracy is not a "myth," as Wilson and Cowell assert, but a reality. What is mythic is the notion that democracy means very narrowly what certain political definitions make it out to mean, that is, a form or style of governance of underlings. The fundamental questions that seem to undercut all the discussion of the viability of democracy in education is what democracy is to mean in this context. Wilson and Cowell set it out as meaning majority rule and then point out that it is often the case that an expert authority is more useful as a head or educational administrator than an ignorant majority. Moreover, we are told that there is nothing to say that a single democratic individual has a more reasonable solution or decision to a problem than an enlightened authoritarian.

What is getting mixed up is the reduction of democracy to some style of administering or managing an institution (e.g., a school). What is paramount is getting things done correctly (reasonably), and groups may not, by their very nature as groups, do much better than an enlightened leader. My point is that democracy is more than decision making and that it is quite a bit better to run the risk of wrong decisions or messy policy making, if we preserve the *right* of members of groups (like teachers) to play a role in that policy or decision. It seems to me that autocrats generally get into power because the masses of men do not want to be bothered with the petty details, are told that they do not have the requisite skills, or some other such rubbish. Actually, the risky bet that one places on universal suffrage is not all that risky if we add the ingredient of freedom.

R. S. Peters writes:

The point is that methods and forms of organization in schools can never just be regarded as ways of promoting particular objectives. For schools are educational institutions, which means that everything that goes on must be regarded as something that can be learnt, as well as an aid to learning. Thus the authoritarian or business-like efficiency of the head cannot be looked on simply as aids or hindrances to learning. They also provide learning experiences for children in how to treat others. (Peters, 1976, p. 7)

Contrast the above with Robin Barrow's comments:

To some people the above issue [should schools be democratically organized?] is of burning importance. I cannot see it that way. At the theoretical level, it seems to me to make little difference who calls the shots, provided that they are called in a competent manner. I do not recognize any obvious weighty point of principle. In practice, therefore, I would see no reason to complain at variations between schools, some autocratically led by wise and inspired heads, others given over to democracy. All that does matter, both in theory and practice, is that decision-making should be carried out by those with requisite qualities, which must include philosophic competence. (Barrow, 1981a, p. 98)

What is surprising about such a view is its avowed a-technological style. Would that we could create an ideologically free context. Actually, when we dip beneath the surface of Wilson and Cowell's argument we find a very classical liberal position at work. The bare bones of this would be, if flushed out, that the best people somehow rise to the surface and become administrators, if allowed to; that somehow public and private distinctions must be kept intact; that fraternity is rather meaningless, or at least it is not as important as governing well; that equality must never be sacrificed to excellence; and that somehow merit is bestowed. Wilson and Cowell's philosophically minded school administrator would be sufficiently gifted with reason such that there would be one right sort of reasonable way of thinking and doing, and not everyone would be expected to know what that is. Certain experts would be shown to have such knowledge and must be placed in positions of power and authority (in schools, etc.) as leaders.

Actually, two notions of democracy and philosophic-mind are seriously undersupported here. Leadership that does not mine both of these cooperative efforts of the governed (one of the tenets of democracy as Thomas Jefferson set it forth) is doomed to destruction, for those who would be subjected to measures they neither understand nor have an opportunity to forge would revolt. Authoritarianism has within it the seeds of its own destruction. Certainly, on the other side, democracy contains within itself a propensity to self-destruct when the majority fails to register its wishes. Actually, Wilson and Cowell seem to collapse the positivist notion of knowledge (that there is one so-called philosophic truth and one such method) with the liberal notion of mild consensus from the governed. It is as if we ought to respect the office holder because of the office, even though he or she is thief or scoundrel. This kind of meritocracy smacks of a status quo ante mentality clearly associated with the rationalizations of Herbert Spencer and other Social Darwinists relative to nineteenth-century empire building (e.g., "white man's burden").

A Popperian argument may be deployed that asserts participatory democracy provides a check against poor decision making stemming from human fallibility (Smithson, 1983, p. 279). A participationist approach to social and cultural organization is quite old, but the notion that Sir Karl Popper added emphasizes the need to protect the social or governmental mechanisms from the unsuccessful administrators. We must have a way of locating and getting rid of the erroneous policy. Never mind trying to find good or excellent policy, the notion here is that we must seek to eliminate errors from policy making. As Alan Smithson puts it:

Democratic policy-making, for all its recognizable warts, does emphasize the give and take of argument and the free play of criticism, it is a structural recognition of human fallibility and value pluralism, it acts as a crucial mechanism for error elimination, and thus shapes and is free to correct policies, be they at school or government level. When this is borne in mind, the claims of philosophic competence can be kept in proper perspective. (p. 280)

The point is that methods and forms of organization in schools can never be seen solely as the ways to achieve the ends of schooling. Rather they are part of the baggage that we find students taking with them when they leave school.

Certainly there is nothing to prevent us from using the term democracy to refer to the kind of rule of experts that Wilson and Cowell seem to be favoring. Carole Pateman (1970) pointed out that the solution to the problems of industrial democracy need not lie in greater participation upon the part of workers in governance. Not enough research exists to tell us if participation in this sense really amounts to much. On the other hand, an argument may be made for education in this regard. For it may be assumed that educating people to participate would probably lead to greater participation on their part (Pateman, pp. 106–107).

A more reasonable view of democracy was set forth by John Dewey. Leadership in the formation of the controlling aims, methods, and materials of the schools must be placed in the hands of teachers or their representatives, democratically chosen, Dewey argued. The gradual realization of this fact, Dewey remarked in 1937, was finally coming into its own. And even if there were "no authorized regular way in which the intelligence and experience of the teaching corps was consulted and utilized, administrative officers accomplished that end in formal ways" (Dewey, 1937, p. 460).

Despite the expansion of democratic principles in educational administration, Dewey saw the major inroads being made in the application of democracy to pupils. Dewey believed that if teachers were subjected to authoritarian treatment by administrators, they would be apt to treat their own students in an autocratic manner. The arguments that teachers were not ready to assume the responsibilities of participation and that some mechanism like natural selection actually placed the "best" people in positions of authority were both faulty. Dewey felt that until and unless teachers were given the opportunity to participate, they could never assume the responsibility to do so: "habitual exclusion has the effect of reducing a sense of responsibility for what is done and its consequence." Democratic theory argues that the best way to produce initiative and constructive power is to exercise it: "Power, as well as interest, comes by use and practice." Dewey goes on to argue that teaching the young requires support for teachers, and that they can hardly expect to understand what they are doing without sharing in the formation of its guiding ideas (Dewey, 1937, pp. 460–462). Teachers are in direct contact with students, while administrators are at their best in indirect contact. Teachers need to be in contact with one another so that they may pool their shared ideas relative to methods and results: to deny this cooperative effort is to promote waste (Dewey, p. 462).

Perhaps more than any other philosopher of education, Dewey stressed the relationship between democracy and education. He wrote:

The political and governmental phase of democracy is a means, the best means so far found, for realizing ends that lie in the wide domain of human relationships and the development of human personality. . . . It is as we often say, though perhaps without appreciating all that is involved in the saying, a way of life, social and individual. (p. 457)

Going on to lay emphasis on the participative nature of democracy, Dewey states: "The keynote of democracy as a way of life may be expressed, it seems to me, as the necessity for the participation of every mature human being in formation of the values that regulate the living of men together" (Dewey, 1937, p. 457). He asserts that "all those who are affected by social institutions must have a share in producing and managing them" (Dewey, p. 457–458). The exclusion from participation is a subtle form of suppression, according to Dewey. For it prevents individuals the opportunity to reflect and decide the methods and means by which subjects may arrive at the enjoyment of what is good for them. The mass of men may be unaware that they have a claim to the development of their own powers. Individuals suffer, but so does the entire social body (Dewey, pp. 457–458).

Dewey pegs his conception of participatory democracy to human nature. He proposes that we must have faith in the capacities of human nature, human intelligence, and pooled and cooperative experience. Dewey finds himself in direct opposition to the view that some autocrat or authoritarian scheme is better. The notion that a select superior few, because of inherent natural gifts, are endowed with the ability or right to control the conduct of others Dewey finds contrary to his ideal of democracy. Although his conception of democracy is relatively recent in history, he states, "men's minds and feelings are still permeated with ideas about leadership imposed from above, ideas that developed in the long history of mankind" (Dewey, 1937, p. 458).

Another criterial mark of Dewey's democracy is a belief in equality. This is not a belief in equal distribution of natural endowments, but equality of treatment by law and its administration. Dewey goes so far as to say that within institutional settings, the individual has equal right to express himself and his judgments, "although the weight of his judgment may not be equal in amount when it enters into the pooled result to that of others" (Dewey, 1937, pp. 458–1459). Dewey also proposed that we require equality of opportunity, because of the unequal distribution of natural and psychological factors. Finally, Dewey added the criterion of freedom to his list. He called not so much for freedom of action, as for freedom of mind. He had in mind the freedom of intelligence rather than the freedom to do as one pleases. He points out that the Bill of Rights sets forth this intellectual freedom (Dewey, 1937, p. 459).

The significance of democracy for philosophic mind is fundamental: the democratic ethos calls for a full and free flow of information, for the open discussion of issues. Being philosophically minded, then, is to be democratic, given this meaning of democracy. But how do the qualities of philosophic mind differ from mere expert knowledge?

THE QUALITIES OF PHILOSOPHIC MIND

There is a brand of argument, set forth in a number of places, and actually quite ancient, that says that philosophy to be really correct or adequate must take place according to the tenets of reason, and that it is never dependent upon the organizational (governmental, institutional, etc.) or temporal character of the setting (see, for example, Bloom, 1987; Siegel, 1988). Philosophical mindedness is, from this point of view, a completely ahistorical or acontextual method of thinking that provides a foundational or privileged position relative to the discourse and sociocultural contexts interrogated.

Critics of philosophy within mainstream educational administration theory argue that philosophy is typically characterized as either embracing certain logical methods for treating all educational matters, with epistemological puzzlements capable of rational unraveling, or philosophy is equated with ideology and taken to be represented in the effort to postulate one philosophical school (e.g., critical theory, pragmatism) against all others. Donald Willower finds the role of philosophy in educational administration "to be salutary because it has helped to legitimate greater variety in inquiry in the field and because it has prompted some scholars to see their work in a broader context" (Willower, 1987, p. 19). It has also provided a place for values and vision. The negative consequences of philosophic application have been, Willower points out, the attempt to apply philosophy naively or without technical skill, and to restrict philosophical alternatives to two or three, or push one view as an ideologue. Interestingly, Willower's characterization of the status of philosophy *in* educational administration provides a bounded view rationality which has been losing favor, even among educational administration theorists. For Willower and followers, philosophy is doubly damned: on the one hand it suffers from the failure to provide a truly objective account (which can only be offered by "science") of states-of-affairs; on the other hand, philosophy fails as it is just another set of relative points-of-view, no one of which is superior to any of the others.

It is possible to misread Robin Barrow's call for philosophic competence upon the part of school administrators in the policy-making function. Smithson (1983) imputes a conception of "competence" that is neither implicit nor explicit in Barrow's argument. For Smithson, "there is a clear technocratic implication in Barrow's position [relative to the philosophically competent headmaster]" (Smithson, pp. 275–276). The clue to this technology is located, for Smithson, in Barrow's remarks relative to the policy-making competencies of heads (Smithson, p. 276). Without penetrating into the finer points of their disagreement, it is sufficient to point out that these two scholars seem to be missing the fundamental feature of the argument. At least one significant difference is found in the philosophic attempt of Barrow to propose through conceptual exercises a state-of-affairs that Smithson refuses to think of except as warranting actual school administrative practice. Barrow engages in the *what if* form of argument, while Smithson treats it as necessarily descriptive of actual administrative conditions in the schools.

Barrow has it wrong, Smithson points out, when he defines "philosophic competence" in the context of curriculum policy making as knowledge about the content of curriculum. Content knowledge, in this instance—for Barrow seems to be more philosophic in nature—that Smithson reads as "technical knowledge." Smithson would have the philosophically competent head having expertise relative to curriculum. But Barrow talks about policy-making expertise relative to curriculum and this knowledge is clearly different (and less significant for Smithson). For Smithson, knowledge of curriculum content is knowledge about curriculum and how it relates to policy making; while for Barrow, it seems that one may be expert in curriculum policy making without being a curriculum specialist in Smithson's narrower meaning of the term "competent" (Smithson, p. 277).

The philosophically competent administrator, as outlined by Barrow, can only be an expert in policy making if he is treating curriculum policies technically (i.e., as a means to ends that have been determined elsewhere). For Smithson, if the head is determining ends, then the philosophically competent head cannot be a policy-making expert, given Barrow's definition of the task. For, according to Smithson, the head is merely expediting the "right" policies determined elsewhere, and being an expert on right policies is clearly nonsense for Smithson (Smithson, pp. 277–278).

Simply put, for Smithson, Barrow's philosophically competent head is a technocrat. This is to say that the philosopher-administrator is one who seeks ways to implement policies set by others. But Smithson wishes his headmasters to be philosophic in a prior sense (ivory tower philosophers), asking basic questions that set the scene for effective policy making but never getting into hard questions of decision making and application (let alone test). In addition, Smithson has a rather naive notion of the policy-making function of the school executive; it is not separate from implementation and testing. Barrow seems to have a more realistic view of the policy-making process, although he stops short of making policy-makers responsible for the consequences of their policies and wishes to elevate them on the formation side only (Maxcy, 1984, pp. 327–336).

Thus, we see two distinct notions of the qualities of philosophic mind as they apply to educational administration and leadership. For Barrow, according to Smithson, the philosophically competent administrator must be a technocrat and an authoritarian, because he or she is an expert in the narrow sense of representing certain interests. Smithson, on the other hand, wishes the philosophically competent head to yield to the democratic interests of participatory governance, making policy responsive to the school-based (teacher) curricular interests (Smithson, pp. 276–279). Smithson is concerned that a technocracy tends to insulate policy issues from public scrutiny and control. Where one has a technocratic view of the philosophically competent head, then he or she fails to recognize the rights of teachers and others to share in the power of curriculum making (Smithson, p. 280). Administrators in the name of "professionalism" wish to retain full control over curriculum (and here we have the British context in mind rather than the American), while teacher organizations wish this function to be shared with teachers. There is a real danger in this, however. For Smithson sees teachers assuming the same sort of technocratic rationale for power and control over curriculum matters that administrators have held. He is distrustful of any monopoly over curricular policy. Once teachers have assumed more of a voice in curricular policy making, they run the risk of becoming technocratic like the headmasters. The consequences would be future parental and citizen resentment, Smithson believes.

THE PLACE OF PHILOSOPHY IN EDUCATIONAL LEADERSHIP

What then *is* the place of philosophic mind in educational leadership and administration? An alternative viewpoint to that of Barrow and others is found in the work of Philip G. Smith (1956). Nothing in Smith's conception of "philosophic minded" points to a requirement for expertise, in the sense of knowledge of some particular domain. This is to say that it is possible to be philosophic regarding a policy area, without being an expert (in the sense of trained as a policy analyst, let us say) in that domain. Philosophy here refers to a set of intellectual skills that may be applied to a wide variety of matters. In Smith's view, philosophically minded administrators are ones who have a generalized or foundational set of processing capacities. He identifies the "philosophically minded individual" as someone who "seems to exhibit characteristics which may be grouped along three interrelated dimensions, namely, comprehensiveness, penetration, and flexibility" (Smith, pp. 30–31). These characteristics are defined as:

COMPREHENSIVENESS

1. Viewing particulars in relation to a large field
2. Relating immediate problems to long-range goals
3. Utilizing the power of generalization
4. Maintaining tolerance for theoretical considerations

PENETRATION

1. Questioning what is taken for granted or is self-evident
2. Seeking for and formulating fundamentals
3. Utilizing a sensitivity for implication and relevance
4. Basing expectations on an abductive-deductive process

FLEXIBILITY

1. Being free from psychological rigidity
2. Evaluating ideas apart from their source
3. Seeing issues as many-sided and developing alternative hypotheses
4. Maintaining a tolerance for tentativeness and suspended judgment. (Smith, pp. 30–31)

Rather than being trained in particular narrow disciplines, we may argue that educational leaders ought to be prepared to be philosophically minded. Smith writes: "It is believed that the truly philosophic educator makes decisions concerning problems of education in the light of a relatively systematic and carefully formulated set of philosophic insights" (Smith, p. 93). These insights are gathered from a variety of sources. A person's philosophic mind is rather like his or her character or personality, Smith argues. Moreover, it is never fully complete, but subject to change and modification over time. As such, a philosophic mind is not simply given or taught to another person: it must be worked at and refined through actual transactions with others. Hence, for Smith, educational leaders ought to be philosophic. As such, they are not narrow experts in curriculum or reading methods, but much more like emergency room medics, capable of responding to the unusual as well as the usual administrative difficulties.

Giroux (1988) characterizes a model of critical pedagogical reform that is built upon the conception of "teachers as intellectuals," by which he means educators capable of critical philosophical discourse. He writes:

> The notion of rationality has a dual meaning. First, it refers to the set of assumptions and practices that allows people to understand and shape their own and others' experiences. Second, it refers to the interests that define and qualify how one frames and engages in problems confronted in lived experience. (Giroux, pp. 3–4)

Here Giroux points up the two uses of "reason" that color the methods deemed appropriate to educational leadership. There is the additional matter of the "problematics," or conceptual structures, which all forms of rationality use to frame their questions and validate their techniques and to limit or omit matters not acceptable to the framework (pp. 4–6). "Ideology" is a set of doctrines, Giroux points out, as well as a medium by which people make sense of their own experiences and those of the world of which they are a part (p. 5).

Paulo Freire casts educators as intellectuals and laments the fact that as intellectual leaders educators reproduced a division between mental and manual labor without ever developing a theory of practice. On the other hand, Marxist thinkers have created theories for practice or technical instruments for reform, but then overlooked the need for dialectical reflection on the everyday experiences of people. Freire frees himself from this bind by redefining "intellectual" to apply to all men and women. Facing repression, groups form their own transformative intellectuals who seek to remake conditions for social change (Giroux, 1988, p. 118).

Douglas Simpson and Michael Jackson (1984) argue that teachers (and we may expect administrators as well) ought to develop philosophic qualities of mind that not only help in school situations but in life generally. Simpson and Jackson identify three dimensions of philosophic mind: analytic, normative, and synoptic. We are told that educators ought to develop along these three dimensions and this development ought to be lifelong. The claim is that these qualities of philosophic thought cut across the disciplines and domains of expertise and provide insights and understanding that narrow training in the fields of knowledge overlook. We are led to believe that in classroom, staffroom, or faculty reports, there is room for this overarching kind of philosophic mind.

Now, one critical hinge upon which the argument over philosophic competence as a feature of administrative leadership seems to hang is that of "expertise." The claim that Barrow and Wilson may be espousing "technocratic rationality" with their injunction that our leaders ought to be primarily "experts" is perhaps no more dangerous than the recommendation that leaders be philosophic minded, if we have in mind just another ideological viewpoint. Certainly, there is a similarity in the fact that both notions provide networks of guiding concepts and normative standards for conducting inquiry and solving problems. This is to say that we really are no farther along by countering a technocratic model of democracy with a philosophic one of Marxist or other orientation. Thus, we may argue that a leader does not remove the taint of ideological mind by assuming philosophic mind. Philosophic mind may be ideological as well. In fact, there are certainly a number of definitions of philosophic mind that could be used in this context.

There is certainly no doubt that today we defer to the authority of experts rather routinely and with increasing regularity. Whether such experts have our best interests in mind is often unknown, yet we are suspicious that it may be the case that expertise is disinterested in the client's individual welfare. Rather than asking for, and/or receiving, "good reasons" for expert authority decisions, we are likely to simply defer to the authority of the expert. Thomas Haskell (1984) writes, "in ordinary parlance one of the best reasons we can offer for choosing a course of action is that it comports with the advice of a recognized expert" (Haskell, p. x). We rely upon experts because we lack the fundamental knowledge that is required. Moreover, it is assumed that in many instances we would be foolish not to follow the advice of the expert (e.g., in the case of a physician diagnosing cancer or legally consulting the construction engineer for girder stress limits, etc.).

We assume (1) that there must be good reasons behind the decision of the expert authority; and (2) that the area of expertise is not that of ordinary experience. We see educational administration becoming a domain of knowledge that is no longer ordinary. In the past, it was believed that school-keeping was commonsense (more like housekeeping than engineering). Today, we find the knowledge level and complexity requires special skills and knowledge. The vocabulary and theory have become increasingly remote from the ordinary language experience of the school teacher. This trend is not unique, having invaded the business community as well. Because our lives are constantly confronted by experts, it may be argued that expert authority and the status deference associated with such authority have become the defining characteristics of modern life (Haskell, p. xii).

In recent years we have become somewhat disenchanted with aspects of expert authority. Malpractice suits in medicine and law mounted at alarming rates. A decided trend of late has been toward a less antagonistic approach toward experts and the social class they inhabit, but there is a continuing raw suspicion that something may be wrong with the ultimate faith and trust we have located in expert authority. Coupled with this distrust is that of the relationship that has emerged between expert authority and power. Critics of expert authority point out that the special privilege that experts have relative to knowledge provides a real opportunity to turn it against individuals and groups. Since expert authority has an interest in preserving its control, it is not entirely unlikely that this authority could be used to subvert the interests of those it purportedly serves. The possibility that such power could be misused is evident.

The general issue of expert authority throws light on the sources of that authority. The role of education (i.e., colleges and universities) in credentialing experts is open to criticism. There is a sense in which the gate-keeping function of the university, college, and professional school is a kind of power or control that requires scrutiny. The curriculum expert increasingly is a graduate (degreed) person from an "accredited" program in an institution of higher learning. The educational institution or credentialing agency determines who and how many experts are produced. Magali Larson (1984) points out that the function of the educational institution is to socialize us into accepting deference toward the experts it produces. The educational institution recruits and trains these experts and in the process undermines efforts to challenge the elite nature of the enterprise (Larson, pp. 28–80). Larson writes: "Expertise, it can be argued, increasingly provides a base for attaining and exercising power by the people who can claim special knowledge in matters that their society considers important" (p. 28). Whether this group of professional experts constitutes a "class" and whether it will provoke an ideological war between elites in the community are open to question; however, in education there seems currently to be no evidence of such a dispute emerging: school boards, for example, seem content with educational administrative expertise as it stands.

In the light of this discussion, we see that Wilson and Cowell, and Barrow, give witness to the replacement of the ideology of participatory democracy in education as a norm with the ideology of expert authority and professionalization. Rather than resting on reason, the doctrine of expert authority is based upon the private monopoly of expert knowledge, originating in universities and colleges and sanctioned by credentialing bodies. There is a group of educated experts, exercising intelligence and drawing upon a knowledge base unavailable to the average person. A new professionalism yields an intellectual strata of society and supports the meritocratic assumptions of this model, further advancing its power to affect decision making and policy in education.

What is questionable is whether educational administration constitutes this unique knowledge domain and the fact that the public cannot gain access to it or—barring this—cannot decide educational policy without it. Whether or not expert authorities, too, have some responsibility for making public the processes used in arriving at policy is a legitimate question. What are the limits of power expert authority may exercise? There is a very real danger that a monopoly over knowledge domains may lead to excesses of political power over social groups (teachers, students, parents, etc).

CONCLUSIONS

From the foregoing it is evident that educational leadership changes its meanings in terms of the type of political culture (in this case democratic) it operates within, and the kind of notion it has of expertise (from narrowly intellectual to philosophic-minded). It has been argued that there are dangers in assuming that democracy is mere ideology and that any ideological context is as good as any other so long as the task of administering is done well. Moreover, I have cautioned that expert authority is not free from crucial moral/ethical difficulties and that philosophic-mindedness may be better seen as a set of skills of thought than a body of administrative theory or knowledge.

On the other hand, it seems that certain conceptions of democracy go well with what one means by philosophically competent. What is surprising is the readiness of some philosophers of education to hamstring philosophic mind in exchange for efficiency of leadership. While the problems of educational leadership are enormous, I wish to argue that we are not better off by trying to make philosophy into a positive science. What seems to emerge from this analysis is that educational administration should be more philosophic first and that such competence may count toward what we mean by leadership. There is, in addition, a need for being democratic, if by this we mean that the avenues of communication and dialogue be kept open and free.

4

Educational Leadership and Policy

Until the 1960s educational policy was left primarily to the states and little attention was given to it by the federal government. However, beginning with the administration of John F. Kennedy, policies came spilling forth as the tentacles of educational reform (Graham, 1984). Today every educational institution orbits around a diverse set of goals, programs, and operating rules and procedures called "policies." Knowledge of the making, enforcement, and evaluation of policy is central to leading institutional groups in any complex western nation.

The critical and pragmatic view of leadership I wish to establish here requires that we face certain assumptions: (1) participants in the institution of the school must have a clear and reasonable perception of the function or role of policy in its day-to-day operations; (2) the policy function must be such as to include the largest share of affected persons, with the outcomes of policy a respecter of human dignity; and (3) a related view of educational leadership vis à vis policy must be nested in a normative democratic conception. It will be argued in the pages that follow that a theory of leadership must be joined with a conception of policy making, implementation, and evaluation as rationally practical, with both a positive view of human nature and a vision of schooling as a democratic way of life.

Strong pressure exists in academic circles to introduce "leadership" into educational governance in response to calls for accountability, competency, and effectiveness; it is often owing to the single assumption that leaders somehow have a special knowledge of policy. It is assumed and anticipated that educational leaders will be able to pull schools out of the doldrums and usher in a new era of educational productivity because leadership somehow brings with it more know-how about the operating rules of an organization than the rank-and-file may possess.

It is knowledge of the policy function that provides the special appeal of expert authorities as leaders. In the following pages I shall examine: (1) the conceptual territory of leadership; (2) policy and its meaning (creation, action, and evaluation of policy as these bear upon the understanding of members of the group); (3) policy making, although requiring some technical knowledge, as it relates to other knowledge domains; and (4) a pragmatic theory of educational leadership, resting upon a democratic ideal, utilizing what we know of how policy operations may be conceived of normatively.

Whether it is the assumption that school administrators as leaders can inspire teachers to become more "productive," and more productive teachers means students will learn more, or the notion that leadership can be taught to school administrators through training seminars, short courses, and other pedagogic means, the standard version of policy thinking rests upon an exclusionary vision. Policy study is taken to be a special form of *techné* (technical knowledge) free of values. Educational institutions, it is often suggested, troubled by economic and scholastic shortfalls (mirrored in drop-outs, lower test scores, etc.), must adopt "policy leadership" as a solution to these crises. Such thinking propels us to consider pragmatically and critically the interface between leadership and policy in education.

Attached to this move to make policy the aspect of leadership as the solution to practical crises facing schools, we find the educational policy operation moving from a more democratic and consensual participatory posture to one of authoritative imposition and dictation. The argument seems to be that since schools face such serious problems over the short run, the normal processes of policy formation and implementation must be amended, with the result that fewer participants in an educational institution are privy to the processes employed in arriving at the operationalizing rules governing the institution.

And finally, policy is currently seen as the arm of social reform with special emphasis upon creating policies dealing with teacher evaluation, student equity, curriculum content, school and system restructuring. Departments of policy, public policy, and educational policy are found sprinkled throughout higher education today. By and large the techniques and resources of the social sciences are being applied in efforts to make policy more scientific and more fruitful. The assumption is that policy has become the single most important means for accomplishing changes in the schools today.

LEADERSHIP: THE CONCEPTUAL GEOGRAPHY

Short-circuiting the normal policy process has become a fashionable alternative for the development of the "new school executive." The popular literature of education and reform sees the various conceptions of leadership sharing a truncated value/descriptive status that leads to confusion and unrealistic expectation for reform through policy. The more scholarly research literature on leadership, as we have seen, forces the concept into three main categories: leadership qua personality traits; leadership qua environmental setting; and leadership qua behavior (Griffith, 1979). These conceptions of leadership have a long history in the world of business, but more recently, the concept has proved of increasing interest to educational administration as it has come to be linked to the creation and implemention of "public policy" scholars. There are, broadly speaking, two recommendations being made today regarding leadership education: (1) It is popularly suggested that for schools to be reformed it is necessary that educational administrators ought to be changed into inspired leaders; and/or (2) it is suggested that there be a restructuring of college or university departments of educational administration to reflect a new interest in "leadership training" (Sergiovanni, 1979, pp. 388–394). It is taken for granted that "educational leadership" is a distinct field of research and teaching and that the typical ways in which educational administrators are prepared must be altered.

It is not altogether clear that either of these views will solve the large problems in education. And it can be argued that such moves will neither release educators and students from bureaucratic repressions, nor fulminate into significant reforms in equitable delivery or receipt of public education.

ADMINISTRATORS INTO LEADERS

As we have seen, from a conceptual standpoint educational leadership is quite murky. "Leadership" is used as an adjunct to policy: it is seen as a way to name certain attitudes aimed at changing educational practice. Leadership training seminars seek to radically alter the values and beliefs of educational administrators in terms of enthusiasm, dedication, responsibility, organization, and so forth so that key transformations may be made in the direction of a school or educational program (W. Schultz, 1977). Little is done in such efforts to explore the often conflicting theories and meanings of "leadership" or the logical bearings alternative conceptions of leading may have upon the day-to-day affairs of schooling.

To designate the head of an organization or institution, we use words like captain, president, CEO, prime minister, head, general, and chief. However, the idea of "leader" seems to carry with it additional weight and importance beyond that expressed by these roles and offices. The conceptions of leadership in use today in business and education have quite a different meaning than the foregoing terms owing to the fact that while these common designations denote a role, "leader" and "leadership" connote a special human being possessed of clarity of vision and appropriate means for accomplishing tasks. The terms "leader" or "leadership" have a halo effect, conferring worth and value to the designate and high regard for the program or plan. It is this peculiar aspect of "leadership" that marks a distinguishing feature of this term. For a person may be a captain without being a leader, for example, but where "leadership" is attached, the role is transformed into a venue.

The point is that current usage seems to place an additional patina of positive value (from the stance of at least some group, not necessarily one's own) upon the role-taker. The notion that there are foolhardy, charismatic, or ruthless kinds of leaders does not detract from the fact that a leader has this weight and value within the group.

As sloganistic concept, "leadership" and attendant arguments for its nourishment often seek to gather followers and supporters (Scheffler, 1960). It is an encouragement to accept uncritically a particular educational policy or set of policies that appears of interest here. There is an assumption that it is counterproductive to the ends of leadership if the inner workings or finer details of the cause are exposed. A "leader" may be hired to "turn things around," or "stir things up," or in some other way to make radical departure in policy. Leadership in this way functions as a kind of eulogized codicil attached to an administrative effort. Credibility and support for a program or policy is gathered through attending to the antecedent values of "leadership" itself. In this way leadership becomes self-reflexive.

In this sense, leadership has a career and can exhibit a history (often from the honeymoon period to termination or retirement). Tyack and Hansot (1982a) discuss leadership in this historic dimension. The sloganistic meanings of "leadership" may begin with an emotional plea for support for a policy direction and later develop into a cult of followership; or the program may encounter rough waters and the leader be demoted, fired, or in other ways separated from the initiation phase of the policy operation. Hence, leaders and their messages are often difficult to separate, and the rational content of the message may be intimately tied to the paradigm they inhabit. "Leadership" seen in this contextual and sloganizing way is endemic to the literature of education. This escalates the confusion surrounding sound educational administration and turns administrators in schools into policy prelates: the policy process is linked to an almost metaphysical expertise that is insulated from critical scrutiny.

CONFUSING ADMINISTRATORS WITH LEADERS

Leadership is often confused with administration: few writers have attempted to distinguish the two. For Christopher Hodgkinson (1983), "administration is philosophy-in-action." This philosophy in action finds its expression, in at least one strong way, through policy. Hodgkinson holds that administrative processes tend to be abstract, qualitative, strategic, and humanistic—hence they are philosophic (p. 26). (Management, on the other hand, is concrete, practical, pragmatic, quantitative, technical, and technological in nature for Hodgkinson.)

Hodgkinson provides us with a model of leadership in which:

Organizational values are articulated by top level administration through philosophical processes (argument, dialectic, logic, rhetoric and value clarification). This is the level of *idea*. The idea emergent from this first phase must be translated into some sort of plan and reduced to a written, persisting and communicable form. This form must then be entered into a political process of persuasion. This is the domain of power, resource control and politics, and we have moved from the level of ideas to the level of *people*. Coalitions must be formed, levers pulled, persons persuaded as power and support are marshalled around project or plan. Each of these three process phases of administration can be subsumed under the rubric of policy making. (p. 26)

There are several difficulties with Hodgkinson's characterization of leadership. First, it is not clear that leadership and administration are co-equal. In fact I have argued that they are both logically and practically separate. Second, while leadership and philosophy seem to be intimately related, it is not the case that leadership has historically entailed philosohy. Not since the days of Alexander the Great have leaders been schooled in philosophy to any extent. This is not to say that leaders should not be so educated. Rather, I wish to propose as a *normative* recommendation that leaders be trained in philosophic thinking. Third, Hodgkinson fails to see *pragmatic* as a school of philosophy that is wider than mere pragmatics. Thus, he overlooks the possibility of a philosophy of leadership that grows out of the practical situations in which leaders find themselves, but is not reducible to expediency (the grossest form of pragmatism).

James Lipham (1964) points out that whereas leaders tend to initiate action, administrators typically do not. Administrators tend to govern small and structured groups, while leaders are usually associated with large, unstructured groups. Finally, the leader tends to have a set of personal goals, while the organization has group goals and administrators are more responsive to them (Lipham, 1964, pp. 139–141). While some of the differences may be argued against, the important point is that Lipham, for one, has begun attempting to sort out the crucial features that mark leaders as separate from administrators.

Within the category called administration it is possible to make further sortings: There is often confusion between leading and management. Robin Barrow (1976a) sees the manager as one who has "responsibility for directing and who concerns himself with the satisfaction of all persons involved as well as with the success of the firm, business or whatever." The manager is one who serves as an overseer, for Barrow. The chairman or chief executive is one "who controls procedure at meetings that may give rise to policy decisions and who has the authority to carry out decisions thus arrived at" (Barrow, 1976a, p. 81). Neither office-holder need be a "leader."

Hodgkinson (1983) argues that leadership and management are one and the same. He found that other studies of leadership failed (1) to distinguish between the logically different categories of administration and management; (2) to acknowledge the intrinsically philosophical nature of administration; and (3) to draw some general implications about differential expertise within administrative processes (p. 26). The result of seeing leadership and administration as distinct and proposing that leaders emphasize newness, change, as well as seeing them as policy implementers, is to somehow view administration as a lower-order activity and leading as higher. Additionally, perscriptive literature which tells administrators how to behave will tend to stress "leadership" behavior over other dimensions of leading. And emphasis will be shifted to talk of leadership "styles" (e.g., democratic, humanistic, Machiavellian). It follows that leadership training may expect unreasonable goals, and administrators may come away from such sessions with a feeling of guilt, anxiety, or inferiority owing to their inability to operationalize the conceptual overlays of uniqueness-producing, radicalization, or innovation (Sergiovanni, Burlingame, Coombs, and Thurston, 1980, p. 7).

Admonitions that supervisors become leaders are equally problem-fraught. Supervision and leadership appear to be fundamentally different. Supervisor status in administration gives us the clue as to why this is the case. Supervisors tend to regulate states-of-affairs and manage personnel. In the educational sphere, supervisors are either administrative supervisors (in which case they tend to do what administrators do) or instructional supervisors (in which case they tend to do what teachers do). While supervisors generally may see it as their task to inspire people, they do not have followers in the sense in which leaders have them. Devotees, advocates, and those won over to the newer methods of teaching do not attach themselves to the supervisor in the way followers become identified with a leader and his/her program. Supervisors help to get the job done, but they do not set agenda or direct the attainment of goals the way leaders do. Like other administrators, supervisors are not at liberty to formulate radically new departures in education, nor do they serve at the behest of their clients (Campbell, 1977, pp. 11–14). Therefore, to call for supervisors to become "curriculum leaders" is to charge supervisors with a mission that is ill-suited to pursue their role. Regulation and rule-interpretation are different activities from rule- and regulation-setting. Often supervisors are viewed with suspicion when they purport to set new directions in teaching-learning, rather than reinforce accepted methods. In an age of accountability, few teachers are tricked into believing that the curriculum supervisor is a leader in any serious sense of that term.

EDUCATIONAL POLICY AND LEADERS

While it is important to sort out the concepts of manager, chairman, and so forth, it is perhaps more vital to see the function of leadership as it relates to policy. Where the administrative position calls for the exercise of policy formulation, it may be argued, we come closer to some more generic requirements of leadership. In this matter, James Lipham (1964) and Sergiovanni et al. (1980) seem to be on the right track when they argue that leadership has associated with it the capacity to innovate or introduce uniqueness. On the face of it, a large number of administrative tasks could be conducted by clerks or other staff members without the loss of effectiveness or efficiency (in fact, with probable improvements in these areas). Thus, it is possible to argue that leadership has as a necessary condition normative matters that have heretofore been neglected in the literature on educational administration.

Whether administrators ought to necessarily be made to feel inferior or guilty because they are not able to measure up to certain defining characteristics of leadership seems less significant than the fact that administrators who are called upon to initiate new directions in education ought to be aware of the normative demands associated with leading. The policy operation is a case in point. I wish to argue that there is a moral/ethical responsibility for the educational administrator as he/she exercises the policy role. However, there are certain dangers in talking in this manner, which I shall address at a later point in this book.

There is perhaps no more singular node of leadership controversy than that of the operation of policy in an institution. Misunderstanding policy, misappropriating policy, or in other ways failing to know when policies apply and to whom, generates a crisis in confidence, confusion in direction, and overall breakdown in daily operations. Leaders must know policy if an organization is to succeed in achieving its goals. Leaders must engage in policy deliberation and formulation, analysis, and evaluation at least part of the time. It is reasonable to expect that since policy is so central to educational institution functions, leaders-to-be are better off knowing about how policy comes into place and how to improve it than not.

For us to understand policy we must see it in its larger paradigmatic network. We must necessarily not divorce educational policy from the inquiry or research method that informs policy. To say this is to admit that the policy process is intimately related to the intellectual means of policy creation and production. Facts do not precede policy. Policy science does not await the accumulation of facts before developing policy. Rather, policy and method are interspersed and interwoven. The values that govern both the so-called "policy science" approach and the resultant policies are recursive and reflective. The old "grounded theory movement" in educational administration, as a research strategy, was ill-conceived owing to the fact that fact-gathering may be interminable and, as the Quine–Duhem thesis has demonstrated, we may (and do) adjust our theoretical nets to account for factual anomalies.

WHAT IS EDUCATIONAL POLICY?

Educational policy is a form of social policy and has grown in importance since the 1960s as a field of study. Educational policy operates relative to the social institution of the school. And when we argue for or against an educational policy, we engage in a peculiar type of discourse. Although policies are supported, Stephen Toulmin et al. (1984) tell us, as a form of managerial argument, with management being inherently teleological (i.e., concerned with the achievement of organizational goals or ends), for Toulmin it requires formal skill in argument analysis. Israel Scheffler (1985), on the other hand, cautions the educators of future policy leaders that policy is not mere technical knowledge. Policy argument as subsumed beneath managerial thinking is an incomplete model. Following Scheffler (1985), I shall argue that while it has been assumed that policy reasoning is intimately connected with managerial thought, it need not be. This is to say that, following a pragmatic view, educational policy may be seen as a practical discourse that takes its strength not from expediency and efficiency, but rather from concerns for human values that should underwrite any activity that seeks to improve life.

"Policy" may be further defined as a definite course or method of action selected from alternatives and in light of conditions to guide and determine present and future decisions; or "policy" may mark the product of a search for such action. Robert Heslep (1987) argues that much of the contention surrounding educational policy arises from a failure to understand the structural features of policy as a product. He identifies these as: (1) the policy statement; (2) the utterance of the policy; (3) the recipients of the policy; and (4) the course of action and goal. Heslep offers a set of guides for the elimination of controversies arising over policy definition, justification and authority, while admitting that some debate over policies is desirable (Heslep, pp. 423–432). Educational policies are rules for the guidance of or determination of a class of decisions which may (or will) arise in future operations of the institution of the school. Policy regulates decision behavior. Since policies operate in different settings, they tend to be responsive to contextuality. Therefore, policy as normative rule lacks universality. Hence, what may be a "good" policy in one school or school district may be "useless" in another. As rules, policies are designed to regulate a number of decision-situations through reasoned control (Ballinger, 1965).

It is possible to identify at least seven different kinds of policies/rules: (1) "Hard and fast policies," which are narrow and require little judgment; for example, the policy that sets the number of credit hours a student must have to graduate. (2) Policies of a highly judgmental type that use multiple criteria. By way of example, a policy setting student admission standards uses high school grades, test scores, extracurricular activity, parent income, and so forth. A number of variables are applied, but it is not certain how much each counts. (3) Substantive versus procedural policies. A procedural policy would call for steps to be taken to accomplish some end. For example: once a book has beeb labeled "obscene," what must be done to remove it from the library? A procedural policy decides what must be done once something is identified. A substantive policy decides *how* something is to be done. This kind of policy aims at providing the "paper trail" through an organization. For example, a student caught cheating may appeal, under X circumstances. (4) Criterial or deliberative procedural policies. These policies call for reasons to be given at certain points in the process. For example, a faculty member may be fired "for cause." But what the cause may be is open to deliberation. (5) Moral/ethical policies. Perhaps the most ambiguous, policies aimed at regulating ethical or moral behavior appeal to the conscience more than to logical/rational moves. (6) Policies about other policies are "a sort of second-order level of policy." For example, a policy that states that policy-making bodies should be made up of faculty members in a school is a policy regulating policies. And (7) broad course of action policies. These policies tend to mediate between highly abstract principles or ethical norms and specific rules of an institution. Functioning as "institutional goals" such policies bind constituents to actions that aim at achieving the "mission" of the institution (Ballinger, 1965).

A fuller view of the entire "policy process" finds at least four key stages: (1) the emergence and identification of a problem needing attention; (2) the formulation and authorization of policy; (3) the implementation of policy; and finally (4) the termination or change of policy (Harman, 1984, p. 17). Policy as regulative norm is tied to a problem within a tradition and climate/culture. Here we may see myth and ritual playing a role. For example, flag salutes in schools are supported by policies tightly wrapped in custom and ritual. Customs may operate on stated policies. The move to make Martin Luther King, Jr.'s, birthday a holiday in many school districts is warranted by a concern for history and the desire to form a cultural tradition/ritual binding a public institution to a continuous and repetitive gesture of regard. It has been customary in the black community to honor this birthdate, and it is argued that this custom should be compelling enough to be supported by other groups. Custom operates in ways to prevent policy as well. The claim that "this is the way we have always done things" is an argument for retaining a practice often not codified by any rule. Custom, then, serves as a justification for policy or the lack of policy. Leadership, taken in the light of this relationship with custom, tends to mediate between the traditional and the new.

POLICY ARGUMENT

One species of educational argument is that of the policy argument. If concepts form the pieces, the larger puzzle is the framework of argument that gives force and direction to educational practice. Some of the skills used in critical and pragmatic analysis may be utilized in the larger examination of this species of justification; however, the structure of argument necessitates the deployment of tools of a precise and ordinary logic-in-use sort. Toulmin (1984) identifies two types of management reasoning: (1) decision making and (2) policy justification. It is appropriate to add a third dimension: critically pragmatic or philosophic-minded reflection. When we do so, policy study becomes less technical and more enlarged practical analysis. Educational leadership, too, changes from authoritarian dictation to that of critical pedagogy (Hullfish and Smith, 1961; Giroux, 1983). In fact, educational leadership becomes a kind of teaching leadership in which the duty of leading is communication and edification of joint participants in the events under scrutiny.

Stanley Ballinger (1965) stresses that our starting point in policy analysis should be the "Problem Area." Owing to the pluralistic nature of democracies, essential points of disagreement emerge among individuals and groups. These "points of contention" are well documented in journalistic and media accounts. A cluster of related issues becomes discernable. For example, the problem area of church-state and education hosts a range of differences regarding the relationship of these three social institutions. The use of public money for the busing of parochial students, release-time for attending religious instruction, the teaching of the Bible in public schools, and the "scientific creationism" issue all are tied together in this problem area of church-state and education.

Focal points of controversy, or points of contention, represent disagreement relative to key issues within the problem area. It is important to see these differing views as more than merely antithetical or black and white thinking. Often points of controversy contain shades of disagreement. For example, on the abortion issue a person may be against abortion except in certain instances. These shades of difference make the charting or plotting of points of controversy shifting and amorphous.

Given the fact that American culture is pluralistic, we find that Americans therefore enjoy a wider range of choices than in many other societies. Differing views require that we structure our choices as these deal with policy. Policy alternatives become the normative guides for what is to be done growing out of the essentially contested points within the problem area. These alternatives must be mutually exclusive if we are to have an issue. If they are not, then there is no issue and no conflict. The policy alternative that states that religion must be taught in the public schools and the alternative that states that it must not are mutually exclusive alternatives.

Although schools create and use policies, the logical structure of policy is often unclear. We are not taught how to analyze policy. As Jürgen Habermas points out, the primary function of administration is to see that policies are carried out. This function holds no commitment to criticism or rethinking the goals of policies. Habermas calls this the "rational-technical" function of public administration. Thus, although schools as social institutions create some policies and operationalize many others (from school boards and legislatures), the logical structure of policy and the justification of policy argument tend to be viewed as "intuitive arts." It is argued here that it is possible to build and implement better policy; and in part this capacity may arise out of the capacity to judge policies. To do so means we attend to the judgmental dimension of policy operations.

Toulmin et al. (1984) point out that arguments in the realm of decision making require a person to make choices within certain limits or constraints (usually of time and resources or money). An eye must be kept on deadlines; therefore, decision makers (in business settings) must act quickly or profits will be affected. Patterns of decision making differ, ranging from incremental decision making to more studied decisions.

Arguments for specific policies are often addressed to constituent bodies (e.g., stock holders, school board members, etc.). Such justifications rest upon research (facts and values) and revolve around key issues. These are "management issues" for Toulmin.

Leaders face issues of fact, strategy, budget, and system. How will the acceptance of this policy proposal affect our profits or goals? Leaders must be, whereas managers are not typically, interested in deeper questions (e.g., the *values* of selling widgets or educating children); managers are interested in the *strategies* needed to accomplish the ends of the institution or business. The manager deals with facts (numbers of students in a program, success rates, dropouts, etc). Factual estimates impact upon the strategy (larger numbers require different approaches). The strategic matters call for attention to the means used to accomplish the ends. The critical task of the leader is to make claims involving reliable predictions of the future. For example, if we implement this policy the anticipated effect will be to make this improvement/change in student learning.

Both laws and policies are regulative norms. The scope of policy is residual and/or derivative with respect to law. This is to say that some policies are rules/guides within institutions but carry no weight outside of the walls of the institution. Other policies may be derived from law codes. Using illegal drugs may be prohibited by school policy and also prohibited by law. A student can be expelled from school for cheating but taken to court for selling drugs in a school after being expelled for that offense. Policies are more loosely regulative norms than laws, and typically the punishment for violating policy is less severe than that of law-breaking.

THE POLICY OPERATION

The three aspects of policy—(1) policy formulation; (2) policy enactment; and (3) policy implementation—may not be easy to separate. However, more importantly (for Ballinger), they point to the social and institutional contextuality of policy, "underscoring the need for conceptual categories and theoretical frameworks by which it may be studied profitably." To this list must be added that of policy evaluation, or the testing of the results of policy in actual practice.

There is in the literature the explicit assumption that policy formulation and policy implementation are strictly divided. Persons involved in developing policy are *not* to be held responsible if the policy goes bad. Thomas Green (1985) argues along this line, as does Donna Kerr (1976). Kerr writes:

until we decide to hold educational policy makers accountable for the soundness of their policy decisions, rather than for the policy outcomes, we are operating on a confused notion of educational accountability. Contrary to the popular saying, one can argue with success, especially if the luck of the draw is mistaken for success. To be sure, policy researchers should give much attention to policy outcomes, as their role is to uncover what seems to work. And policies themselves should be evaluated in part on their outcomes. But policy makers should be preoccupied with making justifiable policy decisions and should be judged on the soundness of those decisions. Because sound attempts can go awry and shoddy tries succeed, to evaluate any case of policy making on its outcome is both to pervert the notion of accountability and to discourage concern with the grounds for policy decisions. If, instead, educational policy makers were held accountable for the justiciability of their policy decisions, then sound educational policy making would be encouraged. (Kerr, pp. 212–213)

There are several difficulties with Kerr's position. First, what we typically mean by "accountability" is that persons are judged in terms of the results of their efforts. But policy makers who are astute at manipulating the tools of policy creation (making apt policy decisions) are expressing a purely rational/technical grasp of the matter. We would ask of scientists that they not divorce themselves from the ends to which their work may be put. Likewise, we would wish policy formers to attend to the concrete consequences of their policies. Policy making is never made in a vacuum. If an irrational, Machiavellian policy is formulated well, it is insufficient grounds for keeping the leader around if the results are devastating to the group. Bad policy making, like bad chemistry, may lead to horrible results. Both the policy maker and the chemist must be held responsible. After World War II the argument was made by Hitler's lieutenants that they were just carrying out orders. The Nuremburg trials showed us that this is insufficient ground for justifying genocide. In like manner, the policy maker cannot pass on the responsibility for bad policy to the practitioners: teachers and students are not to be held accountable for the bad policies of administrators.

THE FUNCTIONS OF POLICY

Essentially, policy serves as a mediating device between the past and present(future) (Ballinger, p. 13). Policy answers the question: In light of other historic precedent and other experience, what ought to be done in the present class of situations? "[A] basic function of educational policy is to enable, within a more or less stable institutional or similar situation, the experience of the past to be brought to bear normatively (regulatively) upon the problems of the institution within the developing present" (Ballinger, pp. 13–14). Policies mediate, but they also are interpretive devices as they draw upon memory of past experience. However, this reliance upon memories points up the values that underwrite such experience and demonstrates the noncognitive elements in the warrant for policy.

Policies also function to provide continuity between one segment of an institution and another, both synchronically and diachronically. This is to say that policy glues successive administrations (principals or superintendents, for example, inherit the policies of their predecessors) and joins principals and teachers, or schools, together in a system. Policy may become a form of *institutionalized habit* and hence lead to traditions that are themselves kinds of operating rules. Christmas is mandated through school policy as a holiday, but the informal traditions that have developed enlarge and expand to include the annual "Christmas concert," "tree lighting," and so forth. Finally, policy may be *interpreted* differently at different times and by different people: Policy thus takes on a life and career of its own.

By the same token, it is important to note that some policies may be "dead letters," or merely inoperative. Part of the task of a critical and pragmatic analysis of policies is to determine the "shelf life" of policies—to examine their viability in the face of institutional interests.

Finally, a thoroughgoing pragmatic critique of policy must explore the netherworld of "unwritten policies." Here institutions may go on for decades, with decisions made based upon no articulated policy statements at all. Followers are in these instances not privy to the methods of policy generation and operationalization; they also never have the capacity to evelute hidden justifications for the claim, "but this is just the way we have always done it!"

Participatory leadership must pay attention, therefore, to existing policy, dead policies, and unwritten policies as they have operated as an arm of an unthinking bureaucracy.

EDUCATIONAL POLICY MAKING

Policy making and using is a normative activity, in the sense that it deals with what ought to be done. But policy is also a normative enterprise in the sense that it entails values (norms)—often of the group. Scheffler (1985) tells us that policy making requires vision. However, rather than a narrow and personal moral picture of what is to be done, makers of policy (leaders, in our instance) should develop policy so as to engender mutual respect for persons and to encourage human dignity. It is an error to equate the program with the vision.

The critical issue educational reformers face when dealing with policy is the extent to which it is *scientific*. Abraham Kaplan (1964) tells us that "what makes policy formation scientific, in a real sense rather than in a purely honorific one, is procedural rather than substantive, as in the case of any other belief: it is not the content [of policy] which is decisive, but the procedure by which the content is arrived at" (Kaplan, pp. 402–403). Citing John Dewey in *Logic: A Theory of Inquiry*, Kaplan emphasizes, "The evils in current social judgments of ends and policies spring from the fact that the values employed are not determined in and by the process of inquiry" (Kaplan, p. 401). The viewpoint that policy science possesses neutral instruments for policy generation is ill-founded. On the other hand, the claim that policy is nothing but tradition, power, or authority is equally dangerous. The scientific approach called for here fully recognizes that crisis situations cannot wait until all the data and evidence are in: decisions must be made. Therefore, we must employ the best methods in policy formulation. "We are playing lightning chess—with this difference, that if we stop to analyze all the variations the move will be made for us, and with supreme indifference to its outcome" (Kaplan, p. 402). Thus, we require critical and pragmatic reflection.

Here too, the democratic ideal comes into play. For policy makers should so structure the institution to maximize the free consent of the members. Teachers may thus come to reshape themselves through the exercise of choice. Education is necessary for the survival of democracy and to free the mind's critical powers (Scheffler, 1985).

THE CRITICAL PRAGMATIC ANALYSIS OF POLICY

Hodgkinson (1983) tells us that the administrator/leaders must be philosophical:

whatever the variations of context and role, the philosophical theme will persist and certain philosophical skills will be desirable and appropriate even for rudimentary survival. At its lowest level, organizational life is a sort of daily combat. Even here, however, the deadliest weapons in the administrative armory are philosophical: the skills of logical and critical analysis, conceptual synthesis, value analysis and commitment, the powers of expression in language and communication, rhetoric and, most fundamentally, the depth understanding of human nature. (p. 53)

The study of policy, its analysis and application, is necessarily multidisciplinary and best served by a critically pragmatic mind-set. A formal analysis of policy allows us to dissect it into parts. As we have seen, policy is made up of three large blocks: policy formation, policy analysis, and policy evaluation. Each of these is subject to reasoned analysis. Ballinger (1965) states that existing policy is made up of seven components:

In institutional setting S, in dealing with decision-situations of the class C, employing the value-base V plus asserted and/or assumed factual positions F . . . policy P shall be followed (as guide *or* determinant) . . . with predicted-and-desired results RI which are asserted or assumed to be consistent with F and a valid expression of V as interpreted in the light of institutional setting S; and further, that RA, while perhaps not identical with RI, (1) will contain nothing incompatible with V or RI or (2) if it does contain elements incompatible with V or RI, is sufficiently counterbalanced by RI elements. (Ballinger, pp. 22–23)

This formal characterization of the structure of policy is a beginning for "criticisms of adequacy." Certainly this model is oversimplistic, but it may be helpful in providing useful focuses in dealing with the problem of language and content of formulated policies. But policies also mediate between our values and our acts. Policy then becomes a means of expressing or actualizing values. And policy analysis thus becomes the act of determining if a given policy, in a rationally defensible way, serves as an expression of or actualization of the value and belief system of the group or institution (Ballinger, p. 26).

Here we would like to take issue with Ballinger's generality. It is possible to locate policies that are *not* expressions of group values, but rather narrow expressions of a leader's or group's desires. For example, a principal who writes a school policy requiring teachers in a public school to say a Christian "grace" before their class at lunch would be expressing a personal or localized group value in direct violation of law and social values. Yet, it is possible to conceive of such Machiavellian leadership dictating policies of an idiosyncratic type. Certainly, much in the way of controversy stems from school boards setting up policies (dress codes, length of day, etc.) which express business values of the community rather than teaching/learning values derived from research. The point is that we must be careful to distinguish who values what in policies.

Ballinger admits (1965, p. 29) that no simple relationship exists between a basic cultural value on the one hand and policies seen as extensions of that value on the other. We find that this relationship is so highly ambiguous, and plural groups made such diverse demands upon the school, that it is virtually *impossible* to locate *the meaning* of value applicable to a given policy. This is not to say that it is impossible to locate the value(s) driving policies, but rather that it is naive to think we can find their singular meaning displayed.

While Ballinger offers the caveat that "in view of the fact that the educational policy operation is a practical enterprise immersed in the major social and political currents of the time, I do not see educational policy study as capable of the degree of systematic ordering which we usually associate with a science" (Ballinger, p. 29). Here Ballinger states that the basic values in our democracy are undergoing change, but he sees values and policies so tightly interdependent that we must study both to gather any sense of policy at all. Nonetheless, he calls for the study of educational policy to be given special emphasis.

If leaders/administrators are to make educational policy, it is further argued, then a closer look must be taken at the value dimension of the educational policy operation and the role of actors within it.

A critical and pragmatic view of leadership stresses the role of socializing adjustment in leadership. In the essay "Great Men and Their Environment," William James (1956) observed that the great man modified the community in original and peculiar ways, but the community remade the great man in turn. This was owing to the fact that both the leader and the community at any particular moment faced ambiguous opportunities for development. The leader's individuality and sense of self grew out of his "being with" others. James tells us that the leader, as a creative self, extends himself to others, and could never be known in isolation (Rosenthal, 1986, pp. 167–168).

Scheffler (1985) points out that those who engage in policy making need more than technical know-how, such as knowledge of methods of analysis, statistical savvy, or knowledge of evaluation (although these are all important). Policy has certain humanistic aspects attached to it: Knowledge of the backgrounds for logical bases and methods; an integration of a number of disciplines; access to the ways in which people understand themselves; and a self-consciousness relative to values (Scheffler, 1985, p. iv).

Heslep (1987) cautions that in the formation, adoption, and implementation stages of policy, policy leaders ought to reduce the risks of controversy by making certain that they pay attention to such matters as having good reasons for creating and adopting the policy, that it matches the goal, that the likely consequences are explored, that its terms will be clearly defined, and that they have the authority to implement. I find that one of the most neglected guidelines, which Heslep notes, is the necessity that policy leaders "be sensitive to the related recipient's values, interests, and prior policy commitments and violate none of these unless there is a good reason for so doing" (Heslep, pp. 431–432).

LEADERSHIP AND POLICY

Leadership is to be seen as correlated with the policy operation, and at this juncture some specification of this linkage needs to be made. Kurt Wolff (1976) sorts out "surrender" from "catch," and by so doing reveals a dimension of leadership that has been largely overlooked. For Wolff, surrender refers to the suspension of received notions, embracing risk. Catch points to capture of the everyday world. The leader, given this characterization, engages in pulling things together, marshalling strengths, gathering followers, and gaining support. Rarely do leaders let go, engage in self-revelation, or surrender. Therefore, it is this catch dimension of the leadership concept that finds leaders logically engaged in policy making. Leaders set nets of meaning (policy) to accomplish key tasks for an organization. They seek to catch rather than surrender.

The language of "leading" and "leadership" is tagged by a statistical or quantitative meaning. Leaders, it is assumed, generate gains, increases, or other measures of worthwhileness. Leadership is conceptually connected to ledger sheets and accountancy. Calls for "competence," "excellence," and "accountability" seem to logically relate to the interest in acquiring, capturing, and securing (the catch). While there is no "leadership policy," it is patently the case that leaders will not be leading without some agenda or plan (often evaluated through statistical means). Leadership is programmatic in at least two ways: First, leading is logically related to some set of policies (programs); and second, leading is programmatic in the fact that it is forward looking. Leadership is programmatic in the sense that although it fails to denote a specific program or plan, the generation of a policy or set of policies must be manifest. Leaders are working toward some programmatic goals and are purported to have insight or grasp of the program/policies as they fit into the "big picture." The leader, to be a leader, must be moving the group or organization along some vector, and movement in its most gross sense is a prerequisite.

It is frequently sufficient that a leader (at least initially) be following some step-by-step procedure, and it is assumed that the grand design or final goal will be delineated. Without goals and procedures in policy operation, the leader loses credibility and followers. Thus, it is argued here that leadership is logically bound up with policy at several points and some of these must be clear to followers, if success is to follow leadership.

The task requirements of leading cannot be understated. Imbedded in the notion of leadership is the critical requirement that the leader get things done, be engaged in a great effort or mission, and have vision or insight. Leaders cannot do the same things as followers, nor can they share the same epistemological base. Some would have it that leaders tend to do things better or faster, stay on a task longer, and so forth (see, for example, Blanchard, Oncken, and Burrows, *The One Minute Manager Meets the Monkey*, 1989). Other researchers stress the point that quality distinguishes the leader's efforts. In the case of educational leadership, we find management and administration to be those activities not conventionally performed by teachers or staff. Thus, it is relatively easy to say of educational administration that it is synonymous with leadership. For example, educational administrators may be leaders in organization, although the teacher may be called upon to do some work of an organizational nature. The claim is made that leadership is a kind of patina term that is added to administration (much like murder is to killing), rather than a designation of uniqueness. Teachers are not regarded as leaders when they engage in certain administrative acts, where school administrators are so regarded.

Leadership must be connected to some mission or gameplan. Good leaders come to be seen as representatives of their goals just as much as they are judged in terms of their skills of decision making or negotiation. Interestingly, leaders are more often judged relative to matters of facilitation (e.g., whether or not the administrator/leader has good personal relations with staff or parents, or whether or not he/she is "humanistic") (Foster, 1980). The irony comes about when leaders are involved in significant front line battles but judged according to the rules of etiquette.

As I have indicated, we can and should judge leaders in te.ms of their success or failure in achieving goals A formal analysis of policy formulation is incomplete.

To propose that policy writing is distinct from policy consequences is to commit the theory-practice fallacy, that is, a split that underwrites and justifies a normative administrative bureaucracy in schools. We need to measure theoretical success in pragmatic terms. The explorer found what he searched for, the scientist discovered the cure sought. In education, however, we are told that it would only make sense to evaluate leaders in terms of their good intentions and skills in theorizing: I wish to argue that this is precisely what is wrong with public education today in this country. Too many bureaucrats have escaped the scrutiny of evaluation entirely, because their failures have been swept under the rug by logical and linguistic distinctions rather than real ones.

Another dimension of the pragmatic that needs mention is the pragmatic context in which educational leaders as policy thinkers must operate. Hodgkinson (1983) cites Scott and Hart:

The organizational world of management is one where complex problems of short-term duration must be dealt with expediently in order to advance the a priori propositions (of the organizational imperative). Pragmatism demands that managers direct their energies and talents to finding solutions for practical, existing problems within an immediate time frame. The language, reward systems, and activities of management demonstrate this concern for the present. Its attention to putting out fires, meeting competition, adjusting to inputs from the public, insuring the smooth day-to-day running of departments, and short-range planning horizons indicate its devotion to securing an orderly, purposeful world composed of interesting, narrow puzzles to be solved. This pragmatic puzzle-world encourages managers not to reflect on larger, less immediate issues of long-range effects or needs. (Scott and Hart, 1979, pp. 45–46)

But to so characterize short-term problem solving as pragmatic—as dissociated from concern for larger long-range consequences or needs—is to embrace the "vulgar pragmatism" noted by Cherryholmes (1988). This common mistake can be corrected by a more scholarly investigation into the philosophy of pragmatism. Leadership is not always derived from or contingent on the goals of the institution. At times, leaders have held no interest in institutional goals, and may even obfuscate institutional ends. One would question the ethics of the leader so oriented, but the fact is nonetheless true. Brent (1983) has noted that at least part of administrative leadership strategy has been to merely play the game, without concern for institutional ends. But Allen Brent seems to go too far when he states that individuals have personal goals, while institutions per se have no mission. It would be incorrect to say that organizations do not manifest goals beyond any one set or interpretation of goals by an individual. It is precisely the complex nature of organizations and the ways in which missions are held and implemented that make the leadership-policy questions so difficult. By its very nature, policy regulates large states-of-affairs rather than individual behavior: policy involves collectivities of individual persons (organizations) whose interests and needs tend to surmount individual personal interests.

Finally, one of the key pragmatic considerations for understanding the notion of leadership is to see the requirement that leaders as policy practitioners exercise moral responsibility. Some philosophers, such as Barrow and Kerr, seem to argue that it is sufficient that the leader make adequate policy decisions: the success or failure of policy is not important, or at least not as important. When viewed from the position of a "consequence-oriented leadership," this view seems unreasonable. Just as the captain remains with his sinking ship out of a sense of moral obligation and responsibility of command, so the educational leader is morally obligated to remain in the wake of successful or unsuccessful policy decisions to accept their consequences.

This call for moral/ethical responsibility continues in the case of the leader who makes policy but either fails to be committed to it or supports an irrational policy (leading to unacceptable consequences). There is a strong moral requirement that administrators who function as leaders pay the piper when they call the tune.

LEADERSHIP, POLICY, AND EDUCATIONAL REFORM

Is all education political? The study of policy in education reveals the interweaving of the political in education. To deny that politics and ideology drive the enterprise is to avoid the day-to-day evidence of power and control as they are exercised in the schools (Wirt and Kirst, 1989). Harvey Siegel (1988) has argued that Freire, Giroux, and other critical pedagogues are wrong-headed to propose that education is political throughout. Arguing that the liberationist and empowerment ideals are at heart based upon reasons, he proposes a primacy of reason in all cases. Politics and ideology are then always derivative. We are led to conclude, following Siegel, that all education is reason (Siegel, pp. 76–77).

The difficulty with positing an exclusive norm of rationality so abstract, a priori, and pervasive that all thought and action stems from it is to miss the point of the role of critical social science. Siegel would have reason elevated to a transcendental signified and have us embrace an "all or nothing" conception of rationality (Selman, 1988, p. 263). Citing Paul Taylor on justification, Mark Selman points out that Siegel fails to see that our judgments are (or ought to be) justified by appeal to broader principles or consequences, which are in turn justified by a chosen "way of life" (i.e., our beliefs and values). This way of life must then be justified in terms of how well it contributes to maximizing the potential for rational choice. Following Selman, we may argue that any educational policy (here taken as an ideal) justification may arise out of an ideology. However, this does not prevent its acceptance unless the ideology is irrational and would not (or could not) be chosen under conditions that are maximally informed, impartial, and free from compulsion (pp. 263–264).

Brian Fay (1987) points out that there are epistemological, therapeutic, ethical, and power limits to this ideal of reason (pp. 144–145).

Looking to the context of policy, in its fuller historically social and political shadings, it is possible to see the operative fact that we may in practice justify policies in terms of the abstract ideal of rationality, but only where we see such policy as imbedded within patterns of belief and value. But to do so is to translate Siegel's concept of rationality into a pragmatic rationality that reveals the relativistic nature of reasoning. Some ideologies may be more reasonable than others and here we could utilize some maximizing criterion, a la Taylor, to run a check on policies within competing ideological frames. But the point to be made is that the meaning of policy can only be understood from a pluralist perspective: Different world views or ideologies may have differing warrants for policies operative within them. No transcendent rationality is evident that makes sense of the practical differences in these cases.

CONCLUSIONS

"Leadership" as typically viewed is not the panacea for educational ills as currently depicted. Two concerns have been noted: (1) the conceptual territory of the leadership concept has been uncharted in educational work; and (2) the relationships between leadership and educational policy may provide a more fruitful way of seeing leadership functioning in educational administration.

It is the case that considerable work needs to be done in the analysis of "educational leadership" if we are to avoid some of the pitfalls that have dogged earlier educational campaigns. In addition, I have sought to stress the essentially value-laden character of "leadership" by illustrating what I take to be the moral/ethical requirements of educational administrators engaged in policy-generating operations. The requirement that leaders as policy makers be held responsible for the consequences of their policies has been argued for here. Thus, I wish to claim that administration in education is transformed into educational leadership where administrators are engaged in innovative or initiating operations, and that the making of policy is one such area. Moreover, I wish to hold such administrator-leaders morally responsible for not only the decision-making phase, but the ultimate consequences of policy as well. Where "leadership" is used in this manner, it would appear to be more fruitful for the improvement of educational governance.

We have charted a kind of reflective image of leadership as it relates to complicated organizations like schools; however, following Derrida, it will be necessary to reveal the map of that terrain. Sokoloff points to the need for a more generic set of requirements for leadership beyond mere mapping, where the metaphorical calls for leading and the informal nature of leadership role and context are acknowledged (1984, pp. 339–341). Given Sokoloff's view of leadership, educational administrators, teachers, and supervisors may be leaders and never deal with policy (except perhaps to implement it unthinkingly) or critical decision making at all. There are ways in which "leadership can be exercised through collecting and interpreting data" for school officials, he argues (p. 341).

By moving the focus away from leading and normative issues, leading and ethics, leading and goal setting, Sokoloff denudes leadership into a kind of subservience role. Leaders are taken to be working in the background engaging in "underlaborer" tasks: leaders become "philosophers" in the worst sense of modernist carriers of water for kings. By focusing on formal leadership and moving informal leading into the spotlight of formal organizations such as schools, I wish to argue, we democratize leadership and through empowerment via self-initiating structuring create a kind of problem-solving leader who will make a difference in schools and communities throughout societies. Purely analytic philosophic moves will never bring this into being, solely because analysis "leaves everything the same." Rather, we need a reconceptualization of leadership that looks to teachers, students, parents, and community participants for the kinds of thought and effort that will turn education around, placing it on a firm foundation of phronesis. Finally, the pragmatic theory of leadership outlined here calls for: (1) participants in the school to have a clear and reasonable perception and means of critically thinking about the day-to-day operation of policy; (2) the policy function to be such as to include the largest share of affected persons, with the outcomes of policy a respecter of persons' dignity; and (3) the end result to be a view of educational leadership settled in a democratic conception of socio-political life.

5

Leadership and the Education of Young Children

One of the difficulties facing any democratic society is how new leaders shall be nurtured and developed. Writing in 1950, R. Bruce Raup et al. characterized the situation facing the schools in the United States relative to this need.

There is a growing interest today in selecting boys with promise for public leadership and giving them special educational advantages and training in that direction. Privade secondary schools are increasingly eager to get such students. The inspiration of some of these attempts comes from the example of England, where boys with high honors in certain schools have been selected and disciplined for government service with remarkably good results. We must expect the demand for such a leadership to grow apace in this country and to induce the proper schooling for it.... The development of such leadership today sets one of the foremost tasks of the public schools. (Raup et al., 1950, p. 274)

The precise way in which future leaders (without the gender specificity of Raup et al.) are identified and developed clearly becomes an educational question of serious ethical and practical significance (Trawick-Smith, 1988). Certain descriptive and normative questions emerge. For example: What is leadership and how do we go about identifying it? What phenomenal characteristics in children are to be equated with leadership? What institutional conditions best yield leadership? Can and should leadership be taught? Do child leaders become adult leaders? What role do the school and teacher play in the development of leadership in early childhood? What is the relationship between the selection and nurture of child leaders and the adult elites that serve as models or support groups for selection? These questions begin to probe the surface of this larger issue.

Some childhood and youth development agencies ostensively are more centrally focused on the development of leadership than others. Certain extra-school organizations such as the Boy Scouts, Girl Scouts, Boys' State and Girls' State, the 4-H, YMCA and YWCA, and other groups offer training in leadership for children and youth. But to what extent do schools and teachers, as the most intense institution and most centrally educative persons in children's lives, influence leadership development in children? A simple examination of school accreditation philosophies reveals schools as being less likely to identify youthful leadership as an aim or goal of primary or secondary education. Do schools and teachers, through some kind of "hidden curriculum," transmit values regarding leadership? In what ways are leadership attitudes, skills, abilities, or behaviors impacted by school climate, teacher expectations, or school culture? The answers to such queries are not to be found in the examination of school documents, but rather in the observation of leadership in school settings.

The problem of how leadership may be nurtured and developed within institutional settings has long intrigued researchers in the fields of public administration, business, and religion. While the bulk of these leadership studies have focused on adults in fairly constrained environs, such as offices and factories, little attention has been directed to leadership among the very young in structured learning situations. During the 1930s, progressive thinkers sought to open up discourse concerning educational leadership. Marion Brown (1933) did a study of leadership among some 259 high school students who held offices or positions in such groups as Student Body Council, Girl's League, Boy's League, and other clubs and organizations. Brown charted the advantages and disadvantages of holding leadership positions by students. She discovered that there were more advantages than disadvantages, but that students believed that leading cost them time that could have been used to achieve better grades, work on relationships at home, and foster outside interests. When Jones (1938) looked at the education of young people for leadership, he found that leadership developed largely by environmental factors, and the school was the institution most powerful in this respect. He wrote: "If a school is to be an effective agency in developing the potential leaders that have been discovered, it must offer a program wide enough and varied enough to provide for the development of all types of leaders needed" (p. 203). His survey of schools and curricula worldwide, but especially in the United States, found promise, but he predicted that more was needed in the way of opportunities for children and youth to learn leadership.

The celebrated Eight-Year Study of progressive schools in the United States, published in 1940, served as a culminating evaluation of the liberal programs that flourished in the schools in the 1930s. In comparing 1,475 matched pairs of students, the evaluation found that the graduates from thirty "progressive schools," when compared with traditional school graduates, participated more frequently in organized student groups and earned a higher percentage of nonacademic honors (Cremin, 1961, p. 255).

When we look at leadership in education, most studies deal with the principal's administrative leadership in schools. Teacher and supervisor leadership comes in a close second. However, there is little significant work done on early childhood leadership in school contexts. The present effort seeks to discover, through anthropological and hermeneutic methods, how early childhood leadership is influenced by kindergarten teachers in classrooms. Chanan Alexander (1983), in discussing the LTF (Leaders Training Fellowship) Ramah camps and the United Synagogue Youth (USY) approaches to identifying potential leaders for American Judaism, points out that current thinking goes against earlier notions that certain children were "natural leaders" and that the LTF and USY were in the business of developing these into community leaders (rabbis, etc.). According to Alexander, leadership has come to be seen in a new light, not as the possession of an elite cadre, but as a set of attributes any youngster could acquire. The test of leadership is in one's dedication to the ideals of conservative Judaism and in the acting out of one's beliefs so that others may follow them. This newer notion of leadership is not elitist and tends not to focus on recruiting future rabbis, Alexander argues (pp. 4; 25). Alexander's contribution to the literature is to demonstrate that the historic elitist attitudes toward youth leadership instantiated by the perceived needs of organized religion have now given way to more democratic instruction in leadership for all children.

While restricting his research to adult educational administrative leadership, William Foster (1982) provides some clues as to how child leadership studies could be improved. He writes: "leadership studies must be conducted on three levels and within three dimensions. The societal, the group and the individual seem to be interacting levels where leadership is found, and it is not found exclusively at any one level. It remains an interactive phenomenon. At the same time, leadership studies must reflect empirical, hermeneutic and critical dimensions" (pp. 25–26). Our own research study benefitted from Foster's insight in the fact that it looked at childhood leadership in groups from anthropological, hermeneutic, and critical pragmatic points of view.

Most empirical research on leadership among adults has been studied through three constructs: (1) leadership style; (2) psychological characteristics of leaders; and (3) conditions or settings wherein leadership emerges and operates (Maxcy, 1983). However, the mass of data generated from studies along these lines is both confused and contradictory. Despite decades of empirical research, we are no further along in the depiction of adequate leadership training procedures than we were in the 1930s. I feel a problem lies with this naive empiricism: Little work has focused on the more philosophical dimensions in leadership research (Maxcy, 1985).

Pondy (1978) tells us that it does not help to speak of leadership as a social influence, nor do we know the elements common to all forms of leadership. Leadership style is not useful to us as it leaves out deeper meanings of leadership. Therefore, Pondy argues that we should not try to collapse all the various leaderships into a few constrained categories. What has been sacrificed is the *creative* aspect of leadership (p. 90). Pondy argues that since leadership is more a matter of *communication* than anything else, we must study it as a language game. For our purposes, I was interested in learning what kindergarten children name "leadership," and how this semiotic dimension squares with teacher perceptions of leadership instruction.

Sergiovanni (1982) talks about "quality leadership" and identifies leadership skills in adults to be a function of leadership antecedents, leadership meanings, and cultural expression. A ten point model is developed to show how these interlocking and interdependent elements form a network. When leadership is tested against excellent schools, Sergiovanni finds a need for leadership *density*. Rather than having leadership located solely in the principal's office, it must penetrate throughout the school. Sergiovanni identifies five leadership "forces" that impact on schools: technical, human, educational, symbolic, and cultural (p. 6). Unfortunately, it is difficult to find student leadership within Sergiovanni's matrices, and were it to be found, it would be extremely difficult to nurture given the desire for control exhibited by teachers, supervisors, and administrators. We find Sergiovanni's concern to stretch the density of leadership admirable: we only wish that his conception of density would penetrate to capture very young school children as well.

The vast majority of studies of leadership tend to focus on the more practical dimensions of administrative leadership in schools (Griffith, 1979). Calls for curricular change and improvement often cast the teacher or curriculum supervisor in the role of leader (Campbell, 1977). We have been warned that consultants were "robbing" the schools when they assured administrators they could turn them into "leaders" (Sergiovanni, 1979). The assumption has been that the critical areas of education were those involving educational administrators. The solution was to retrain lackluster managers into "educational leaders." To rush leadership studies so as to install programmatic administrative change has blurred the multiple meanings leadership has generated. Leadership training has become *the* focus of a growth industry, with consultants and corporations dedicating themselves to its nurture in the private sector. However, efforts to validate the popular theories of leadership have failed (McCall and Lombardo, 1978). Therefore, what thinkers are calling for are new conceptions of leadership that can account for the ways leading works (McCall and Lombardo, 1978). I shall argue that what has occurred in the studies of adult leadership should be informative, but not axiomatic, for the study of childhood leadership. Simple characterizations are apt to become slogans rather than reforms. We are interested in learning how teachers, rather than administrators, deal with leadership among kindergarten children. In most of the empirical research, the focus is too pecuniary and practitioner-oriented; and is not sensitive to conceptions of leadership among the politically powerless young.

It is reasonably clear from any cursory review of the literature that not only do new studies of childhood leadership need to be done, but that there is a demand for deeper understandings of how leadership is imbedded in teacher-learner situations (Mintzberg, 1982). Certainly it must be acknowledged that adult leadership and the frantic push to develop administrative leaders rather than managers in the schools impacts upon students. The cultural demand for excellence has forced leadership onto center stage, with school boards and citizens equating leadership with improved education. In part we shall be interested in detecting which teacher-leader models, in the kindergarten setting, seem to generate what kinds of leadership in children.

It is important to keep in mind that the context in which leadership is viewed is one of a school culture. The degree to which this school culture relates to childhood leadership and the ways in which teachers deal with such impacts is an untapped research area. If the school culture climate plays any role in student leadership, and I expect it does, then how must this cultural context be taken into consideration in the present analysis? The study centered on kindergarten classrooms, and while these classrooms formed part of the larger school culture, the study did not go beyond the confines of two classrooms. A study of school culture would enlarge the present study beyond reasonable limits, but no study of child leaders would be complete without analyzing, to some extent, the culture within which they flourish. To some extent kindergartens are more insulated from the larger culture than the other grades. The narrower focus is justified owing to this more protected environmental nature of kindergarten life.

THE 1986 KINDERGARTEN STUDY

In working out this project, anthropological field techniques (observation and note-taking) and hermeneutical philosophical analysis were selected as the most appropriate methods of study. It was decided to inform neither the teachers nor students that they were being observed during the preliminary stage of this research activity. After collecting observational reports and conferring regarding them, a set of initial generalizations regarding leadership meanings, activities, and teacher influence were set forth. A normative approach was more fruitful owing to the elliptical nature of leadership concepts and youthful vagaries exhibited on survey sheets. Following Henry Mintzberg (1982), excessive reliance upon constructs as a priori structures within which to fit data would be artificial. He gives five recommendations. First, "do your research *in order* to create richer, more relevant constructs" (p. 255). Second, Mintzberg rightly cautions researchers who deal with leadership to "get rid of instruments" so that you may keep yourself open. "What matters is being there, with your eyes wide open" (p. 255). Third, Mintzberg recommends we "get rid of measurement, or at least, if you insist on it, measure in organizational terms." It is more important to focus on *how* things are done than *what* is done (pp. 255–256). Hence, what became important in the 1986 study was the *quality* of teacher-student leadership interaction, and measuring instruments are not sensitive to this view. Fourth, Mintzberg tells us to "get rid of variables"—dependent and independent— and come to see the world as a system. Finally, he recommends that we get rid of a priori definitions.

While Mintzberg's recommendations have a radical tone to them, his open-textured approach is more genuinely appropriate to exploring the less structured world of the kindergarten. The lack of artifice upon the part of the young subjects called for an openness upon the part of the researcher. In this study I saw "leadership" to be so ill-defined that part of the responsibility was to generate a stipulative definition of our object (pp. 256–257). Following Mintzberg, the study was careful not to allow artificially structured methods to get in the way of finding out. This research project was underwritten by the maxim: Keep it simple. As Mintzberg states it: "the best methodologies to study organizational and managerial phenomena are usually the simplest, most direct ones, the ones that give full vent to the researcher's imagination" (p. 257). The hermeneutic dimension emerged quite early in the study when it became apparent that conventional definitions of "leadership" failed to do justice to early childhood leading. The investigation sought to enter the hermeneutic circle and attempt to explicate what might count as "natural leadership" among children in light of what was observed in the kindergarten classrooms. "Leadership" was therefore reduced to background modes for the purposes of the present study. Drawing upon hermeneutical techniques, the effort was one of providing an understanding of the ways in which a kind of leadership "world view" influences perception and our own thought arguments. The limits it imposes on the roaming about of the imagination when dealing with leadership were probed. The general notion of *Verstehen* as it has been used in the hermeneutic tradition helped. Nonetheless the fallacy of thinking that since there are no fixed rules regarding what counts as best and worst in leadership interpretations, there is thus no rational way of making practical judgments regarding it was found to be too pessimistic an attitude. Avoiding the extremes of romanticism and ethnocentrism, this research study was steered through conception and observation dimensions. A radically different understanding and explication of leadership was required if the present study was to succeed. The hermeneutic dimension brought into play the linguistic discourse. This was recorded by patient observation of the relationship of language to the unobtrusive presence of historic traditions regarding the ways in which pupils are dealt with in schools in the United States. Leadership behaviors were in part language behaviors. To understand and to come to explicate these matters was the hermeneutic task. The study dealt with such questions as: Are the children we identified as leaders in the early phases of the study involved in leadership at the end of the semester? Has teacher interaction changed with regard to kindergarten leaders? We wanted to know if those children the teachers found to be leaders would square with those we saw engaging most often in leading.

Characters

Two kindergarten classrooms in a Louisiana city were studied. Both classrooms had two teachers each. While both teachers in each classroom are officially "teachers," it is clear that one teacher functioned in the capacity of a head teacher, while the other was a helping teacher. In the two classrooms, the dominant teacher did most of the academic teaching, directed children to centers, and in other ways functioned as a team leader. At times one or two high school or college-aged student aides assisted in the two classrooms. These aides functioned as "go-fors" and were largely ignored by the students. Each kindergarten held twenty-six students, aged five and six. There were thirteen boys and thirteen girls, white, black, and Oriental. Since this was a university laboratory school, the students tended to be drawn from university faculty families as well as wealthier members of the community at large. The average intelligence level of these classes was above the norm. No handicapped children were enrolled.

Setting

The two kindergartens were divided into three geographical areas: first, in the rear and near the washstands and toilet was the art center; second, in the middle and along the wall was the housekeeping center, and next to it in the center of the room was the blocks and toys area; third, and finally, the rest of the room was broken up into learning centers, with tables, caged animals, storyboards, tapes, and records. One teacher desk was next to the art center, the other near the door. Closets and alcoves held coats and supplies. The students had low cubbyholes along the window in the room to hold their mats and school work. There was an office for the teacher near the door.

Events

Routinely, the students were rotated among the centers during the day. At times the full class was gathered together for directions or group work. The centers held from three to eight students. After about fifteen minutes, the head teacher rang a bell or in other ways indicated a change in the routine or shift to another activity. When the students had completed a task, they raised their hands, had it recorded as complete, and/or were allowed to go to toys and blocks, or to the housekeeping center. These latter areas were most popular. Some students would move to the caged animals area and feed, play with, or observe the pets. Students frequently stopped and cleaned up their work. This was particularly important in the art center.

Observations

One of the first difficulties encountered was that of locating the "natural leaders" in the classrooms. Three or four children could be said to be leaders owing to their size, demonstrable effects on the other children, and the ways in which the teachers dealt with them. Certain children were more willing to seize command or move to dominant positions in the classroom. In addition, the notion that leadership was a set of linguistic and motor activities seemed to fit logically with what was observed. A conception of the "natural leader," although a rough notion, provided a starting point for observation. This notion was refined over the course of many weeks. Examples of assertiveness, efforts to take charge or command, and other signs of dominance in play and instruction centers were looked for. More subtle indicators of leading, such as gestures, and eye and head movements, came into play as the study continued.

Kindergarten leaders were observed almost exclusively from the beginning. Teacher leadership models affected kindergarten children. Teachers seemed to provide strong role models of leadership for the children. The school culture, too, provided reinforcements for leadership ideas. Teachers in the other elementary grades tended to reinforce this modeling process.

THE PROBLEM OF DEMOCRACY AND EQUITY IN THE KINDERGARTEN STUDY

Repeated observations revealed that whichever children may have been natural leaders, they were in effect only so if the teacher allowed them to continue to lead. In classroom situations, teachers sought to control children, but also selectively reinforced leadership actions on the part of some of the less assertive children. Perhaps in the spirit of democracy, the more vocal, bigger, stronger boys were purposively discouraged from assuming leadership in certain activities. The result was that the students researchers identified as peer leaders tended to become discipline problems, required more verbal commands, and in other ways expressed their frustration.

Whether consciously or not, the interactions between the two teachers in each classroom took on leader-follower patterns as well. The relationships between the two teachers (both females) resembled traditional dominant-submissive relationships. For example, the submissive teacher tended to work almost exclusively with the art center, wore an apron-smock, and worked at the sink or near the washroom. The dominant-submissive role interactions were so pronounced we believe they either reaffirmed traditional parental roles or provided students with a school-based model for domestic life in which the male dominates.

The two teachers rarely interacted directly. Each teacher monitored her own "territory." Mrs. P in Alpha classroom is the head teacher; Mrs. A is second in command. When Mrs. P approaches Mrs. A, she does so with hands on hips, and/or with hand raised in gesture: Mrs. A remains submissive with head lowered, nodding in affirmation. In our observations the head teacher tended to walk with more authority and positioned her hands and arms so they were above those of the second teacher. This body language communicated control and command. One must wonder if it did not send leadership messages to the class. Mrs. A was the younger of the two teachers, acted less authoritatively, and tended to defer to Mrs. P without hesitation. We suspect that the age difference was not great, and that the deference was a function of role definition or position in the teaching hierarchy (untenured beginning teacher).

In Beta classroom the head teacher, Mrs. W, is a larger woman than Mrs. P in Alpha and is not as active or demonstrative in the classroom. Nevertheless, she manifested similar head teacher characteristics. Mrs. X is in charge of the art center, wears a smock-like covering, and tends not to interact with Mrs. W or invade her territory. Mrs. W, like Mrs. P, has full access to any part of the room, but her second-in-command rarely leaves the art area unless she has a specific assignment (e.g, conduct group reading in reading semi-circle).

When students must pass from the room to lunch or recess, the teacher leadership may be shared. For example, Mrs. A may take the students out to recess while Mrs. P remains in the classroom to tidy up or do work. At dismissal, Mrs. P walks the students out to the waiting automobiles, while Mrs. A is at the end of the line. Thus, when the two teachers are involved in an activity (such as leading the students out of class to another location), Mrs. P is at the head of the line and Mrs. A is at the end. This indication of leader-follower relation is consistent and serves as a reinforcement for other role-playing in the classroom.

There were displays of brinkmanship which reinforced leadership of teacher over student. For example, on one occasion, Mrs. A asked a girl to help her pass out cookies. When two other girls stood up, they quickly took their seats when Mrs. A made a sweep down their aisle. While teacher brinkmanship was often evident, student brinkmanship was discouraged. In fact, student to student interactions were carefully monitored. When one student went to join a second at the animal cages and the first instructed him about the animals, Mrs. P quickly intervened and sent boy number two away. Peer teaching is one way in which leaders may exercise their leadership skills over followers. The teachers intervened to maintain control in this domain, frequently, we would suspect, at the expense of student learning as well as leadership.

Rules and the learning of rules are an important aspect of the kindergarten culture. At times there was inconsistency in teacher attitudes toward rules. The teachers in Alpha classroom insisted upon students raising their hands to be called upon before they spoke. However, this practice was not systematically followed. More rule-oriented students continued to raise their hands, but the teachers called on other students, ignoring those with raised hands. The more eager students came to shout out answers to teacher questions, with some being disciplined and others not. The hand-raising rule would seem to be essential to the conduct of the class, but it was not attended to by the teachers with any degree of consistency. This ignoring of rules by the teachers to control the class or in other ways accomplish their ends operated against a democratic equality of treatment norm that was ostensibly a part of the teacher-goals. In addition, the almost catch-as-catch-can approach to rule enforcement tended to throw student leaders off pace: they often were unable to time their efforts effectively to assert command. So many aspects of daily life in the classroom (and outside the classroom) were subject to rules, that little opportunity arose for students to make decisions on their own. One thing that young leaders do is decide for groups. Teacher rule-enforcement inconsistency and overly rule-structured activities disallowed student leaders freedom to make such decisions.

Girls were often hugged and praised for their work, while the boys were not. Girls were called upon by name to perform special leadership tasks; boys were not. Yet, when girls misbehaved, punishment was swift. Importantly, most of the time teachers followed up punishment with words of praise. One was led to believe that everyone wound up being disciplined at some point, so the other students did not seem to be disturbed if one of their number was singled out to sit in a chair and do nothing while they were busy at their centers. Disciplining was one of the most effective ways teachers had for enforcing group norms. Leaders were squashed easily when they sought to "act out." Doing nothing (sitting in a chair on the circle while the others played and worked) reinforced a peculiar notion of punishment. If the child was "bad," he or she was restricted to ineffectiveness and inactivity. This particular kind of punishment may well be a function of the regional culture. While in other parts of the country, one is punished by having to clean the erasers or stay after in school, in Louisiana schools and culture, to do nothing is severe punishment. Some teachers designate a "do-nothing chair" and force students to sit for long periods of the day. The impact on assertive and activity-prone leaders is more serious than for the more laconic students: Doing nothing, for a leader, may be intolerable.

While leadership roles could be a function of reward, I found that initially student leaders, displaying what is labeled "natural leadership," became quite frustrated when they were not called upon to fulfill such tasks. The opportunities for assuming such roles were few and the more docile students occupied such roles so frequently that the more leader-like children came to either disvalue these jobs or deal with their frustration by "acting out." Toward the end of the study, I found these leaders less interested in overtly seeking these tasks. It was evident that teachers used leadership jobs as vehicles for drawing out the less leader-like children: the effect was to discourage the more assertive leader-children. When a high leadership type child was rewarded with the job of "Wake-up Wizard," he mentioned it with moderated voice and said it was "my turn to be the Wake-up Wizard, because I had been the quietest during naptime." One possibility may be that the teacher-delegated job was seen as routine and as a reward for following the rules, not as a source of power or authority over others.

An interior landscaping fault seemed to generate discipline problems. In Alpha classroom the toys and blocks area was located in the middle of the classroom. In most instances, boys gravitated to the play center after they completed learning tasks. When two or three boys began to interact in the toys and blocks area, Mrs. P would regularly verbally discipline them regarding the noise level. One of the boys indicated to the other children that they ought not to play with a particular spaceship toy, because "it's a noisy toy." The likelihood that you would be disciplined if you chose to play with particular toys was known; however, students continued to play with them, compete for them, and so forth. Neither teacher in Alpha classroom made the connection between "noisy toys" and the number and rate of disciplinary actions they engaged in during the day. The Beta classroom also revealed difficulties with its play area, but it was located on the back wall of the classroom and tended to be less noisy. The larger, physically more aggressive children tended to gravitate to this play area, despite the likelihood of disciplinary action there.

The more recent literature emphasizes one aspect of kindergarten life: the use of play in preparing youngsters for the rigors of instruction. This study found that play was a negative activity for the teachers, and that they sought to wean children from the play areas to more serious (less noisy) learning center activities. The opportunities for children to fantasize leadership roles in play was rather routinely discouraged by the teachers. On the other hand, the housekeeping center was a safe sanctuary from discipline. Most of the girls went to the housekeeping center. The play there was quiet and unobtrusive. Neither teacher would intervene in the housekeeping area. When they did it was brief, of low intensity, and without incident. The sharp contrast between the two areas (housekeeping and toys) and the kinds of role models worked out in them seemed to shape leadership acts as well. Thus, students were more apt to be directive and at times dictatorial in the toys area; in contrast, the housekeeping center produced few altercations among students. The fact that toys were located in Alpha classroom in the geographical center of the room perhaps compounded the problem. The noise was more evident than if it had been located in one of the corners or near the art center. All teachers tended to discourage noise of any kind as my observations progressed through the semester. In addition, the students were discouraged from using the toys area entirely at times. Academics was the focus in both Alpha and Beta classrooms with a progressive effort to reduce playtime.

Power and control of the leader teacher was evident in the manner in which children were disciplined. For example, when a boy played with a gun-like toy and made noise with it, Mrs. P turned in her student chair in a learning center and told the class that "S may not play with that noisy toy." This impersonal objectification of the child made him an example to others. She neither moved toward him nor away from him. The child "S" was directed to sit in the reading circle. As a display of power it seized the attention of the entire class. It reestablished a hidden assumption: the blocks and toys area is one in which disciplining will occur. Also, toys are real potential troublemakers. When the child plays with one and interacts with other children, he is disciplined. Whether the teachers were aware of this impression is not known. Clearly the student learned that play was unrewarding.

In our efforts to identify leadership among the kindergarten children, at first only male children appeared in observation reports. The identification of leadership with male sex was stereotypical. Then a conscious effort was made to search for female leaders to counterbalance this bias. However, as the semester progressed, those characteristics that were felt to serve as indicators of leadership (aggressiveness, size, desire to direct or control, eagerness, voice level, willfulness, and positive self-concept) came to be modified or changed by teachers and school culture. Thus, the largest girls and boys in physical terms, for example, did not turn out to be leaders all the time. Of course the teachers, in choosing leaders for various activities, tended to pass responsibilities around.

It may be that what is referred to as the "natural leader" fails to develop in democratic contexts because such children are given fewer opportunities to take command. Playground activities too became structured so that inter-actions that could produce leadership reinforcement were extinguished. A shift in emphasis from raw, aggressive "seize control" type leadership to orchestrated and delegated leading resulting from teacher initiative was charted during the course of the semester.

The kindergarten leadership problem area resolved itself down to a number of issues as a consequence of the study: I deciphered one complex issue centering upon what Alexander had earlier identified as a need on the one hand to identify "natural leaders" and nurture them in an educational setting so that adult institutions can be strengthened, versus a situation in which democracy is invoked as a pedagogical rationale for passing leadership tasks around to all children so that each shall have an opportunity to learn to lead others, again with the consequence that adult institutions shall be strength-ened. These alternative approaches were found to be based upon certain philosophic assumptions as to what "leadership" amounted to, how it was engendered in others, and the bearings such attitudes would have on the democratic American society. While it is too early to conclude what this may mean, if it is the *philosophical* level wherein the analysis needs to be conducted, and the daily workings out of these presuppositions goes on without reflection, then it is clearly the case that fuller and deeper work must be done if we are not to commit near ideological damage to kindergarten children in our teaching of leadership.

CONCLUSIONS

First, most traditional strictly empirical methodologies and definitions of "leadership" did not appear to fit the cases of kindergarten children very well. Drawing upon hermeneutic-anthropological methods, this research sought to observe and record student life worlds in the cultural context of the school to determine if we could redefine childhood leadership and how it comes to be frustrated or nurtured by teachers.

Second, early observations revealed that teachers impact significantly on student leadership by (1) serving as role models for such leadership, and (2) reinforcing or extinguishing extant leading in the children through teaching and discipline, as well as through a kind of leadership hidden curriculum. The function of the various centers illuminated the fact that discipline could be used to separate boys from girls and to reinforce teacher control and extinguish pupil self-initiated actions, some of which were leader-like.

Third, student leadership was perhaps most significantly influenced by teachers, while the domain of the school culture also came to exercise effects. The present study did not focus on the entire school culture, but those features of that culture that supervened and did so with a heavy hand. It became clear after a number of weeks that if all the significant influences exercised on children in early childhood were to be located, the total school community would need to be examined.

Fourth, sex role stereotyping played an enormous part in the modeling of teacher leaders. This was so striking in the interactions of the co-teachers and the interior landscaping of the classrooms that it became apparent to this researcher rather early in this study. The body language, territoriality, and communications between teachers and visitors seemed to bear out our generalizations. Co-teachers took on a dominant-submissive role relationship which worked its way into the geography of the classroom, the arrangement of the centers, and the control exercised over various sections of the room by the teachers. We found that children without conventional dominant households might find the leadership model difficult if not impossible to decipher. More liberal or radical parents would not identify with the role relationships exemplified by these teachers.

Fifth, discipline was the most effective way for teachers to form and reform student leadership, while rewarding children with leadership positions proved to be ineffectual over time. Forcing student leaders to "do nothing" had the result of cutting them off from their role as leader from the group they had controlled. A diminished interest in leadership "jobs" among the children emerged as the year progressed.

Finally, philosophical features of this inquiry increased rather than diminished over the course of the study. What teachers tend to do regarding the reinforcement of leadership in the kindergarten class, consciously or unconsciously, is linked to two prevailing philosophies of education: Either teachers assume that leaders are born and not made, and the function of school is to nurture outstanding potential adult leaders; or they presuppose that leadership is something a democracy requires its institution, the school, to be "passing around," so that all children should share in it. I found the latter philosophy evident most profoundly in this study of these kindergarten classes.

Certainly more needs to be learned of childhood leadership. Fictional heroes such as Huck Finn, Billy Budd, Dorothy of Oz, and David Copperfield provide rich means of characterizing the learning of leadership (and its extinction) in children and youth. Leadership classes for adults aimed at fostering leadership growth and development in children and youth should be offered to Boy Scout, Girl Scout, Campfire, and other leaders. And more studies should be done that trace the practical teaching of democratic leading (overt and covert) in institutions like schools.

6

Moral Imagination and School Leadership

Two different strategies for the solution of most, if not all, the problems in public education have been set forth by critics: One group I shall term the "moral visionaries" argues that current educational difficulties may be solved by stronger, more imaginative educational leadership. Such leadership is best seen placed in the hands of school administrators, rather than teachers or parents, they assert. To lead effectively, school administrators must have a dedicated following (teachers, parents, children). To gain this following, the leaders must set forth a *moral vision* or plan invested with commitment and warranted by "moral imagination." Such moral thinking ought to yield plans, policies, and goals, all of which are beyond reason and are so compelling subordinates are expected to eagerly follow. Finally, it is argued that principals and superintendents can be taught to be leaders with moral vision by colleges and schools of education (W. Greenfield, 1987a).

A second set of critics, the "personal relationships" group, suggests quite the opposite solution to the problems facing the schools. These thinkers argue that leadership ought to be diffused throughout the organization. Vision drops out of the discourse and is replaced by dialogue and deliberation among parents, teachers, students, and administrators—to provide a community plan for school improvement. While various names are used for this process (more recently it has been called "site-based management"), the effect is similar: moral vision is replaced by value-driven human relations psychology, resulting in policy and practice of a caring nature (Smith and Blase, 1987).

In this chapter, I shall argue for a third approach—a middle road—that avoids the extremes found in the "moral imagination" and the "personal relations" views. Here I shall examine and critique both positions in the interest of establishing a critical and pragmatic perspective on leadership. It will be argued that it should be required of leaders, if they are to be good leaders, that they help followers identify and further what is of value. Hence, a theory of value is essential to any normative theory of leadership.

MORAL IMAGINATION

What has been meant by "moral" has varied greatly historically. While some authors have sought to distinguish "moral" from "ethical," the tendency in American pragmatic philosophic circles has been to subsume both under the category of "value." However, older notions of moral, which carry with them aspects of principles, ideals, and superordinate religious rules, continue to get played out in modern academic works. In part, the call for "moral imagination" as an aspect of educational leadership suffers from this misappropriation of an archaic meaning of moral. This move is abetted by the literature on imagination, which is abundant and significant.

Elemire Zolla (1978) distinguishes between daydreams and imagination, lamenting the loss of the latter and connecting this demise with the decline of the West. It is important to distinguish these two kinds of imagination at the outset: imagination that deals in revery, deja vu, or remembrance; and imagination that is inspirational, creative, innovative, and problem-solving in nature. While the first may be made up of memories and earlier impressions, the latter is more fruitful for creative work as it provides visions and images of a changed and improved future condition or situation. We are interested in the inspirational and creative imagination here, because it is this meaning of the term that is implied in most of the talk about moral imagination in the literature of education.

Forrest Williams (1962), in the introduction to his translation of Sartre's *Imagination*, points out that a strict behaviorist rendering of imagination is wrongheaded: The psychology of the imagination must be phenomenological (p. vii). And it is to Husserl that one must turn for the first work of this sort. As Williams states: "Only the recognition that there are structures of consciousness which can really be observed, but in reflection alone, rather than by the senses, permits a phenomenological approach to the nature of imagination" (p. viii). Sartre credits Husserl with providing the first adequate psychology of the imagination with a phenomenological approach to the subject suggested.

Christopher D. Stone, in *Earth and Other Ethics* (1987), argues that moral imagination is necessary for us to ever question a moral principle that we have received uncritically. He claims that we need to employ imagination to move beyond the small community of persons we know to the concern for the devastation of the forests of Brazil or the rivers of the world. Familiar patterns of relations with persons can only be superseded by imaginative attention on a new plane or framework. Moral thinking seeks an image, Stone argues (pp. 244–246).

` Current research into imagination has taken a decidedly phenomenological turn. However, it is the phenomenological interpretation of imagination that poses the greatest threat to mainstream educational research in general and administrative research in particular. Most studies of administrative leadership eschew talk of "imagination" because the concept fails to be substantiated by traditional scientific procedures. On the other hand, since imagination is not subject to such verification or validation procedures, it has come to serve as a unique warrant for educational proposals as these are linked to "qualitative" or "naturalistic" inquiry (Phillips, 1987, *passim*; Eisner, 1979).

At the interface of education and imagination, Harold Rugg (1963) provided a Jamesian account of imagination occurring at "a critical threshold of the conscious-nonconscious continuum on which all life is lived" (p. 39). Rugg attempts to provide a theory of the creative imagination which warrants a new approach in education, one in which teachers are taught to teach creative discovery (pp. 310–314). H. Gordon Hullfish and P. G. Smith (1961) argued that imagination was an important part of reflective thinking and that teachers ought to provide time for students to engage in imaginative thought (pp. 141–143). They suggest a strong tie between morals and imagination, where imagining is seen as exploring choices. They propose a more narrow definition of imagination when they write: "Imagination is nothing more or less than the ability *to make the absent present*, and it is this ability that leads men to the stage of the hypothesis in their acts of thought" (p. 141). Here moral imagination functions as a kind of logic of discovery and precedes inductive and deductive reasoning. One of the primary assumptions in current theories of moral imagination in school administration is that imagination is as legitimate a mechanism for hypothesis formation as any scientific procedure. We find the work of Rugg and Hullfish and Smith important but overlooked by contemporary writers in discussions of moral imagination.

The prospect of transforming administrators and teachers into morally imaginative leaders is not a recent notion. John Dewey was not free from this sweeping kind of social rhetoric. He wrote in the pages of *The Social Frontier* in 1935 of the school administrator that "his leadership will be that of intellectual stimulation and direction, through give-and-take with others, not that of an aloof official imposing, authoritatively, educational ends and methods. He will be on the lookout for ways to give others intellectual *and moral responsibilities*, not just for ways of setting tasks for them" (p. 10) [emphasis added]. The view that school administrators could provide moral leadership and that this role was superior to routine decision making has deep roots in the literature of school reform.

Imaginative leadership was needed, post–World War II educators believed: "To solve problems in community life educators are needed, first, with vision, second, with ability to further vision, and third, with courage to follow through—to see that the application of vision makes a difference in community living" (Campbell and Koopman, 1952, p. 19).

Russell Kirk (1978) popularized a conservative conception of moral imagination which linked educational leadership to the humanities tradition. For Kirk, moral imagination was to be located in the "great ethical poet" (e.g., Homer, Plato, Dante, Shakespeare, and Cervantes) (p. 270). Kirk distinguished three kinds of imagination: moral, idyllic, and diabolic. He wrote:

The idyllic imagination responds to primitivistic fantasies—to the notions of Rousseau, for instance; it roused the radical emotions of young people in the 'Sixties, even though they knew Rousseau only at third hand, if at all. The diabolic imagination loves the violent and the perverse; one need not go so far as Sade to find it; it runs through D. H. Lawrence, for one. (Kirk, p. 271)

Interest in literary moral imagination encouraged William Foster (1986) to apply a hermeneutical approach to the study of educational administration, focusing on the school leadership as text. He proposes that "a school administrator should look to a literary, rather than scientific, model to guide his or her work in part because literature deals with human events, with tragedy and comedy" (p. 29). Like Kirk, Foster supports a literary approach heavily invested with moral value: "Morality . . . belongs in the center of work; and it can get there only if social scientists are morally alive and make themselves vulnerable to moral concerns—then they will produce morally significant works, consciously or otherwise" (p. 32).

The poetic voice in moral imagination is highlighted by Thomas F. Green (1985). He writes: "For our moral education, all of us need—in addition to the conscience of skill, membership, and sacrifice—the formation of conscience by prophets, that is, by poets and by the literary giants of our experience" (p. 22). The moral significance of the conscience of imagination, Green points out, "is nurtured in conversation with the great writers of imaginative literature" (p. 24). This position is mirrored in *The Closing of the American Mind* (1987). Allan Bloom argues that *only* liberal education develops imagination (p. 79). The writer's muse is an imaginative conscience that reaches for moral standards. The literary mind, Bloom demonstrates, is in the business of moralizing about human life and society, providing mirrors and images for the reader to ponder.

Former U.S. secretary of education William Bennett argued that teachers and principals must not only "articulate ideals and convictions to students," but should also "live the difference [between right and wrong, good and bad] in front of pupils" (Gutmann, 1987, p. 57). Here Bennett calls not for indoctrination of moral views, but for setting moral examples to follow through moral discipleship.

School administrators utilizing "value leadership" resting upon "moral imagination" ought to "raise teachers' consciousness regarding the connections between their personal motives, needs, and values and the collective interests and welfare of the school's community," William Greenfield proposes. He goes on to say, "Value leadership rests upon the exercise of moral imagination and interpersonal competence and is viewed as integral to the principal's ability to administer the school in a distinctly moral manner" (W. Greenfield, 1987a, p. 1).

Understandably, this argument is attractive at the outset. Better schools and better school administrators are needed. If morally imaginative leadership can help toward this end, then it is a good idea. It is further assumed that leaders ought to have programs or plans, and if they are accepted by followers, all the better. Being imaginative, if taken to be inventive and creative with respect to plans and programs, is perfectly acceptable, for we are only interested in results. And finally, injecting morally imaginative visions into our immoral schools is seen as superior to other modes of educational change. But this shell of a moral argument obscures a multitude of sins. What is clearly dangerous about proposals for "moral imagination" and "school leadership" lies in the assumptions supporting them and the consequences that follow.

The discourse of morality and leadership will be explored in this chapter. The notion of morally imaginative school administrators qua leaders, although seemingly beneficial, may have serious and detrimental impacts on the way educational institutions are operated in the future. The present effort will take issue with this vision of moral imagination as a guide to administrative value leadership. On the other side of the issue, I shall examine the arguments for a human relations view of school leadership that stresses "caring" and "empathy" as guiding educational administration. A third position shall propose replacement notions of "critical imagination" and "democratic value deliberation."

MODELS OF MORAL IMAGINATION

The unifying link between all of the authors discussed here is the importance that they all place on the centrality of morality and imagination in education. However, lurking within their various conceptions of moral imagination are four different, but related, conceptions of moral imagination. Each has its failings, and individually or together they may lead to a number of abuses in the hands of school leaders.

Four distinct meanings of "moral imagination" are to be found operative in the literature of education.

Moral Imagination as Discovery

Moral imagination is often touted as a superior method of arriving at plans and policies. Comparable to intuition, moral imagination, in the hands of the school administrator, is a method of discovery of hypothetical states-of-affairs that stand as "visions" of the future (W. Greenfield, 1987a and b).

Moral imagination as an engine of discovery has the problem that it must compete with other, rational procedures for arriving at a policy or plan. This is to say that in any situation the leader must accept the notion that, were a competing rationally deduced plan to present itself that was fundamentally different from the imagined one, the former would have to be rejected on the simple ground that visions are better than reasons. This kind of argument is likely to lead to all sorts of irrationalities in education. Given this view (imagining first, critical thinking second), the situation could emerge in which the valid, justified, true belief in science was rejected in favor of what the imagined vision tells us. Running the school from behind a crystal ball is not a new idea, but it pales in comparison to the proposed model of moral imagination as discovery.

These imaginative visions are not contestable. Imagination has attached to it a radical personal relativism that excludes it from the normal processes of rational discussion. Your image is as good as mine. If images were subject to the same rational procedures of criticism as logically derived plans, there would be less need to twist followers into acceptance. The heavy-handed need to make followers accept the image is proof of the shaky grounds upon which this method of discovery rests.

And against Bloom (1987), T. F. Green (1985), W. P. Foster (1986), Kirk (1978), and Bennett (1987), it is important to see a literary moral imagination yielding fictional value-laden images. That the literary version has invaded talk about moral imagination for administrators is all the more dangerous for its hidden alliance with literary classicism. Literature-driven moral imagination is not a reliable tool for developing plans and policies, owing to the fact that (a) such images are derived from fiction and are more likely to result in unanticipated outcomes; and (b) such fantastic imaginings are seen to be above the level of critical and openly discursive scrutiny. Plato ejected the poets from his republic because they distorted the truth, so too should we vanquish fantasy and prophetic vision from the school policy process.

Moral Imagination as Moral Authority

Moral imagination may mean moral authority. Dewey (1935), Hullfish and Smith (1961) and W. Greenfield (1987a and b) propose that school administrators function as moral models for teachers and students. Here there is a subtle move from seeing the school administrator as being *in authority* to viewing him/her as *an expert authority*. School principals exercising moral imagination possess superior moral knowledge and certitude.

It is questionable whether moral imagination conceived of as setting forth moral traits of leaders is appropriate for the moral education of youth. Having children model the moral imagination (read moral authority) of the teacher or administrator may lead to children mimicking a conservative set of notions, none of which may be fruitful for new situations they face. Kirk (1978), for example, argues for the teaching of dogmatic truths to students in schools (p. 255).

The literature on moral education is extensive and John Wilson is an articulate spokesman for a view we would suggest here. For Wilson (1961) it is far wiser to teach children to reason morally than to indoctrinate them into some moral viewpoint. Leaders as moral authorities are apt to dictate a kind of morality that serves their purposes, and not necessarily those of teachers, students, or parents. Following Wilson (1961), moral reasoning as a process to be learned seems to be superior to the induction of the young into one leader's moral vision.

It is possible to disagree with the notion that *anyone* may be an expert in morality, in the sense of having more or superior moral knowledge than anyone else. And it is clearly not going to follow that if I know the good: (a) I will know how to induct others into it; or (b) that they ought to follow my lead anyway. There is a Pied Piper notion of moral leadership operative in tandem with W. Greenfield's view (1987a and b) of "value leadership" that is highly suspect along these lines.

There is an additional danger in posing the school leader as moral expert: Were the school leader to adopt a moral absolutist view (e.g., often displayed by religious fundamentalists), there is no guarantee against religious dogma invading the public schools. A religious fundamentalist school administrator of a southern public elementary school revealed that he had designed the perfect personnel handbook for his teachers based on the Ten Commandments. The length to which *moral* imagination, can be taken given this sort of misappropriation would be curious to say the least. Any school policy could be taken to be a moral edict of God (or Allah, etc.) as delivered by the school principal. Moral imagination as moral expertise in this way would take on an irrefutable source for policies of the most parochial sort. There would be no way the administrator could err, no caution against moral school administrator leaders operating as dogmatic ideologues, nor any room allowed for conflicting moral visions in the school.

Finally, the notion of moral expertise of school leaders must be seen as overlooking the gap between moral thought and moral behavior. The claim upon the school administrator as moral expert, following this sorting, finds a principal a moral expert in theory rather than in practice. Here the leader may be seen as an expert *in talking about* morals rather than a superior practitioner. However, moral character would have to be demonstrated as well as be talked about by teacher or administrator. On the other hand, this call for moral action may lead to a new difficulty: How would morality be demonstrated by the leader? For example, would the moral leader have to have had a religious conversion experience—to have been "saved"—in order to qualify for a post in the public schools? Or would some other moral test be administered to school leaders?

Moral imagination as moral authority fits with modern views of school administration as deeply affected by the current psychic troubles visited upon our culture. There is a very real danger that moral imagination qua authority may become the narcissistic vision of "inspired" leaders, unchecked by democratic consensus or external criteria of rationality. We would caution against viewing moral imagination in education as moral authority of school leaders.

Thus, moral imagination taken as moral authority cuts off the pedagogical possibilities of teachers and students growing as moral agents, involved in selecting options and making decisions about educational futures. While moral reasoning, following Wilson (1961), enhances this end.

Moral Imagination as a Faculty of Mind

It is possible to see moral imagination as a mental faculty. This psychological category of mind (moral imagination) would have all the trappings of any other faculty but would be invested with moral certitude. The exercise of the moral faculty would lead to the discovery, through imagining, of the proper moral course of action to take. Thus, imagination, rather than being playful or deceptive, is a psychological category in action, under proper incentive and freedom. Like intuition, it functions without our full willfulness or intent. Moral imagination is a kind of sixth sense that is profound and beyond rational monitoring or correction. We either get the vision right or we do not. The error is not in the moral image, but in the cognitive effort to understand it.

This kind of reasoning about moral mind invests it with a profound and primitive wisdom, much like mythic mind. Irrational or super-rational, moral imagination produces extraordinary visions which are profound and illuminating. Like myths, such images may be primordial (Jungian), reaching down into the deep recesses of the collective psyche. As an alternative and in many ways superior rendering of reality, moral imagination, like myth, is to be looked to as the trusted, "true" view. In some versions of the moral imagination argument (e.g., W. D. Greenfield's view), it is implied that moral imagination renders a more truthful and adequate account than do other means of inquiry.

Arguing that an image or vision is moral owing to its source (imaginative mind) may lead to the acceptance of *any* normative claim regardless of its impacts. A moral imagination in this view is moral precisely because it functions as part of moral mental entities. We wish to argue that elevating mind to the status of a moral faculty slights the role of judgment in morality. Minds of themselves are neither moral nor immoral; judgment makes them so.

Moral Imagination as Super Science

One way to interpret the current demand for a morally based administrative program (search for a morally justified basis for social policy) is to see the effort arising from a frustration resulting from the inability to ground public administration on some natural or social science base. Criticisms of positivism and logical empiricism in educational research have provided a fund of support for alternative views of research called "naturalistic" or "qualitative." And these new research efforts seek to base their work on the realm of human values, moral and ethical in part. Moral philosophy has come to replace science as the foundation for educational research and practice. We find difficulties with this trend.

The argument seems to run something like this: Since there are no law-like generalizations in administrative "science," and since we cannot predict the outcomes of particular educational policies, strategies, and so forth, there is little prospect that we can scientifically intervene to shape or mold the instructional process; and since we cannot scientifically master the technical process, the image of the educational leader as a technical or scientific expert is to be rejected (T. B. Greenfield, 1986; Smith and Blase, 1987). The difficulty with this argument is that it rests on the effort to discredit naive empiricism and simplistic positivism, only to substitute a naive notion of moral philosophy.

As D. C. Phillips (1987) has argued, there are a number of notions of empiricism and positivism that currently underwrite educational research. Most researchers do not hold to this simplistic version of positivism (D. C. Phillips, 1987). Despite John K. Smith and Joseph Blase's protesting to the contrary, most educational researchers do not search for "law-like generalizations," and few see predictability as their goal. On the other hand, it seems hardly advisable to seek to ground educational administration on moral philosophy (although this may add a heretofore overlooked dimension). Moral theory cannot replace administrative theory. What is needed is not a softer science, but a firmer one. Following Phillips, we would argue that the essential need is for educational research to look to successful long-term research programs for warrants for administrative conduct, not to some value image that eschews efforts at either confirmation or refutation.

Positivist science has failed to deliver certainty to educational administrative praxis: moral philosophy will not provide this either. But we are easily entranced by quick fixes, and moral imagination, proponents argue, surely cannot hurt.

PERSONAL RELATIONS LEADERSHIP

On the other side of the debate over morality and educational leadership we find a non-principles, individualistic moral/ethical model for schools. An early example of this "personal relations" model of educational administration states:

Formal delegation of power to the superintendent is disappearing in some communities. Board members, administrative officials, parents, and teachers often operate as a cooperative group and disdain formal line and staff relationships. Fixed status in these cases becomes less important. The "least" individual may express his ideas for school improvement and be heard. This trend may lead to many new patterns of group action and a new pattern of human relationships. (Koopman, Miel, and Misner, 1943, p. 49)

This second approach to moral/ethical decision making is explicit in Nel Noddings's *Caring* (1984) and in Alasdair MacIntyre's *After Virtue* (1981). Essentially, what this view holds is that morality and ethics are matters of character. Instead of asserting that a leader's behavior is to be pinned to the task of deciphering or developing a normative set of ordered principles to guide moral decisions (Kantian), these thinkers propose locating values in human character development. While MacIntyre moves his ethics of virtue back in time to an Aristotelean tradition; Noddings differs by locating her argument in the feminist insight that ethics grows developmentally over time in the interchanges we have with others.

For Noddings, these relationships yield interesting questions about obligations we may have toward generations in the future. Using educational theory and practice, she provides a non-principled view of moral/ethical operations. And looking to parenting she sees examples of ways that caring may be practiced in institutional settings, like schools. Her position has it that as human beings we are involved in concentric circles of persons: the inner rings are made up of intimate relations. It is from our connections with these inner circle humans that we learn to care for others. The reciprocal nature of these relationships is important: we learn to care by being cared for ourselves.

Noddings rejects the notion of principled decision making on the ground that any principle can endanger those for whom one has a caring regard. Some principles may lead to the sacrifice of one's children, as found in the Bible, for example. Or in the case of the child who asks his mother for a note to gain permission to stay home from school for a reason both mother and child believe to be worthwhile. The school will punish the child unless the mother lies and states that the child is ill. There are two options open to the mother: either she can dismiss the school rule on absences as silly; or she can simply act in what she and her child agree is a caring way and not attempt to justify her decision in terms of principle at all. For Noddings, the latter choice preserves ethical integrity.

It is important, in the development of caring, for the one caring to be receptive of the cared for and their situation. To attempt to walk in the shoes of the other, so to speak. Reciprocity is crucial to her theory of caring. The model may be logically depicted thus:

(W, X) is a caring relation if and only if

   i. W cares for X (as described in the one caring) and
   ii. X recognizes that W cares for X.

When we say that "X recognizes that W cares for X," we mean that X receives the caring honestly. He receives it: he does not hide from it or deny it. Hence, its reception becomes part of what the one caring feels when she receives the cared for. We do not need to add a third condition and a fourth, as in, "W is aware that X recognizes," "X is aware that W is aware that," and so on. (Noddings, p. 69)

Noddings goes on to suggest that schools should be organized for caring. This caring-type organization can only be brought about through the "de-professionalization" of education, by which she means the elimination of the special language that separates educators from the community. This is not to say that they do not need preparation in their subject matter areas, but rather they ought to be prepared to care for their pupils. Circles and chains would be formed to define structures in schools, wherein teachers would rotate in and out of administrative roles. The effort would displace "career administrators." Noddings writes, "There is no reason to believe that the existing mass of principals, deans, supervisors, assistants, directors, counselors, and consultants has really contributed to either efficiency or effectiveness. The enterprise can be organized differently" (p. 199).

The crucial issue, one which Noddings seems not to handle successfully, is how to determine personal responsibility to fulfill general social obligations. This responsibility, it may be argued, is an obligation which defines the person's individual moral/ethical identity (Neville, 1989, p. 11). The circle of morality is localized and impoverishes one's capacity to think along global issues: The starving children in Africa have neither the means nor the inclination to call upon me in my office in urban America. Since the equation is truncated, for Noddings, caring cannot take place. Here the moral imagination people seem superior, as they can envision the starving populations and operationalize a moral/ethical course of action (see Stone, 1987).

In the arena of educational administration, Smith and Blase (1987) focus on the moral insensitivity of contemporary school leadership. They take issue with W. Greenfield's notion that educational administrators ought to be viewed as experts who use teachers to accomplish their ends. They write: "Leadership is . . . much more than a strategic planning which calls upon the supposed law-like generalizations of empirical inquiry; leadership is rather an openness to issues of human significance" (p. 36). Like Scheffler (1985), Smith and Blase draw upon Kant's categorical imperative to warrant a more humane theory of school leadership.

Interestingly, for their characterization of leadership to succeed, Smith and Blase must launch a frontal attack on "positivism." Contrasting their view of leadership with that warranted by empirical science and traditional notions of educational administration as expertise, Smith and Blase argue for a human relationships view. Leaders function morally by treating teachers and others as parts of a moral community, and as ends in themselves and not means to a scientifically determined end (Smith and Blase, pp. 36–37). As a solution, the writers propose what they call a "significance view" of individuals, which "demands that people see each other as ends in themselves" and accept the fact that administrators and teachers inhabit a "community of moral discourse" (pp. 17, 36).

SCHOOL LEADERSHIP

"Value leadership" has a special appeal in organizational reform. "Leading a school requires that the principal deliberately influence teachers and others to adopt the principal's vision as their own, and this should be a distinctly moral act guided by moral principles" (W. Greenfield, 1987a, p. 28). We are led to believe that the principal can justify almost any action provided that his decisions are based on "moral principles." For as Greenfield puts it, an action is justifiable if "it is perceived by others as grounded in deliberate reflection guided not by the principal's personal preferences, but by moral principles" (W. Greenfield, 1987a, p. 2). Greenfield shifts his definition of "moral imagination" later when he adds, "[imagination] . . . is 'moral' in that it is the application of some standard of goodness that illuminates the discrepancy between the present and what is possible, and better" (1987b, p. 62).

There are several difficulties here. We are not any further out of the woods if the principal grounds a vision on personal moral principles or a perceived "standard of goodness." There are countless sets of moral principles, any one of which may be used to warrant administrative decisions. Again, there seems to be little protection afforded teachers and pupils who face an administrative policy authorized by a fundamentalist religious moral code, a Nazi set of moral principles, and so forth. Furthermore, W. Greenfield's notion of moral imagination as resting on moral principles fails to address the issue of the relativity of moral principles and the likelihood of administrative intolerance toward competing moral principles.

As we have seen, as a counter to the call for moral *principles*, Nel Noddings's philosophy of *caring* seems a likely candidate. The novelist Dorothy Sayers once wrote that the first thing a principle does—is kill somebody! In place of rational principles of moral dictation we may place a premium on regard for others. This emphasis upon caring is essentially feminine in nature and challenges the male philosophers to give up historic control over the literature of philosophy, a literature that has emphasized the masculine regard for principles. Certainly, the domain of educational leadership has suffered from an excess of principles-driven models for educational governance. Followers are subordinated by fear of failure. Since the administrative head does not care for the follower as a person or individual, but only insofar as the worker is productive and active in the organization, we find a resultant bureaucratic mentality that lacks a clear conception of human nature. Hodgkinson (1983) warns that it is essential for the administrator/leader to have a philosophic view which includes a knowledge of human nature and how it plays a role in organizational success. Administration ought to adopt this credo. Hodgkinson asserts: "I believe in the potentiality of individual free will, in partial determination and degrees of freedom, and in the possibility of enhancing human autonomy, for ourselves and for others" (p. 44). Scheffler (1985), too, places supreme importance upon the regard for human dignity in the governance of education.

On W. Greenfield's account, school leaders should influence others to adopt their vision and thus tacitly approve the moral code that underlies them (W. Greenfield, 1987a, p. 10). Hence a double claim is made: teachers and students must accept not only the administrator's vision of how the school should eventually evolve, but the principal's theory of morality as well. There are several problems with this notion, not the least of which is the assumption that the principal is somehow invested with a moral superiority by virtue of his/her position as principal.

Speaking of "raising teachers' moral consciousness" as a central duty of "value leadership" finds leaders cast as reformers and change agents. However, it is not clear that educational administrators need to be *reformers* to properly administer. To argue that a successful principal is one who "taps latent levels of motivation and morality among teachers" (W. Greenfield, 1987a, pp. 16–17) is to become more tent-meeting leader than a real visionary. Raising moral consciousness and surfacing moral latency are functions better left to ministers and priests: It is a serious question whether school administrators ought to be placed in the role of spiritual leader.

Nor is it the case that the "principal as leader is operating at a broader level of understanding and motivation than teachers" (W. Greenfield, 1987a, pp. 16–18). This claim discounts the professional expertise of teachers. There is need to call for a caution against the pretense that school administrators are instructional experts, "in the sense of knowing precisely definable ways (based on research findings) to more effectively and efficiently teach" (Smith and Blase, p. 39). I shall argue, following Smith and Blase, that school leaders, to exercise "value leadership," need not be subject matter experts.

An equally dangerous notion proposed here is that value leadership includes "rewarding" and "reinforcing . . . those orientations which are consonant with the goals represented in one's [the principal's] vision" (W. Greenfield, 1987a, p. 18). The implication is subtle but clear: those faculty members who, for one reason or another, choose not to share in the principal's moral vision will be discriminated against in one fashion or another. We have seen a national growth in dictatorial school principals as reported in *Time* and elsewhere. The grand irony of it all is that the whole issue of value leadership and moral imagination is thus placed in the same context as "the pursuit of democratic and universal values" (W. Greenfield, 1987a, p. 21). The "democratic" and "universal" dimension in Greenfield's position seems to evaporate upon closer examination, for teachers and pupils play a role so long as they agree with the leader's moral image: when they disagree they have no standing.

The entire administrative agenda of value leadership and moral imagination rests upon the assumption of a subordinate/superordinate relationship between the administrator and the teachers, and this implies among other things that somehow principals "know what is best" in instructional and other matters, owing to their position. Smith and Blase (1987) correctly identify the failure of this version of the moral imagination theory to provide a sound human relationship model which sees teachers treated as ends in themselves rather than the means for administrator-generated visions. It is necessary, I wish to argue, that we reconstruct the *role* of administrators by viewing leadership as a *complement* rather than a right of office. On this account, educational administrators would be leaders only insofar as they: (1) exercise self-restraint in using power to obligate followers (a Machiavellian potential is to be guarded against in which the value leader could exercise *any* means to the leader's own end—talk of reason and moral principles notwithstanding), and (2) give up the warrant of supposed scientific expertise, which Smith and Blase see as seeking the status of a god. With this latter point I disagree. While it is one thing to criticize administrators who posture as experts in the teaching fields, it is quite another to discount the entire body of research regarding educational administration. What is needed is a proper filtering of educational administrative knowledge by the leader, not the total rejection of research done.

At the heart of the moral imagination view criticized here is the naive assumption that values are matters of personal preference and intuitive understanding and are not subject to any kind of rigorous reasoned scrutiny. In place of this assumption, I wish to argue that if imagination and leadership are to be accepted dimensions of school governance, then they must be subject to rational discourse and open to critical pragmatic test. The canons of critical reflective thought are no less required here than they are in reading, math instruction, or social studies teaching.

Studies of leadership in education have revealed a hydra-like concept that resists all efforts at analysis (Maxcy, 1983; 1984; 1985). The concept of "leadership" may be ill-fitted to the discourse of educational administration, owing to the fact that it is not clear that when administrators direct subordinates that they "lead" them in any clear sense; and proposals that administrators become leaders (secure training in leadership, model leading behaviors) or adopt certain traits or techniques of leaders in other fields (military, politics, etc.) fundamentally confuse the task nature of leadership with achievement of desires.

Just as the failures of research programs in cognitive science often throw researchers into metaphysical justifications for continuing inquiry, so educational administration researchers are beginning to turn to moral/ethical discourse to warrant *praxis*. The difficulty is that we are no better off in jettisoning insufficient canons of scientific rationality by adopting insufficient canons of moral philosophy. Morality may be a port in the storm, but it is not a safe one—not safe from serious criticisms.

Moreover, following Gabriele Lakomski (1987), I wish to argue that the work of Hodgkinson (1978) and T. B. Greenfield (1986) to "treat *all* values as ethical and moral ones" and as subjective and non-cognitive (never true or false, but only "good" or "bad") is to make the comparative evaluation of *competing* values virtually impossible (Lakomski, p. 71). As Allan Bloom (1987) tells us, we are awash in a world of relativism where anyone's values are as good as anyone else's. In a sense, the value subjectivist position of the moral imaginationist is as dangerous as the earlier logical positivist claim that value claims are mere ejaculations: both camps insulate values from rationality.

CRITICAL IMAGINATION AND DEMOCRATIC VALUE DELIBERATION

Can we steer a middle course between the excesses of both the moral imagination theory and the human relations view? Here I wish to develop the moral/ethical/valuative dimension of the pragmatic leadership model that I have been advocating. First, it is important to say something about pragmatic value theory as the advance guard for our theorizing.

The pragmatic view of values neither deduces morals/ethics from some other world, nor does it propose that we may simply read them off of nature: more is required. The pragmatist points to human intelligence and the processes of scientific thinking as the source of morals and ethics. As values, morals and ethics may be seen to change from culture to culture or era to era. What is ethical or moral today may be unethical or immoral tomorrow.

When we fuse democratic processes with the scientific method of critical intelligence, as Dewey argued we ought to do (1916), it is possible to arrive at acceptable (valued) behavior. Moral vision and ethical vision are subject to intersubjectively arrived-at evaluation. We need not listen to dictators, like Lenin, or inspired leaders, such as Jim Jones.

Critical Imagination

Living in a democracy causes us of necessity to deliberate about choices. This would appear to make any effort at moral leadership in the schools sensitive to democratic processes. Rather than the conception of moral imagination, I wish to suggest a critically pragmatic imagination, that is, the use of creative imagination tempered by reflection to determine ends-in-view. This is not to argue that imagination is (a) a special mode of discovery; or (b) moral authority; or (c) a psychological faculty; or (d) a super science. As we have tried to demonstrate, imagination is neither moral nor immoral. Following Hullfish and Smith (1961), imagination may be seen as leading to hypotheses; however, it is not valuationally separate or superior to other modes of thought. Like intuition, imagination is a process of thought and not thought itself.

We can have morality only when we have others. Shared imagination of course involves others. We take it that current conceptions of moral leadership arising out of imaginative skills stress the private and personal character of discovery, not the public and democratic side. The prime necessity of the public school administrator arriving at policy from an open and rational path rather than a personal course is overlooked in most views of moral imagination.

T. F. Green (1985) finds imagination to be linked to conscience, in part moral, but as: (1) rooted in membership in a group (in this case the school); (2) carrying a critical tone; and (3) proposing new possibilities for the future (pp. 22–24). Unlike Green, Foster, or Kirk, I can find no rationale for deriving critical imagination from poetic or literary writings. It is entirely conceivable to exercise imaginative thinking without lapsing into prophesy or parable. In school administration, we would argue that what is required is a rootedness and connectedness in the school community (teachers, students, parents, bus drivers, etc.). And the school leader ought to allow for criticism (by self and others) of policy images. As Green states it: "It is only imagination that allows us to speak to other members about the chasm that exists between the hopes and fair expectations of the community and the failures of our lived lives" (p. 23). And finally, we would find inspiration for dreams and visions stemming from all kinds of everyday experience, not just literary writings.

Democratic Value Deliberation

Morals are one species of value. Imagination is moral only in part. Morality results from judgment. A variety of preferences, desires, interests, and goods play upon our minds. However, it is important to see discussion and deliberation about the importance of such values as a vital part of what we are calling "critical imagination." Moreover, such value deliberation in schools should be public rather than private. Leadership, whatever else it may mean, should be lodged in the collective deliberations of those most affected by the choices under consideration. The locus of control is not in a remote authority, but in the collective consciousness of users. Rather than an unconscious prototypical intuitive source of moral ideals, we would have the moral component emerge in the active deliberation of the publics involved. In practical affairs, the teachers and students affected by policy ought to be empowered and have a say in the source and content of such policy.

While schools may be seen as moral institutions, they are only partially so. The duty of the school administrator or teacher is not to introduce private and personal imaginative moral propositions into the school social world. Rather, it is the requirement of the enlightened school officer to be value deliberative. Rather than a single morally imaginative leader directing schooling, we wish a collective of value (and here we mean ethics, morals, wishes, and desires, etc.) deliberative teachers, students, and administrators.

The difficulty is furthermore seen in the fact that if the moral school leader is the only one invested with moral authority, then it is difficult to see how children or teachers will develop moral leadership. Children need moral skills if they are to operate as successful adults, parents, and citizens; teachers need moral skills if they are to instill them in children. The point is that we are advocating morality as responsible value-rational deliberation here.

An analog to the present argument is found in Richard Pratte (1988), following T. F. Green (1985), for the development of a public as opposed to a private conscience. Pratte points out that although a conscience is uniquely private in the fact that it speaks for a single individual, it may be "formed for participation in the public sphere. Thus a public conscience refers to an inner voice formed for telling us what to do in a situation having consequences which go far beyond the individual, what are called public acts" (Pratte, p. 214). Imagination, we wish to argue, is like conscience in the fact that it refers to a private enterprise. However, when it is adopted for the purpose of informing policy, we wish to argue it must be *formed* for the public and institutional administrative purpose. Pratte and Green argue for moral education of the private/public conscience: I propose we add a moral/value education for administrators for the purpose of reshaping the private resources of the so-called "moral imagination" into the public democratic critical imagination.

Interestingly, W. Greenfield (1987b) seems to have been influenced by T. F. Green's concept of "conscience" in the formation of his own notion of "moral imagination." However, this position mistakenly elevates the authoritarian and inspirational component of imagination in the name of morality, while overlooking the need for the imagination to be rooted in school membership and open to criticism by participants in that community. W. Greenfield's moral imagination is incapable of moving from a private to a public conscience.

The imagination of the leader should be public and open-textured. Because there are impacts on students, teachers, and parents owing to visions and goals implemented, it is reasonable to expect the institution's participants to share in deliberation regarding these images. As Pratte argues: "The public good cannot best be served by the inherent confidentiality of private conscience" (p. 215). Public education cannot be served by private moral visions. Moral imagination takes on the character of a kind of religious conscience in which are spawned "moral principles informing conduct that is confidential, particular, intimate, sectarian, offering not only guidance but hope, faith, and so on" (Pratte, p. 215). Rather, the school leader, having decided not to give a moral patina to images of what the school and its inhabitants ought to be, must now turn to the more rigorous practical judgment. For the school administrator must make decisions resting on judgments that are informed by reason. With the current craze for "naturalistic" inquiry in the social sciences, it is not surprising that such a rational twist may be suspect. Moral and ethical values need not be stripped from the schools. On the contrary, there is a need for the proper identification and treatment of value positions in education. To identify moral values with some privileged position owing to their method or source, however, is tantamount to grounding administrative praxis on metaphysics. *No matter what the source or method of derivation* of administrative plans or policies, it is vital to evaluate them on rational grounds—grounds that are not undercut by the irrational authoritarianism of origins, whether they be imagined or dreamed. To further assert that moral imaginings must be acceded to by others *owing to their source* is the worst form of authoritarianism. Educational administration, if it is to survive the current crises of confidence, had best turn away from occult or super-psychic groundings to democratically discursive *phronesis.*

Administrative leadership changes its meaning relative to the type of political culture or climate in which it operates, and the notion of expertise (narrowly intellectual versus philosophic minded) adopted by the leader. If we are to have reflective leaders, then a knowledge of critical thinking methods (some of which are democratic in nature) would be helpful. It has been asserted that the current penchant for expert authority does not free administration from value concerns. T. B. Greenfield (1986), W. Greenfield (1987a and b), Smith and Blase (1987), and others are correct in their stressing the importance of moral-ethical values in doing good administering. However, educational leaders have no monopoly on values.

The critical and pragmatic perspective on leadership that is advanced here finds democracy to be the most congenial social arrangement, or way of life, offering a middle ground between abstract moralizing found in the moral imagination view and the atomistic individualism of the personal relations model.

Leadership should be reconceptualized so as to profit from the pluralistic cultural settings within which it operates and to recognize that it may be shared and that leadership in a democratic society requires followers be treated as ends in themselves, rather than as means. Schools are special types of organizations that have particular cultures/climates in which both values and caring are important parts. But the extremes that caring theorists and moral imagination thinkers propose seem to overlook the communal and rational bases of school societies. Despite the serious problems schools face, the answer is not in suspending human rights and establishing Machiavellian dictators operating under "visions," nor is it to be found in emotionalism and personalism. The solution is to be found in moving beyond dictatorship on the one hand and laissez-faire naturalism on the other. "Value leadership," whatever else it may mean, is no different from rational leadership in its demands upon us: values that are irrational and nondiscursible are totalitarian and to be rejected. The plea is for the "open society" of open institutions with options openly arrived at: we can only see privileged access to visions and forced compliance with images as undemocratic, unethical, and vicious.

The British "headmaster" solution to governance seems superior to the principalship idea favored in the United States. The administrative functions are taken to be additional duties assumed by one of the teachers in the school. Educational administration and leadership are not elevated to the status of a special role in the schooling process. Since the headmasters teach and share responsibilities with other teachers, they tend to respect teachers and students as persons, become involved in deliberative discussion with all involved in the institution of school, and exercise restraint in the use of power. The redefinition of the notion of "principal" would thus eliminate all need for talk of moral imagination in school governance.

It is necessary to distance ourselves from T. B. Greenfield (1986) and Smith and Blase (1987) regarding the role of research in informing administrative action. T. B. Greenfield and Smith and Blase overreact when they narrow their notions of educational research to simple positivistic inquiry. To argue, as Smith and Blase do, that "a moral leader refuses to allow discussions of major pedagogical issues to be dominated by what the research supposedly demonstrates" seems to disenfranchise rational dialogue (p. 39).

CONCLUSIONS

This chapter has attempted to lay a course between the two extremes of "moral imagination" and "personal relations" as theoretical frameworks for supporting leadership. Moral imagination has been found to isolate and privilege administrative choice. It is suggested that "critical imagination" is superior. By stressing the "democratic value deliberative" dimension of educational leadership, it is argued, leading will become more reasoned and inclusive relative to values.

Human caring, we have discovered, fails to provide the social glue that allows private personal feelings to be directed to social organizations like schools. The emphasis upon character is important, but dialogical reciprocal relations seem insufficient grounding for community choices that impact upon both the development of the young and the future of society generally.

I have proposed a pragmatic theory of value that stresses the importance of democratic cultural consensus in the arriving at plans and policies that affect the school community. By enlarging rather than limiting the participants in the deliberative process, I wish to argue, the quality of life is enhanced and pedagogical responsibility is fulfilled.

7

Postmodernity and the Preparation of Educational Leaders for the Future

A rather recent self-consciousness of the temporal nature of the modern era has caused theorists to propose that we are either about to enter a "post-modern" age or have already arrived. This historic reflection on the assumptions of modernity sets the stage for a critical inquiry into the fundamental questions of education for this new time period. Since there is no more critical practical problem facing Americans today than the question of how teachers shall be educated for their task, postmodernity stands as a new mirror of possibilities for teacher preparation. The popular press often comes to locate the source of all the malaise in our society in our schools and teachers.

In this chapter I wish to discuss contemporary proposals for teacher education reform, as they relate to educational leadership, located in the modernity/postmodernity debate. It will be argued here that most talk of reform of teacher preparation is rooted in the discursive mode of modernity. Further, rather than improving the caliber of teaching in the United States, the current reforms are susceptible of perpetuating many of the present difficulties. Finally, the present effort will develop a new approach to critique, one in which postmodernity is shown to be a useful intellectual and heuristic device for understanding and redirecting educational leadership and teacher education reform for the future.

Earlier we mentioned the need for a "critical pragmatism" to be used in the understanding of "leadership" in educational settings. Such a philo-sophic view must be coupled with other postmodernist strategies if we are to see our project clearly to the end. In this chapter we will explore more fully what such a social philosophy may mean for educational governance and teaching.

MODERNITY AND POSTMODERNITY

It is difficult to understand the new discourse of postmodernity without a grasp of what is meant by "modern." Simply put, modernity is the effort to implement the project of the Enlightenment and Cartesianism. Lawrence Cahoone (1988) defines it thus: "the ideas, principles and patterns of inter-pretation, of diverse kinds ranging from the philosophic to the economic, on which western and central European and American society and culture, from the sixteenth through the twentieth centuries, increasingly found itself to be based" (Cahoone, p. 1).

Common patterns and tendencies have cut across these cultures, some of which coexist during certain historic periods: democracy, the nation-state, science and "the scientific method," secularism, rationality as the method of thought, secularism, and humanism (Cahoone, p. 1). While modernity has only recently come under scrutiny, this tardiness may be the result of western cultures' accepting too readily the fundamental value of these characteristics.

An interest has emerged recently in critically examining modernity and its agenda with the goal of deciphering the legitimacy of modernist values. Under the rubric of postmodernity, scholars and writers have come to challenge modernism and propose discourses that go beyond the Cartesian and Kantian legacy. The notion of postmodern is not entirely free from ambiguity, however. There seem to be at least three strong uses of the term as currently employed: (1) postmodernity, in the sense of a populist attack upon elitist modernism; (2) postmodern, taken to be a resistant and critical deconstruction of modernist tradition; and (3) postmodern, in the sense of a neoconservative antimodernism (H. Foster, 1983, pp. ix–xii). Of these mean-ings, the second seems most fruitful for the present project. Foster writes of this version of postmodernity:

A postmodernism of resistance, then, arises as a counter-practice not *only* to the official culture of modernism but also to the "false normativity" of a reactionary postmodernism. In opposition (but only in opposition) a resistant postmodernism is concerned with a critical deconstruction of tradition, not an instrumental pastiche of pop- or pseudo-historical forms, with a critique of origins, not a return to them. In short, it seeks to question rather than exploit cultural codes, to explore rather than conceal social and political affiliations. (H. Foster, p. xii)

I find the potential value of postmodern liberation (in this case of leader-ship) to rest in the critical and pragmatic attempt to explicate the meanings that late modern society and its social reformers attach to the teaching profession (Dumm, 1988, p. 211). In this way, postmodernity offers a conceptual stance and counter to the assumed Cartesian notions supporting contemporary reform discourses in teacher education such as the "Holmes Report" and *A Nation at Risk*. An opposition or resistance model of post-modernism challenges: (1) the idea that there is a single *foundational* epistemology by which all objects and events are to be judged; (2) the view that "rationality" and "scientific method" are singular modes of thinking; (3) that "progress" marks the history of Western civilization; (4) that institutions are somehow committed to ends, goals, and aims—while means are free from ethical/moral considerations; and (5) that only two stances face us—objectivism or relativism—as we seek to create better institutions and people in the future.

One postmodern approach, pragmatism, has resurfaced in recent years as a philosophic tool for the analysis and reconstruction of contemporary thought. Following the impetus of Richard Rorty's work (1979), theorists such as Bernstein (1983) and Cherryholmes (1988) have added significantly to the power of postmodern thought by appending pragmatism to other continental philosophic orientations. Bernstein mixes pragmatism with hermeneutics to provide a postmodern vision of social science reform "beyond objectivism and relativism." Cherryholmes joins poststructuralism, deconstructionism, and radicalism to pragmatism to develop his own unique "critical pragmatism." Cherryholmes writes:

the meanings we ascribe to our lives, texts, and discourses-practices are continually dispersed and deferred. Our texts and discourses-practices continuously require interpretation and reconstruction. We choose to act, furthermore, without the benefit of positive victories. Our choices and actions, in their totality, are pragmatic responses to the situations in which we and those around us find ourselves. They are based upon *visions* of what is beautiful, good, and true instead of fixed, structured, moral, or objective certainties. Poststructural analyses contribute criticism, that is sometimes radical, to our pragmatic choices (Cherryholmes, pp. 229–230)

Neither Bernstein nor Cherryholmes recognize an Archimedean or foundational view from which to judge human choices and practices. Rorty moves from hermeneutics to praxis and in the process drops epistemology as central to his project. Distinguishing "vulgar" from "critical" pragmatism, Cherryholmes argues that critical pragmatists reject a pragmatism based upon "unreflective acceptance of explicit and implicit standards, conventions, rules, and discourses-practices that we find around us" (Cherryholmes, p. 230). However, where Bernstein, following Arend, would have us engage in judgmental acts, Cherryholmes, following the lead of the deconstructionists, seeks to move beyond judgment to *criticism*.

Cherryholmes writes: "When being judgmental one forms an opinion or makes an estimation or decision by applying given criteria or standards. When being critical one treats such criteria and standards themselves as problematic" (Cherryholmes, p. 230).

Following Gadamer and other hermeneuticians, a postmodern view would see the school and teaching acts as species of *texts*. Deconstructionists such as Derrida and Deleuze would support the idea that a single view of the text (in this case teacher education) needs a mirroring such that differences could be depicted in "tracings." What is required is a new "map" of language, in particular what Deleuze calls "order-words," operating from deep-seated human speech. The relationship between linguistic statements and the act of leadership would then be seen as internal and immanent (Deleuze and Guattari, 1980 (1987), p. 79). Every statement is related to implicit presuppositions. The "voices" support the option of a problem-opening middle range set of activities. Here one could argue, following Jacques Daignault, that teachers be seen as architects for the space of meanings staged for students that lies between the individual text (life world) of the student and the mirror of that text (the curriculum and culture of the society and beyond that the "general text").

What is to be called for in a postmodernist rendition is that the educator (teacher, counselor, or administrator) be a "performing artist," rather than a "narrator" of the specific text of the organization of the school. Another way of saying this is to argue that educators are artists and not middle managers responsible to the corporation for producing children. Pedagogical education that results in the management vision of teaching fails to generate a critical "voice" for teachers. Postmodernism divests the self of subjectivity and generates a tension between nihilism and authoritarianism. Educators, then, have the option as practitioners of either turning their backs on the agendas of social change or entering into reform and hence destroying the freedom of their charges.

The deconstructionist finds that teachers are losing that voice, but that it may be regained by mixing teacher and student empowerments. We would argue that through a deconstruction of the text of teacher education, we may identify the disabling elements and reform programs so as to restore the polyvocal and critical nature of education. This move implies resistance, and power must be reconceptualized toward hope and reconstruction.

Cherryholmes argues that critical pragmatism focuses first upon attempting to read these institutional "texts," followed by efforts to evaluate and criticize them. Bernstein would have us seek to move beyond a foundational epistemological stance (whether it be "rationality" or "scientific method"), while avoiding a vicious relativist perspective that sees no way to judge the differences among such texts or discourses. And Deleuze would propose looking to the internal pragmatics of speech to see how our actions become what they are.

The postmodern approach, in the present instance, seeks to uncover the modernist agendas that current reform rhetoric manifests as they apply to teacher education proposals, to resist these modernist characterizations, and to move beyond them. Let us turn to one concrete proposal for teacher education change to test the postmodernist strategies outlined above.

THE REFORM PROPOSALS OF CLIFFORD AND GUTHRIE

There are a large number of education reform reports that have gained public attention (including *A Nation at Risk, Tomorrow's Teachers*, and *A Call for Change in Teacher Education*). These critical analyses have been widely discussed by people inside and outside the teaching profession. One reform work has been published (*Ed School*, by Geraldine Clifford and James Guthrie, 1988) which reflects the earlier analyses, while attempting to provide an historical treatment of the creation and development of the institution of the "school of education" in the United States along with proposals for reform. The book displays the institution of the education school, with its goal of preparing teachers for the schools of the nation, as sandwiched between the demands of research-oriented graduate school dictates and the real world of professional practitioners and the community. In light of current criticisms and efforts to dismantle schools of education across the country, the authors propose four strategic changes for schools of education in the future: (1) adherence to national professional standards for teacher preparation; (2) concentration upon graduate professional preparation (and concomitantly the end of undergraduate teacher education majors); (3) building upon revised and strengthened undergraduate liberal arts and subject-matter major requirements; and (4) focus upon the professional doctorate (Ed.D.) rather than the research Ph.D. All of these proposals rest upon traditional conceptions of the educational leader as goal-setter and policy-achiever.

There are five conditions that must be met, for Clifford and Guthrie, if these suggestions for the reform of education schools are to be implemented: (1) such institutions must have a clear sense of organizational purpose; (2) strong leadership and competent followership must be encouraged; (3) external relationships with professional educational organizations (unions, NEA, etc.) must be nurtured; (4) high levels of productivity must be developed; and (5) an effective alignment between organizational purpose and organizational structure must be created (Clifford and Guthrie, 1988, pp. 348–367).

ANALYSIS

First, by way of analysis, the Clifford and Guthrie proposals seem to buy into the meta-narrative of one version of positivism, and by so doing thwart the needed self-consciousness of modern tradition. It is assumed, in the sense of being taken for granted, that certain external standards or rules exist (sociocultural codes), or can be brought into existence, such that teacher education programs can be judged and evaluated, and hence accepted or rejected. Such an intra-institutional evaluation rests upon an embedded code of "rationality." Beyer rightly criticizes such an epistemological view in his work *Knowing and Acting: Inquiry, Ideology and Educational Studies* (1988). Bernstein (1983) goes to great pains to show how social science must reject the Enlightenment commitment to external standards and norms of rationality if it is to improve in the future. Paul Feyerabend rejects the twin values of "the scientific method" and "rationality" when he writes: "We, on the other hand, retain the lesson that *the validity, usefulness, adequacy of popular standards can be tested only by research that violates them*" (Feyerabend, 1978, p. 35).

It is significant for the true reform of teacher education that the modernist meta-narrative of external standards and values be critically scrutinized. Bernstein and Cherryholmes would have us look closely at the embedded nature of such norms in the "rationality" of science and social science. I wish to argue following Feyerabend (1978) that only by violating such standards are we to see what really works pragmatically in the leadership of educational futures. National norms and standards of assessment are external and artificial to the concrete instances of teacher preparation that require remedial work. Each instance must be pragmatically tested in light of fruits.

The Clifford and Guthrie proposals for the reform of teacher education are rooted in a tensional positivistic meta-narrative of cause and effect, means and ends, and concept and object. There is a naive foundational epistemological view underwriting their position that sees in the discourse and codes of modernity the standards and norms leading to the solution to the current crisis in teacher preparation. By tacitly accepting an Archimedean point from which to judge teacher education programs, the authors effectively counter the possibilities of alternative discourses and differing agenda.

In addition, the acceptance of external rational standards of judgment propels educational programs into the acceptance of socially derived knowledge. The goal of teacher training is thus to reproduce the inherent values and norms which the programmatic evaluation instruments tell us are legitimate. The inadequacies of current teacher education practices are continued.

Second, Clifford and Guthrie, as well as *Tomorrow's Teachers*, suggest that the professional side of teacher preparation be stressed and that the undergraduate teaching degree be abolished. This is not a new argument historically. What is new is the acceptance upon the part of insiders (Clifford and Guthrie are members of the education school establishment) of the uselessness of the professional education degree.

There are two difficulties with this proposal. One is that the "professional" nature of teaching is ill-defined and tends to suffer in comparison with medicine, law, and other fields. This is largely owing to the fact that teachers have not succeeded in self-defining whereas the other "professionals" have. Clifford and Guthrie point out how other fields suffered and turned their image around by active efforts (lobbying, creating organizations, etc.). It is argued that teachers could do the same.

We would counter-argue that the business of teaching is typically viewed as a mediating function ("midwifery") and the teacher is not empowered either as a curriculum maker or textual interpreter. Scholes (1985) and Cherryholmes (1988) show how the development of this "textual power" can enhance the teaching profession, transforming educational followers into pedagogical leaders in control of pedagogy and understanding.

Another difficulty with this proposal is found in the increased use of "parallel professionals" as teachers. People holding degrees in fields other than teaching and with no educational instruction are moving into teaching positions across the country. John Pullium tells of the economic decline in the forestry industries propelling students to education (1987). He rightly questions the motives of such transfer and points to the differences in aims and attendant skills required. The Clifford and Guthrie proposal does not help us in addressing this kind of problem.

The professionalization of teaching must be seen for what it is: an effort at "gatekeeping" and domination over a field that is more representative of a "helping" field than a profession. William James argued against the licensure of physicians at the turn of the century. His argument seems antiquated today given the professionalization of everyone from truck drivers to carhops. James pointed out that such licensing inhibits the freedom doctors would employ in healing the sick. External standards were seen as idealized Germanic absolutes that hindered rather than helped the advance of medicine. I would argue that professionalization of teaching, in modernist terms, would have the same effect. Rather than promoting the experimental and intellectual development of better teaching, national standards become the minimal requirements for practice.

Third, focusing upon graduate preparation rather than undergraduate education seems to present little difficulty here. Beyer (1988) points out that at what juncture teachers-to-be receive teacher education preparation may have little influence on the quality of teaching. However, there is concern regarding the kind of preparation they are to receive. The conceptual difference between techné and praxis is informative here. Much has been written about these notions by the postmodern social science theorists (e.g., Bernstein, 1983).

The concept of techné is critical to our pragmatic understanding of teacher preparation. Gadamer (1975a) argues that the meaning of techné has been transformed in modernist culture from its ancient notion (found detailed by Aristotle). As he puts it:

In a scientific culture such as ours the fields of techne and art are much more expanded. Thus the fields of mastering means to pre-given ends have been rendered even more monological and controllable. The crucial change is that practical wisdom can no longer be promoted by personal contact and the mutual exchange of views among citizens. Not only has craftsmanship been replaced by industrial work; many forms of our daily life are technologically organized so that they no longer require personal decision. In modern technological society public opinion itself has in a new and really decisive way become the object of very complicated techniques—and this, I think, is the main problem facing our civilization. (pp. 313–314)

If leadership in education is to be transactional rather than Machiavellian, teacher preparation programs must work for a future in which teaching is no longer defined as mere technical knowledge. Beyer (1988) writes: "Teachers must not be reduced to technicians whose commitment is to competence, isolated proficiency, and the skillful manipulation of means and ends." Beyer gives us three reasons why a technical competency is incomplete. First, it overlooks the complex nature of the classroom experience. Teachers are not able to operationalize a scientific rule to fit each situation. Second, seeing teacher training as vocational preparation limits the possible future growth and development of teachers. And finally, the technical definition of teaching plays into the hands of those who see education as simple promotion of social and cultural reproduction at the expense of a more democratic school practice and social transformation (Beyer, pp. 175–176). In short, teachers need to become real leaders in their teaching.

I would argue that because the concept of techne has been reduced to mere technical know-how, there is little value in appropriating it for teacher preparation programs. "Experts" in education are all too willing to subsume educational expertise under the model of a very narrow standardized technical efficiency. Additionally, the discovery of "teacher-proof" teaching materials and equipment has so removed educators from the role of "craftsman" that there is little hope of their regaining a sense of skilled workmanship.

Fourth, Holmes, Clifford and Guthrie, and other reports argue that teachers-to-be must be inducted into the liberal arts and the subject matter which they will teach. Beyer (1988) argues that what is overlooked here is the fact that teacher education courses may already contain liberal knowledge. He points to the "foundations" courses such as philosophy of education, history of education, and so forth as examples. Teacher education courses, then, need not in principle be different from the liberal arts offerings (Beyer, p. 180). There is, further, a view expressed in Clifford and Guthrie as well as *Tomorrow's Teachers* that assumes a separation of theory and practice. Teacher knowledge (practical knowledge) is different from and can be added to "liberal education" (theoretical knowledge). Beyer (1988) correctly argues: "the dichotomization between liberal and applied study, theory and practice, is itself the result of epistemological, political, and institutional pressures and patterns that we must transcend" (Beyer, p. 177).

The rejection of the theory-practice polarization and the adoption of a view of knowledge as understanding aids in reconceptualizing educational leadership in light of teacher preparation. Teachers need both theory and practice, and efforts to separate these are artificial as well as dangerous. Here we wish to introduce the concept of praxis. Yet there is a danger in adopting this notion, owing to the fact that praxis has been deformed in present-day culture and reduced to mere technical control. The "authority" of experts is divorced from the older notion of praxis as requiring choice, deliberation, and decisions about what to do in concrete situations we face (Bernstein, pp. 148–150). W. P. Foster (1986) writes of a postmodern praxis for educators:

The administrator, the teacher, and the student of administration and schooling work not to reproduce a given social world, but to remove the limits set by it. To achieve this task theory must become practical, must inform our methods of dealing with the world and influence our ways of framing our condition. (W. P. Foster, 1986, p. 191)

Finally, Clifford and Guthrie argue that the Ed.D. must be resurrected if a truly professional force is to be developed for the future. The controversy surrounding the Ed.D. versus the Ph.D has erupted many times since the first introduction of the Ed.D. There is evidence that despite the Bennett and Bloom criticisms of educators, there is a tendency for more education degrees to be granted in the future. The Carnegie Foundation reports: "the figures for education degrees granted will be on a pronounced upswing because there is an increasing number of students entering elementary and secondary schools" (Carnegie Foundation, 1988, p. 32). However, if the number of undergraduate degrees in education were to be seriously curtailed as Clifford and Guthrie, Holmes, and others recommend, it would obviously have a profound effect on future numbers of Ed.D. degrees (Carnegie Foundation, 1988, p. 32).

What Clifford and Guthrie seem to overlook is the fact that elements of their other proposals auger against their last proposal ever becoming a reality. Increased emphasis upon the liberal arts may well shift emphasis away from the goal of attaining an education doctorate. At least one part of the puzzle centers on what should count as "educational knowledge." Where education is viewed as nothing but techne, a set of learned methods, the effect is to reduce education to technical knowledge and to reduce pedagogical leadership to followership. However, as we have seen, postmodernists point to the need to view "education" as more than this. Beyer (1988) argues for teachers to be prepared in true praxis, or "teaching as empowering—involving self-reflection, critical analysis, moral debate and practical wisdom, continuing opportunities for creativity, autonomy, and academic freedom in the classroom—that is a result of teacher preparation based on praxis" (Beyer, p. 202).

THE CONDITIONS

Clifford and Guthrie, Holmes, and other national reports have focused upon certain enabling conditions that must be met if the project of teacher education reform is to succeed. For our purposes, the Clifford and Guthrie conditions will be used here to illustrate these recommendations. Clifford and Guthrie propose: (1) such institutions must have a clear sense of organizational purpose; (2) strong leadership and competent followership must be encouraged; (3) external relationships with professional educational organizations (unions, NEA, etc.) must be nurtured; (4) high levels of productivity must be developed; and (5) an effective alignment between organizational purpose and organizational structure must be created (Clifford and Guthrie, 1988, pp. 348–367).

The essential ingredient in these conditions is that of the organization. Postmodern theorists William Pinar and Madeleine Grumet (1976) argue that significant change in teaching will not come through organizational dictates, but rather through the reconceptualization of individual teaching. They advocate the use of autobiography and other literary techniques to reform teaching practice. Scholes (1985) reinforces this vision of the teacher by showing how a reconstruction of the teacher as textual interpreter may aid in empowering pedagogy.

Even educational administration theorists, long wedded to organizational theory as the single most successful explanatory net, have turned to postmodern critique. W. P. Foster (1986) tells us that organizational theory has too long relied upon the data from business and industry. Newer models of organizational thinking reveal the fact that the human variable has been neglected. Foster writes:

While traditional approaches to organizational study have focused on the individual organization as the unit of analysis, we should also look at micro-processes to discover how individuals construct their own realities, and macro-processes to understand the relationships between organizations in society. Finally, process itself is relevant. Traditional studies have focused on the organization as if it existed in a time warp. A processual analysis would attempt to look at the organization over time, and to analyze the processes of change and innovation to see how they occur in relation to other changes in the social system . . . look[ing] at the organization not only through a variety of frames, but also in a dialectical manner, moving between individuals and structure and relating them to wider or perhaps more constricting perceptions of the nature of organizations. This gives us a new way of conceptualizing schools and school systems . . . organizations [are seen as] human constructs. (W. P. Foster, p. 146)

Unfortunately, Clifford and Guthrie are guilty of conceiving of education schools according to an outdated modernist view of structural-functionalism. Having accepted an organizational view of teacher preparation, their reforms perpetuate the inadequacies of this self-defining sociocultural set of codes. Unless teaching is seen as something other than the followership and organization that permits it, the ideological and political forces that dominate and reproduce teacher powerlessness will continue. Unless a post-modernist resistance to limits is adopted, little change will result.

Locating a sense of purpose is also set in the meta-narrative of positivistic organizational theory. To be legitimate, an institution must have "institutional goals." Clifford and Guthrie write: "Having a well-specified sense of purpose clarifies judgments and provides a base against which to assess progress" (p. 360). To have such a sense of purpose helps an education school define itself and to aid in warding off hostile incursions and appropriations from rival segments of the academic community, they assert (pp. 360–361). What is interesting about this kind of talk is the degree to which the authors have accepted uncritically the assumption that schools of education are organizations that *ought* to be in the business of producing some commodity (teachers) and that process is open to objective scientific determination and evaluation. The rational-technical interest in modern societies that has been so thoroughly criticized by Habermas and his followers is here tacitly accepted for teacher education (W. P. Foster, 1986, ch. 4).

LEADERSHIP AND EDUCATIONAL REFORM

"Strong leadership" is used in a cliché manner in the Clifford and Guthrie modernist image. Elsewhere I have argued that educational leadership is a conceptual maelstrom that refuses clarification. The essential tension in the position advanced here rests in the move to make administrators leaders when in reality what is required is management. Leadership operates as a kind of value gloss here. What Clifford and Guthrie are really searching for are expert accountants who will fight off the invasions from the liberal arts and sciences by posting ledger pages filled with statistics proving the teachers college has delivered the required enrollment numbers.

A postmodern vision of educational leadership links the concept with the notion of *power*. Here leaders seek to release, teachers and teachers-to-be from ideological and political constraints that function to reproduce pedagogical impotence. Teacher *empowerment* is also linked to critical pragmatism. Teachers need to adopt a critical stance along with their practical wisdom. Shifting the locus of control from the organization to the teacher would go a long way toward releasing the potential of teaching for social and cultural good.

Improving the relationship between teaching and external organizations such as unions and professional groups has long been advocated by liberal reformers. It is not the case, however, that such affiliations automatically bring improved professionalism for workers (teachers). Some professional groups are vital and progressive, attempt to advance the profession by providing benefits to members, and in other ways enhancing work. However, other external groups are lackluster at best, tend to take more than they give to members, and fail to move the profession forward vis à vis the future social and cultural changes (Strauss, 1988). Like Dewey's view, critical pragmatism finds the necessity of communities of like-minded individuals forming and reforming on the basis of shared interests and goals. The difficulty with present-day educational reforms is to be found in their top-down, non-democratic, efficiency-driven positivistic assumptions. Connecting up teachers-to-be with these sorts of external communities can be a dangerous mistake. The danger lies in subversion and co-option.

Clifford and Guthrie fail to see the similarity between their view of the education school as a product-oriented mechanism and the older "banking notion of education." The slip from one to the other is easy. We have seen how elementary and secondary schools have been characterized as mini-factories and micro-businesses whose aim is to produce a product, that is, educated persons. The analogy with the world of business has been popular since the early part of this century, when Franklin Bobbitt and W. W. Charters, Charles Peters, and others sought to adapt Taylorized methods to the schools.

Critical pragmatism has attacked this vision before. Dewey and his followers showed how the epistemology of educational banking was illicit, how it failed to provide for the full and reconstructive nature of experience. For the pragmatist, then and now, the human being is not an empty container waiting to be filled with "facts" by the educator. Clifford and Guthrie lead us to believe that somehow the education school must embrace the banking notion of pedagogy, even though it has proven unsuccessful in the elementary and high schools of this country.

The argument that the education college must exhibit a sign of organizational purpose that fits organizational structure is part of the same thinking that sees teachers as powerless resultants of organizational ends. This structuralist-functionalist, positivist view has been heavily criticized in the postmodernist literature. The meta-narrative is laced with assumptions about the role of human beings and the power of organizations over them. W. Foster (1986), drawing upon Habermas, argues that purposive rational action has undetermined the role of critique in organizational culture. Teachers are unable to be self-reflective or to develop self-understanding. The emphasis upon rewards of the system finds them marching to a succession of drummers. The Clifford and Guthrie criterion of fit is as fruitful for a concentration camp as it is for an education school.

CONCLUSIONS

In this chapter I have attempted to demonstrate how the problem of how teachers may be educated in the future requires a mode of inquiry that goes beyond that of modernist jingoism. I have proposed that we look at proposals for the reform of teacher education through the lens of "postmodernism" viewed as "critical pragmatism." What is so patently evident, as John Pullium (1987) has so aptly put it, is that we talk of the future in medieval ways. The future of teacher preparation programs hinges on our ability and desire to resist modernist discourses and to transform shopworn methods of inquiry into newer, more fruitful methods; to cast teacher education in a new light; to see our task as critical and pragmatic philosophers of education to be one of reconstruction of praxis, or as Henry David Thoreau put it, "to solve some of the problems of life, not only theoretically, but practically" (Bode, 1947, p. 270).

8

Empowerment and Educational Leadership

Witnessing the crises in schools in America, educational experts have moved toward the encouragement of the articulation of an "empowered" authoritative teacher's voice. Albert Shanker, president of the American Federation of Teachers, calls for a "true teacher professionalism," with an emphasis upon expertise, autonomy, independence, and decision making. Theodore Sizer (1985) writes: "the existing teaching force has substantial strength. We must empower and enhance the abler folk within it. Our experiment absolutely depends on able teachers. To plan otherwise is to give up" (p. 235).

On the other side of the ledger, advocates of stronger educational administration push for a restructuring of schools, with greater emphasis upon the supervision and evaluation of teachers, and greater attention to "effectiveness" by all educators. Buffered by structural functionalist research, these thinkers find the question of "empowerment" to be concerned with the authority and position of the principal or superintendent—not the teacher. Where this group may suggest the empowering of teachers, it is always and only against the backdrop of a formal conception of institutions and the ends they wish served. (The neo-Marxist criticism of this power position argues that empowerment of teachers can never be emancipatory owing to the ideological commitment of the powerful.)

Power is taken to be the common sense catalyst for both factions in the current rhetoric of educational reform (Nyberg and Farber, 1986). Proper and prompt exercise of power in the name of educational change is central to specific arguments for reconfiguring schools (Barrow, 1984).

Prior to the adoption of strategies for educational reform, it is important to analyze the assumptions supporting these plans for change. Certain prior questions need to be dealt with here: (1) What is meant by "power" and "empowerment"? (2) How may "empowerment" be seen as the solution to the crises that plague our nation's schools? (3) Once settled upon a definition of "power," in what ways are power and "power structure" related to the larger issues of educational reform? (4) How are power and leadership connected and what bearings do their relations have on education?

CONCEPTIONS OF EMPOWERMENT

The first task of this chapter is to treat the meanings of "power" and "empowerment" found in the literature of philosophy, education, and social science, and to reconstruct those meanings so as to help form a pragmatic theory of leadership that is rational, democratic, and emancipatory.

Against the multiple uses of the term "empower," it will be argued, is a *conception of "power/empower" that is transactional*, involving persons (or a person and himself/herself) in a (educational) setting. We should note that this use of "transactional" is derived from a view of John Dewey and Arthur Bentley (1949, pp. 103–143) and not from James MacGregor Burns's conception of "transactional" versus "transformative" leadership. Simply stated, what I intend to argue is that empowerment is dialogical, in the sense that it involves two or more persons involved in an exchange and interchange of reasoned choice. There is no linearity or unidirectionality in empowerment as commonly assumed—where some transferral of power, read "force," or authority from one person (or persons) to another (or others) takes place. This commonsensical meaning of empowerment is mechanistic and sees power as a *behavior*, potential and actual, latent and manifest—a kind of molecular and energized "matter in motion."

This Newtonian view of power is a "one-dimensional view" and operates in the political science literature. Robert Dahl's (1957) "intuitive idea of power" is a pluralist account in which "*A* has power over *B* to the extent that he can get *B* to do something that *B* would not otherwise do." Or if *A* makes a successful attempt at this, a power relation is evident. The first definition, Steven Lukes (1974) tells us, illustrates the potential power view, while the second points up the actual power behavior. In both definitions, the one-dimensionality is evidenced through a stress upon power as a study of concrete, observable behavior, and the focus of *decision making* as the primary job of the powerful with *conflict* resolution as the test of success. Political pluralists, such as Dahl, evidence a one-dimensional view of power when they focus upon behavior in the shape of decision making relative to an issue over which there is observable conflict of (subjective) interests (Lukes, pp. 14–15).

A more sophisticated version is the "two-dimensional view" of power. This definition sees the pluralist view as restrictive owing to its reliance upon behaviors such as intiation and decision making. Power is not only the making of decisions, but also the creation and sustenance of barriers to the effective airing of policy conflicts. Peter Bachrach and Morton Baratz (1962) argue that "organization is the mobilization of bias," and part of this bias is the formation of an elite group which seeks compliance and promotes their vested interests. Power, for Bachrach and Baratz (1962), as a two-dimensional concept entails coercion, influence, authority, force, and manipulation (Lukes, pp. 16–17).

A better analysis of two-dimensional power involves looking at both *decision making* and *nondecision making* activity, where nondecision making is the capacity to stifle or suffocate demands for change in the existing allocation of benefits and privileges within an organization or community (Lukes, pp. 18–19). Lukes correctly points out that both one-dimensional and two-dimensional models share a concern for actual observable conflict: both views are conflictualist.

In the "three-dimensional view" of power, we see the emphasis on behaviorism to be too strong in models one and two. In addition, the bias dimension is too narrowly construed as a function of individual actors, decisions, and actions. Both models one and two, moreover, are too tied to Weber's vision of power as the probability of individuals realizing their wills despite the resistance of others. And model two is incomplete owing to its emphasis upon power as actual observed conflict (Lukes, pp. 21–22).

The three-dimensional view of power involves a "thorough-going critique" of the behaviorism of the other views, the individualism, and the overt conflictual characteristics of the situations. In the three-dimensional view, Lukes expresses a focus upon the decision making and control over political agenda (but not necessarily through decisions); the importance of issues as well as potential issues; the observable (overt and covert) and latent conflict; and the subjective and real interests of the parties involved (Lukes, p. 25). For Lukes, "power is one of those concepts which is ineradicably value-dependent." By this is meant that both its definition and any particular use of the term are tied to a given set of (probably unacknowledged) value-assumptions. These value postures order the range of "power" in empirical application (Lukes, p. 26).

The essential core meaning of power in all three models is that A in some way affects B in a manner contrary to B's interests. The difficulty, however, resides in the methodological and epistemological handling of this transaction: the applying of primitive (causal) features to this relation (Lukes, p. 26). A better definition of the concept of power may be: "*A* exercises power over *B* when *A* affects *B* in a manner contrary to *B*'s interests" (Lukes, p. 34). The trick is in determining what "interests" may mean. As Lukes puts it: "any view of power rests on some normatively specific conception of interests" (Lukes, pp. 34–35). A search for "power interests," like that of a tracking of "power motives," is apt to relocate the discourse of empowerment in the realm of psychology of mind: a dead end for any pragmatic theory of leadership.

A second set of meanings of empowerment and power finds these terms identifying situational or structural features of organizations. Weber writes, "All political structures use force, but they differ in the manner in which and the extent to which they use or threaten to use it against other political organizations" (Gerth and Mills, 1958, p. 159). Here power is attached to the bureaucracy *within* the organization in the search for higher offices, more sinecures, and better opportunities for advancement; while outside of the organization, power is in the organization's exercise of force over neighbors, foes, or competitors.

With these two kinds of definitions, power and empowerment take on the characteristic of either (1) molecular entities or matter in motion (the billiard ball view of power), where power is force, weight, strength, or some other measurable quantity of mechanical influence, systematically reduced to variables or data, and measurable; or (2) force, in the sense of muscular influence, located within organizations, which can be "wielded" or "exercised" in the struggle for existence.

The foregoing theories of power/empowerment are interactionist. I wish to argue for a view of power/empowerment as a matter of *transaction*. Here, following Dewey and Arthur Bentley (1949), the term "transaction" denotes the fluid activity side of power; the impossibility, except through some conceptual "freeze-frame" device, to locate power in any one person or place. The analog may be found in the word "loan." For a loan to be had, there must be a loaner and a borrower, some set or agreed upon sum and pay-back schedule, a transfer of funds, and so forth. The complexity of the loan-operation is such that at no single place may we effectively say that the interactants "loan." (Phillips, 1987, argues against this position in his *Philosophy, Science and Social Inquiry*, but not persuasively.) The transactional nature of loaning seems clear because the parties engage in some kind of business. By a similar token, the empowerment of agents is not an interaction (in which A gets power from B, for example), but a transaction, in which A provides opportunities for B to use power, while B takes it upon himself or herself to take power; however, power resides neither in A nor B, but in the complexity of actions involved in power itself. Rather than a classical mechanical and vitalistic view of empower as interaction, I propose a more pragmatic epistemological stance.

The emergence of power provides a serious threat to conventional uni-linear and mechanistic theories of power. It is not clear how power gets out, develops, or grows, given the mechanical view. For this, we must have at our disposal all of the characters and events that make power manifest. Dewey and Bentley (1949) talk of "hunting":

If we watch a hunter with his gun go into a field where he sees a small animal already known to him by name as a rabbit, then, within the framework of half an hour and an acre of land, it is easy—and for immediate purposes satisfactory enough—to report the shooting that follows in an interactional form in which rabbit and hunter and gun enter as separates and come together by way of cause and effect. If, however, we take enough of the earth and enough thousands of years, and watch the identification of rabbit gradually taking place, arising first in the subnaming processes of gesture, cry, and attentive movement, wherein both rabbit and hunter participate, and continuing on various levels of description and naming, we shall soon see the transactional account as the one that best covers the ground. This will hold not only for the naming of the hunter, but also for accounts of his history back into the pre-human and for his appliances and techniques. No one would be able successfully to speak of the hun*ter* and the hun*ted* as isolated with respect to hun*ting*. Yet it is just as absurd to set up hun*ting* as an event in isolation from the spatio-temporal connection of all the components. (Dewey and Bentley, 1949, p. 133)

Another avenue worth pursuing in highlighting the transactional nature of power is that of the political manifestation of power as derived from science. Joseph Rouse (1987) argues persuasively for the characterization of political power as an emergent of laboratory science. Just as the laboratory worker seeks to measure, mix, count, analyze, decompose and recompose, separate and isolate, the social actor must do similar things in the laboratory of society. The laboratory microworld is one in which power is seen as "capillary power relations" over things; while the society is taken to be a laboratory (writ large) in which power relations are typically attached to the state or the owners of capital (Rouse, pp. 243–244). Rouse proposes that "we should describe laboratory practices and their extension as embodying *power* relations" (p. 244). Here laboratory practices are overlapping and mutually reinforcing the forms of disciplinary power or biopower that Foucault talks about. Power over human beings and the control and manipulation of things are the same, while the discourses have been unfamiliar. Moreover, Rouse points to the impact of laboratory power upon our ordinary lives, changing what and how we think (e.g., the daily rituals of washing our hands, checking the labels on our foods). In addition, the laboratories have exerted power over our lives by leading us to institutionalize new scientific understandings (electricity yielding companies; petroleum propagating oil industries). These new systems require constant service from us, if they are to work (Rouse, p. 245). At this point in his argument Rouse invokes a more transactional view of power:

These [power] constraints have a very different shape from traditionally understood power relations, however. They do not take only the form of power *over* particular things or persons, possessed and exercised *by* others. They circulate throughout our relations with one another and dealings with things and pervade the smallest and most ordinary of our doings. They shape the practical configuration within which our actions make sense, both to ourselves and to one another. (Rouse, 1987, p. 246)

Beyond the mere compelling us to act in certain ways, these power transactions also "reconfigure the *style* and interconnectedness of what we do," Rouse points out (p. 246). Increasingly, our options and self-under-standing are colored by the laboratory microworlds. Enclosed, isolated, or partitioned, the things we encounter and do are subject to careful measure-ment, enumeration, and scheduling. We are now doing things that are more visible and accountable than ever before: increasingly we are compelled to produce *signs* of efficiency and effectiveness (Rouse, p. 246).

Rouse points to our social organizations, which, owing to scientization, have become more artificially complex in the face of increasing isolation of individual human beings within them—all with the aim of making human actions physicalistic causal connections. Hence,

scientific knowledge is embodied in practices that in a sense come to possess us. . . . The power relations that interest me [Rouse] are not the power *over* nature that scientific practices provide us, although this aspect has also figured prominently in my account. I have been arguing instead that it is the effects of these practices upon us and our form of life that need to be understood in terms of power and that call for explicitly political interpretation and criticism. The forms of power/knowledge embodied in the natural sciences help reshape our world as a field of possible action and fundamentally influence what is at stake in our lives. (p. 247)

John Dewey subscribed to something similar when he argued that the techniques of the laboratory scientist could be carried into the society at large in helping resolve social problems. No democratic culture, to Dewey's mind, had ever made adequate use of scientific method in determining policy. He therefore suggested that the scientific mode as amended to the democratic method would stress the freedom of inquiry, toleration for diverse views, free communication, and the free distribution of findings of such inquiries to all individuals. It was to be the nature of this new method to welcome and tolerate alternatives and conflicting points of view in the search for a consensus of conclusions, and to make whatever was concluded subject to public knowledge and further inquiry (Dewey, 1939, p. 102).

By focusing upon the *methods* of the scientist, rather than his/her findings, a set of techniques of thought could be adapted for the use of schoolchildren. Thus, the society was viewed like a large scale laboratory, where ideas could be tested out. Human inquiry, then, became the instrument for the active probing of social problems, with students learning the methods of science as applied to the social sphere. Dewey wrote: "The general adoption of the scientific attitude in human affairs would mean nothing less than a revolutionary change in morals, religion, politics, and industry" (Dewey, 1930, p. 155).

"Power" in educational discourses/practices, following Rouse and Dewey, is best understood by a fuller social philosophical analysis that is sensitive to the rational scientific and critical transactional features of action/thought. For a new conception of "empower," as it relates to educational leadership, going beyond the earlier functionalist/interactionist groundings, we must take into consideration at least these conditions: (1) rational authority or expertise; (2) teacher collaboration and collegiality; and (3) the democratic culture/climate of school settings.

Rational Authority

Kenneth Benne (1970) distinguishes expert authority from rule authority and proposes a third type of authority, which he terms "anthropogogical authority." Benne tells us: "There is a widespread tendency among scientific students of behavior to assimilate authority to power. . . . Where sociologists follow the tradition of Max Weber and treat authority as a species of power—legitimate and formal, as over against informal power—they tend to reinforce the popular identification of authority with established power." The upshot is that authority, in education in particular, is linked with conservative force, while reformists become committed to the overthrow of authority. Interestingly, as Benne perceptively points out, such educational reformers (at least in the 1960s and 1970s) did not question power (pp. 386–387). In fact, the reformers wanted power.

Benne turns the authority and power relation into a triadic condition. Authority is a function of concrete human situations in which "a person or group, fulfilling some purpose, project, or need, requires guidance or direction from a source outside himself or itself" (p. 392). This need Benne calls the "field" of the authority triad. The individual or group thus *grants obedience* to a person or group (or a rule, method, or way of coping), Benne proposes. This granting of assistance is based upon claims of *effectiveness* in mediating the field of conduct or belief. The authority relation is a social relationship "between subject(s), bearer(s), and field(s)" (Benne, pp. 392–393). The bearer of authority, then, must receive the willing obedience from the subjects of his (or its) authority. The bearer exercising authority must help in mediating the field of conduct or belief in which the subjects feel uneasy and ill-prepared. Out of this condition, the authority should provide advice, leadership, guidance, or direction (Benne, pp. 392–393).

For Benne, "power" is human influence. Each person, as he/she occupies a community, defines the human powers in terms of that community. There is a definition of the working community in this regard. The human will speaks to the wills of other wills who are dependent or alienated. Claims of obedience, power over others, claims of authority—all implicitly offer service to the dependent in satisfying some human need (while also exercising a threat of power over others) (Benne, p. 392).

In the present cultural crisis in education we find arguments for "teacher empowerment," pitting teachers as authorities against school administrators as powerful (but efficient) bureaucratic managers. In this equation, *authority* has received insufficient attention as it is attached to questions of power and leadership (Cherryholmes, 1988).

Scheffler (1985) tells us: "To enhance an agent's capability to perform is to empower him to perform" (p. 59). For Scheffler, empowerment is tied to capability (potential), hypothetical outcome, and positive or negative value (good or bad). To empower is to transfer expertise to the uninitiated.

> To empower a student to learn the arts of healing is at the same time to empower him to learn methods of poisoning. To keep the learning of poisoning out of his range of decision would also keep the learning of healing out of his range of decision. . . . potentials, construed as capabilities of acquisitions are surely not intrinsic to the person; they must be developed or constricted over time. Finally, the principle of relativity of potential earlier mentioned holds here as well. (Scheffler, p. 62)

Scheffler is interested in showing the direct link between a task and the power concept. However, empowerment also has attached to it a strongly moral dimension: to empower is to inculcate a *potential* to do harm. Here the agent is confronted with the equivalent of a moral education where power is released to do good, but also to inflict harm where wrongly exercised. This definition admits of the common misconception that empowerment is a function of others, and is strongly related to knowledge (in Scheffler's example, of medical expertise). It is doubtful that empower may stand up solely on a logical account, one that overlooks the discourses/practices wherein empowerment is played out. By drawing upon analytical philosophical tools to the exclusion of critical and pragmatic considerations, empowerment continues to operate as a sedimented epistemological concern and fails to become connected to any emancipatory or reform agenda. We must ask of Scheffler—What is the meta-narrative of empowerment?

Empowerment certainly has attached to it a knowledge dimension. It is not clear, however, that it is a didactic pedagogical act of passing on of knowledge from an expert to the novice. Like the slave boy in Plato's example, knowledge as power may well be the self-realization that control over data and explanatory concepts lies within, not without. The empowerment of educators does not imply *force* or *compliance*: We must assume that a reasoned embrace is necessary if the discourse/practice is to be infused with power. Additionally, as Scheffler points out, empowerment is connected with *choice*. Decisions of practice are essentially reasoned ways of proceeding in action. To empower is to reflect the capacity of the object of empowerment to be a potential bearer of knowledge within a particular setting or context (Scheffler, p. 63). In educational empowerment, the domain of knowledge is more significant and plays a larger role. Empowered teachers are not less expert as a result. But empowerment need not generate good (or evil for that matter) in any stronger sense than does simple cognitive reflection. All choice has the capacity to go sour, degenerate, and lead to less than noble ends: empowerment does not of itself insure that this will not happen. In this meaning of empowerment, teacher empowerment must not be seen as a moral panacea for the ills of schooling.

We must ask—How is it that the advocates of empowerment think the way they do?

Burbules (1986) points to traditional efforts to offer typologies which itemize forms that power takes, but which assume that power is something an individual or group has and uses, with differences found in the *means* of exercising it (Burbules, p. 96). Burbules draws upon Anthony Gidden's definition of power to support his own view.

Power within social systems can thus be treated as *involving reproduced relations of autonomy and dependence in social interaction.* Power relations therefore are always two-way, even if the power of one actor or party in a social relation is minimal compared to another. Power relations are relations of autonomy and dependence, but even the most autonomous agent is in some degree dependent and the most dependent actor or party in a relationship retains some autonomy. (Burbules, p. 97)

Gadamer in his work *Truth and Method* (1975b) finds power to be incapable of measurement, existing only in its expression as a tension or interplay of power components. Here "empowerment" would mean a transaction rather than a state of knowing. Power for Gadamer, like Giddens, is relational and entails submission and lack of freedom. Nonetheless, there is a kind of unity in this power tension relation.

W. P. Foster (1986) sees leadership as a political act which attempts to empower followers. Drawing upon Burns (1978), he asserts that empowerment in social settings entails: (1) modification of hierarchical organizational structures, and (2) the enabling of unrestrained discourse. Here empowerment is a vehicle for the critical theory agenda of resistance to and release from ideological oppression (Foster, pp. 187–188). More recently, Foster has stressed power as "transformative" and intellectual (1989). Focusing upon school administrators and teachers, Foster calls for educators to become (following Henry Giroux, *Teachers as Intellectuals: Toward a Critical Pedagogy of Learning*, 1988) "transformative intellectuals" by: (a) attempting to change not just students but the social order; and (b) providing models for others to follow in the quest for social change. Foster points out that there are three dimensions for his scheme: (1) the school administrator as intellectual leader; (2) the "virtuous practitioner" striving for an ideal through administering and teaching as a form of the good life; and (3) transformative administration/teaching, in the sense that the administrator and teacher become agents of social science and not just managers (Foster, 1989).

There is a sense in which social science as inquiry may be seen as itself a power relation manifest in discourse/practice. Brian Fay (1987) sees "empowerment" as one of the conditions necessary for a truly critical social science. We shall have more to say about the power relation in educational research later.

Cherryholmes (1988) defines power as a relation as well. He writes: "When I use the word *power*, it will refer to relations among individuals or groups based on social, political, and material *asymmetries* by which some people are indulged and rewarded and others negatively sanctioned and deprived" (Cherryholmes, p. 5). Cherryholmes goes on to say that these asymmetries are based on possessions or characteristics, with power being constituted by relationships among those differences. Power is a relation, Cherryholmes asserts. Moreover, power is important because of its effects: "the effects of power lead us to ask how they may come about and what relations and processes produced them" (p. 5). Ideology is interweaved with power when people accept, believe, and internalize explanations and justifications for the asymmetries of their social world, Cherryholmes argues (p. 5).

Foucault's fundamental contribution to the definitional enterprise relative to "power" is to see power as a "machine" in which everyone is caught (Burbules, p. 97). However, Bernstein finds within the power relation a means to reconstruct community. The machine may work toward reform. He writes:

I want to stress the danger of the type of "totalizing" critique that seduces us into thinking that the forces at work in contemporary society are so powerful and devious that there is no possibility of achieving a communal life based on undistorted communication, dialogue, communal judgment, and rational persuasion. What we desperately need today is to learn to think and act more like the fox than the hedgehog—to seize upon those experiences and struggles in which there are still the glimmerings of solidarity and the promise of dialogical communication in which there can be genuine mutual participation and where reciprocal wooing and persuasion can prevail. For what is characteristic of our contemporary situation is not just the playing out of powerful forces that are always beyond our control, or the spread of disciplinary techniques that always elude our grasp, but a paradoxical situation where power creates counter-power (resistance) and reveals the vulnerability of power, where the very forces that undermine and inhibit communal life also create new, and frequently unpredictable, forms of solidarity. (Bernstein, 1983, p. 228)

Collaboration and Collegiality

Institutional cultures are not islands: There are exogenous variables which play upon the field of any institution. Power transactions involve some tension in the sense that there is usually friction between *compliance* and *resistance*. So long as the tension of resistance and compliance remains it legitimates the person exercising (or capable of exercising) power. And the one agent is empowered by reason of the unempowered recognizing and complying with the powerful one (Burbules, pp. 97–98). Institutional "health" may be gauged by the power transactions within that culture.

This tension can be overemphasized, for it fails to account for the over-throw of the powered by the unempowered. Revolt is impossible. Moreover, compliance may be a more subtle form of empowerment of the unem-powered. F. G. Bailey (1988) speaks of "Svejkism" as a means of undermin-ing role leaders in organizations by making them appear fools. Teachers need not look to a particular role player (e.g., administrators) to empower them. Rather, empowerment, if it means anything in educational reform, points to the capacity for individuals, in *collaboration*, to *empower* themselves. Power is not so much transferred as it is *released* through interpersonal transactions. This is to say that when an agent is empowered, it is not the case that he/she is given power by another, but rather that the power within the agent may be surfaced and expanded. This often takes place through some catalyst (see, for example, Paulo Freire's adult literacy program in *Pedagogy of the Oppressed*). "Empowerment," then, may be seen as a manifestation of the educator's role—that is, teachers are involved in working with groups (often small collections of children or adolescents), and school administrators work with groups of teachers and larger collectivities of youth.

Dewey and Bentley provided a matrix for understanding this social setting in their *transactional* vision of all sociopolitical discourse, of which power and empowerment are slices (Dewey and Bentley, 1949). A pragmatic theory of leadership, then, relies upon the proper amount of collaboration and collegiality among teachers/administrators. This view finds it essential that educators not be isolated individuals. Through joint efforts, using groups and organizations of interest-bearing actions, educators may empower their leadership where they transact business for the purpose of realizing the goals of the organization (school).

"Power" needs clarification and revitalization as a concept in language if we are to reform education at all along ethical lines. Power may be taken to be a "fundamental category of human experience" which arises whenever two or more people are related through some plan of action (Nyberg, 1981, p. 170). Power is partly psychological because it requires a plan or intention; it is partly social because it requires at least two people who are related in some way, and it is always found where organizations are evident; and power is instrumental because it is an action idea, a means in relation to a plan. Power is *pragmatic* (Nyberg, p. 170). Nyberg writes:

My analysis makes power teachable, too. It helps to explain the possibility of practice. As an aspect of all social relations that involve at least people and a plan for action, power has a set of discernible characteristics and four distinct forms. These characteristics and forms can be identified, iillustrated, explained, practiced—in short, they can be taught. And in order to achieve the democratic principle that requires a broad distribution of power, knowledge about power ought to be taught. Clever teachers can use the forms of power (force, fiction, finance, and fealty) in their methods of teaching anything, and then reflect on the different effects caused by each . . . we should recognize that power already exists in the various social relations of the school, even though it does not yet exist as a focus of study. (pp. 172–173)

While everyone has experienced power as a member of societal groups, the discursive nature of the notion of power is silent. More particularly, "philosophy of education has been dogged in its denial of power" (Nyberg, p. 69). If power is an essential ingredient of any organization and if we are apt not to discuss it openly, then following David Nyberg's argument to its logical end-state, we must be culpable when power is used unwisely.

"All power is delegated and is maintained through the consent of those who delegate the power" (Nyberg, p. 170). And "any power-holder is limited by the consent (good will) of those who delegate the power, and by the unpredictability of power's long-term effects" (Nyberg, p. 170).

Against Nyberg (as cited by Burbules, 1986) it is possible to argue that not all power transactions are consensual. But here Nyberg puts a peculiar spin on the notion of power entailing the consent of the unempowered for its proper functioning. In a set of strange remarks, Nyberg asserts that power is maintained by those who have it; or we may say, the empowered are allowed their power by virtue of the powerful. All power depends upon consent, for Nyberg, but it is oddly the consent of the powerful, not the powerless. This equation makes power interactionist and one-sided. It would seem that all power is either autocratic and absolute, or brokered out by the powerful to their delegates (Nyberg, pp. 170–171).

Power relationships so one-sided disable the unempowered. This is the situation we currently see operative in school communities. Administrative power is so often all pervasive, teachers have little opportunity to become empowered. Following Burbules, we see institutional power possessing, in many instances, "a life of its own" (Burbules, p. 102). However, this stultifying sense of "powerlessness" that teachers feel in their schools today, attributed to the institutional culture in which they must operate, does not disable resistance (Foster, 1986). Perhaps too much has been written about "giving teaching back to teachers" (Barrow, 1984); less has been said of the codes of hierarchical leadership in place in the social structure of schools which render those who have the most potential for effecting change and improvement in the classroom—the classroom teachers—"powerless." Nyberg seems to contribute to this characterization.

It is argued here that while the teacher's creative power and ability to provide positive pedagogical leadership is undeniably structurally impaired by bureaucratic mentality, *empowerment* need not wait upon the liberation by those "in power." What is needed in educational discourse/practice is an empowering collegiality among educators that engenders true democratic leadership and power—whether this participation be on the decision, policy, or norm level.

Democratic Culture

National reports on education in the recent past, such as *A Nation at Risk* (1983), have mistakenly focused on recommendations for improvements to only the "outward structure" of schools (e.g., a longer school day, a longer school year, increases in amounts and kinds of subjects being taught). In 1986, the Education Commission of the States, echoing the sentiments of the Carnegie Forum (Task Force, 1986), stated:

Nobody reports to the teacher. The teacher reports to everyone else. Other people decide almost everything—how the day is organized, how students are assigned, what the curriculum will be, what is the day-to-day scope and sequence of instruction, how discipline is meted out. The schools operate in an incredibly bureaucratic culture, at the bottom of which we find the teacher. That makes schools very unattractive to many people with real intellectual skills and the desire for some control over themselves and their environment (Odden, Anderson, and Farrar, 1986, pp. 1–2).

More recent reports are beginning to recognize the importance of the power of the teacher as the real catalyst for change (Maeroff, 1988). For educational change to be truly empowering, it must come from those in the social structure of schools who will be most affected by that change—the classroom teachers themselves.

The "powerlessness" felt by many teachers in schools today is a symptom of a much deeper illness affecting educational culture. Cherryholmes (1988) speaks of "the 'intertexuality' of discourses-practices that constitute and structure our social and educational worlds." The social system/culture operating within a school setting may be thought of as a form of discourse-practice in which the dynamic elements of the text become here the role differences and power relationships which develop between and among administrators and teachers. Cherryholmes further maintains that these asymmetries are based on differences in "possessions" or "characteristics," with power being constituted by relationships among those differences. It is redundant to refer to a "power relation" because power *is* a relation. The "relational conception of power" focuses on power as a means of prevention as well as direction and control. As we have seen, power may serve the interests of persons or groups in preventing others in an institutional setting from manifesting their power. In this case, power is embedded in the codes of authority and organizational role (Burbules, 1986, pp. 103–104).

The dominant power transactions operating in many contemporary school social systems are based upon and emanate from an entrenched sociocultural structure which is both bureaucratic and formalized. This social structure creates and reinforces these power interactions. As Burbules states:

The identification of a relation as a power relation, therefore, has a descriptive and a normative aspect: one is never neutral in calling a relation "power." This identification rests on a presumed conflict of interests. These positions of conflicting interests are the nodes or vertices of the "web." They often preexist the particular persons who come to occupy the relation. . . . Power is not simply a matter of getting people to do things (or not do things), but a relation of human attitudes and activities against a background of conflicting interests." (Burbules, p. 104)

A snapshot research study of arrangements of power in schools typically reveals both hierarchical and sedimented power locations. Bureaucratic culture, as it is found in the social structure of many schools, can be viewed as a discourse-practice embedded in a positivist meta-narrative. It is possible to call this meta-narrative "structuralist" following Cherryholmes (1988). Structuralism seeks to define an epistemologically grounded system of educational truths—an ahistorical, acultural matrix of functionalism and control by and through which common and legitimate educational goals can be realized. The positivist meta-narrative of power in bureaucratically structured school systems attempts to foster and promote educational empowerment through an emphasis on order, accountability, structure, rationality, linearity, systemization, and control. Burbules (1986) argues that "bureaucratic organization is characterized by *hierarchy, specialization*, and *relegated* responsibility" (p. 107). This closed-ended structuralist meta-narrative emphasizing order, structure, and control is antithetical to the realization of any truly liberating and goal-oriented educational empowerment of teachers.

Interestingly, bureaucratic organizations *depersonalize* the precise power relationships that make them operate successfully (Burbules, 1986). In the face of this depersonalization it is possible to hold out hope for a type of organization that emphasizes *participatory* rather than hierarchical decision making, *collective* and collaborative rather than specialized tasks, and *de-centralized*, rather than centralized responsibility (Burbules, 1986, p. 108). This more democratic organizational form is less likely to introduce coercion and manipulation, he argues. Democratic organizations do have a potential to degenerate into models of efficiency, however. Therefore, Burbules (1986) calls for periodic scrutiny of our institutions, because they may well become ends in themselves.

The essential enabling characteristics of this emergent democratic community is to be found in its flexibility and open-endedness. Rorty (1979) states: "It is the commonplace fact that people may develop doubts about what they are doing, and thereupon begin to discourse in ways incommensurable with those they used previously. . . . All that is necessary is the edifying invocation of the fact or possibility of abnormal discourse, undermining our reliance upon the knowledge we have gained through normal discourses" (Rorty, pp. 386–387).

Constructing a normative (in the sense of recommendational) democratic community that empowers all educators to become pedagogic via collegiality is perfectly reasonable. What must be faced is the opposition from entrenched organizational ideologies and social codes. A resistance to the text of traditional (grounded theory) educational power must be developed if empowerment is to take place in education. The layering of traditional administration-teacher relations must be revoked and new *transactional* meanings of empowerment released. To empower oneself, leadership is necessary.

The foregoing relates to the general problem area of professionalism and power in education. This issue has largely been overlooked by educators, and yet if education is to be professional in the fullest sense, inquiry should begin. The term "power" has generally assumed that there is some *locus* of control and that this usually takes the form of agent or agencies which dispense its force through goal-setting, planning, and/or decision making. Power is *distributed* or allocated to agents (individuals, groups, societies, nations), but is more often than not a result of ignorance of the domain or plane of existence upon which plays are conducted. And finally, power is regarded ambivalently in American culture as both unacceptable as it functions to dominate and make submissive human affairs and as acceptable from the point of view of its exercise. A reconstructed view of power, I shall argue, may seek to narrow its meaning in several ways: Power may be seen descriptively as a transaction as it serves to bridge and call into play activities between agents and events. Nowhere is the question of the relationship of power and professionalism more relevant than in the sphere of education. We must sort out notions of power as force, rule, expertise (practitioner power), sociocultural forces, administrative/ managerial control/enforcement, and power as potential for action. There is a dualism between power and powerlessness. Beyond the wider scope of power meanings, there is the narrower notion of power as professional accreditation or licensure. From a normative standpoint, power may be seen as sensitive and intelligent decision making relative to freely associated interaction among participants in a field of play or context. Power is normatively used where it is taken in the sense of calling forth specifications as to what ought to be done in certain circumstances, while power also carries with it a set of "floor authorities" or authorizations for its use. Finally, power tends to function with respect to particular situations (e.g., rule-legal power; economic power; social power; professional power), depending upon the purposes and goals of the agents and the circumstances of decision and reflection.

"Professionalism" is often used elliptically. Here a profession is taken to mean a vocation or occupation calling for an advanced expertise, peopled by individuals who comprise membership of shared interests and skill. The medical doctor is held up as a clear case of a professional; however, the field of medicine and that of education differ significantly. Often professionals provide a distinctive service and their activities involve highly theoretical and analytical components. Also, professionals have an expertise in a certain knowledge domain as well as a facility for implementing this knowledge. And professions exercise control and guidance over their membership, setting standards for ethical conduct and creating facilities for enforcement (Clayton, n.d.).

Professionalism implies a kind of normative power. Educators as organized professionals should generate criterial norms and standards determining admittance into the profession and regulating practice. Educational professionals ought to have the power to form directives for action with regard to problems arising out of the exercise of their skills and expertise. And, finally, teaching professionals ought to have the power to make policy and policy decisions regarding their status as agents of cultural mediation in the society.

Power should not be seen as a drama of dominance and submission, but instead growth and diversification of participation in human association. Facing enormous problems today, the teaching profession should be empowered in the sense of being released and freed to do its job in the schools.

"Power" and "profession" must be seen as tied to leadership. The meanings of power and professionalism are related to the transactional nature of leadership discourse/practice. By professionalization, I have in mind power being placed in the hands of educators such that they may possess leadership in policy and decision making affecting learning in schools. We must not overlook the triadic relationship between power, profession, and leadership.

To do so is to thwart the educator and prevent him/her from exercising skill and moral/ethical judgment (phronesis) in policy forming and judging.

THE RELATION BETWEEN EMPOWERMENT AND LEADERSHIP

Hodgkinson (1983) remarks that:

Leadership thought is now a subdivision of psychology rather than of philosophy. What began in antiquity as a profoundly philosophical concern—how to find the Guardian—has become demythologized, secularized, empiricized and psychologized, and now flourishes as a thickly tangled web wherein notions of values, ethics and morality have been leached away, ignored, or deprecated as irrelevant. (pp. 197–198)

Power is often conceived of as a resident characteristic of authorities (and authoritarians) (Burbules, p. 113). Pedagogical authorities are no less free from the enslavement of power. It is our position that power is intertextual. This is to say that power encapsulates human beings in settings so that, despite their unwillingness to take part, power moves them.

I have stressed the fact that the educative use of power, by leaders, "results in the empowerment of followers" (Foster, p. 186). It is important to see power in a normative pedagogical sense as well, if we are to understand the workings of empowerment for educators in general and leaders in particular. Normative empowerment entails the efforts to empower self in the face of conditions requiring decision making. Certainly, there are constraints and negative factors affecting such autobiographical empowerment. Nevertheless, as a goal or ideal, self-empowerment is essential to the fully operative teacher.

And, as we have also seen, it is important to keep in mind that a preface to empowerment is caught up in the capacity of educators to engage in *resistance* to those individuals and conditions that disable them. As Cherryholmes (1988) stresses, the teacher must, to gain power, resist some of the prevailing codes and sedimented meanings of administered school culture. Following Scholes (1985), he argues that what is needed is "text against text," or the critical pragmatic effort to test one's own against received meanings. Hence, resistance may take the form of refusing textbook interpretations, restyling workbook pages, and so forth, thereby empowering oneself as well as students (Cherryholmes, 1988, pp. 158–167).

One means of reinvoking power transactions for educators is to see the profoundly judgmental activities that form their instructional leadership. It may be argued that because teachers are called upon to make important decisions regarding how and what to teach, they should be informed in the skills of *phronesis*. Working within educational settings, educators engage in judgments of practice, using reason. By this we mean that they are called upon to decide what should be done. According to Raup et al. (1943), judgments of practice are made at three levels: making individual decisions in one case; making a policy where a number of instances must be regulated; and reconstructing the basic norms of conduct in an institution. These three levels are interrelated. This is to say that policies should be made in terms of the cases at hand as well as in light of the institutional norms and standards, and rights and duties. Decisions generate policies, while policies help to shape future decisions. Norms may cut across institutions and touch every aspect of life. There is a continuum, Raup et al. argue: decisions—policy—norms (Raup et al., ch. 4).

Following Raup et al., I advocate that the process of empowerment itself gains legitimacy in and through this same kind of continuum, and that the practical interrelatedness of these judgmental levels, in an "empowering" sense, requires that those who would be empowered in practice be accorded access to each level.

There are two vital and strategic problem centers in phronesis, or practical judgment: the character of the judger; and the community orientation of the judger (Raup et al.). Empowerment, I wish to argue, bears heavily upon the moral character of the person engaged in practical reasoning. Every action involves the self as projected in character. This character is involved by virtue of being the patterned and oriented disposition to act in particular ways. A distinctive aspect of phronesis is the large role played by the self-projecting character of the judges. This character shapes or is shaped by the world in which it works. Even the methods used to inquire form a part of the character of the judger. As Raup et al. argue, the method of intelligence is to work out or to pursue not facts but a more fulfilled and more adequate character. Such character becomes objectified through judgment (Raup et al., ch. 4).

The second component is the community orientation of the judger. Unfortunately, the role of educators in schools is often compromised by the perceived hierarchy and codes of the organization. Rather than face them down, increasingly we hear calls for "efficiency" in educational institutions. Habermas has written about this aspect of administrative thinking which fastens on goals and ends without critical reflection of worthwhileness. The transactional nature of the empowering process is often stymied by the closed-endedness of efficiency. When conflicts arise in institutions in which basic norms are themselves called into question, the community orientation of the judges becomes an unresolved feature of the situation. Raup et al. point out that this dimension has been ignored where problem solvers have attempted to use the method of science. This effort neglects the subjective side of practical judgment (Raup et al., ch. 4).

A society may give voice to incompatible points of view with groups shifting from one point of view to another in an effort to "objectivize" themselves historically through the process of reflection. Once self-doubts emerge, a people may engage in a discourse in ways incommensurable with past use. This is part of the edifying process which undermines past knowledge and unblocks conversation. As Rorty points out, the limited self-confidence is overthrown by ongoing edifying dialogue (Rorty, 1979, pp. 386–387).

Conflicts over judgments may require rebuilding and re-educating the judges' norms and self-confidence. This is not to say that one must overlook the facts of the case. Rather, the goal of practical judgment is to arrive at a common persuasion. Thus, an adequate judgment of practice will reconstruct the normative perspective of the judges by reconstructing the characters and self-confidence of the judges (a dimension most people overlook), yielding a community persuasion or united action (see Rorty, 1979, on "edifying discourse"; and Bernstein, 1983, "abnormal discourse").

We are arguing for the possibility of "abnormal discourse" as a means of releasing new empowering discourses/practices in educational settings. We must be sensitive to the plural and competing interests of the actors, while recognizing that not all practical judgments involve uniform agreement. We are *not* arguing that such phronesis should focus on commensurability (Raup et al., ch. 4; Bernstein, 1983). This democratically driven conception of practical judgment is informative for the problem of empowerment as it relates to leadership. Where the community of judges engages in conjoint determination of outcomes, power resides in the collective deliberative machinery of judgment—not in commonly derived consensual discourses/practices.

It is important to consider the role of self-deception in democratic deliberation. Grumet (1987), speaking of the use of storytelling, indicates: "I suspect the difference between personal and impersonal knowledge, or practical and impractical knowledge is not a difference in what it is we know, but how we tell it and to whom" (p. 322). The stories we tell others may be ultimately less dangerous than the ones we tell ourselves (p. 322). Hence, while the setting in which empowerment transactions take place is of significance, the circumstances never override the role played by the self in deciphering surrounding conditions. It is important to see the logico-rational function of practical judgment to be wedded to personal belief and, as such, human inquiry and feelings.

This insight into the non-rational side of empowerment has ample support in the writings of Jean Paul Sartre and Alfred Schutz. Grumet cites Schutz: "Meaning . . . does not lie in experience. Rather, those experiences are meaningful which are grasped reflectively. The meaning is the way in which the ego regards experience. The meaning lies in the attitudes of the self toward that part of its stream of consciousness which has already flowed by"

(p. 322). Leadership, seen in the light of experience so taken, stresses the role of ego in attempting to decipher events. Raup et al. speak of the "artist leader" and it is the sense of seeing leading in terms of aesthetic understanding that aids us in uncovering the meaning of the leadership/empowerment relation. Here leadership requires not naked imagination, but critical pragmatic imagination.

The view that practical judgment requires a dimension of character calling upon creative imagination and aiming at seeing the "whole" of human situations marks it as an art. However, it is vital to see this creative leadership conception as a function of the group process (a collection of egos) and "not the exclusive possession of top management" (Raup et al., p. 245).

Raup et al. write: "Leadership may be required in emergencies or when the social group is inexperienced" (p. 32). The press of compelling events or the lack of experience of the group may dictate that the group willingly follow the leader or leaders, because they have confidence in the leaders' devotion to the common good, or owing to the leaders' experience and ability seeming manifest at this time. But such leadership must be responsible to the group, subject to review by the group progressively to the point where the program, policy, and purpose are confirmed by the judgment of the entire group or as many members as possible (p. 32).

Leadership must be diversified and is dependent on the integrity of the leader, say Raup et al. Hence, different situations will call for different leaders. Leadership, rather than residing in one person (ego) or one class of persons, is seen as widely diffused among the population. Every person may, in some situation, function as a leader.

At the heart of leadership is *democratic control*. Leadership is not inconsistent with the democratic method. Each type of emergency faced by the group calls for a different kind of leadership. Essentially, leaders should be trying to put themselves out of business by transferring democratic social control to the group intelligence as soon and as smoothly as possible.

For Raup et al. the ideal method of social control is democratic cooperation. However, during the second half of the twentieth century, this ideal has been replaced by the image of the strong Machiavellian leader. The difference is not so much a matter of "style" as it is of morals and ethics.

The argument here is that each of the participants in an educational judgment of practice (whether it be at the decisional, policy, or norm level) comes to be empowered in that judgment insofar as what he/she brings to the judgment is decisive and self-referential. The judgment is an exercise in power where the decision is transformative of the moral character of the judges. Here it is important to see the element of "surrender" and concomitant "risk" emerging (Wolff, 1976). For a judgment to be adequate, the judges (here teachers and administrators) must be willing to give up (surrender) presuppositions, values, and so forth to the end of resolving the problem. This entails risk of loss of some aspect of self qua character as well as loss in the sense of practical consequences that may fail.

Finally, the call for leadership operating as phronesis need not be warranted in some transcendental signified (to use Derrida's notion). We must resist, as Philip G. Smith (1964) points out, the "urge to lay claim to any [moral] base outside democratic principles" (p. 417). And, "teachers having deep and insightful respect for individuality, and backed by professional organizations that are disciplined and responsible with respect to their role in a democratic society, should never feel it necessary to side-step the moral dimension inevitably involved in any attempt to promote the growth of human personality" (p. 417).

INQUIRY AND POWER

This section of the chapter examines the bearing of the new view of empowerment upon the conduct of educational research. Here we wish to demonstrate that educational inquiry, seen as a species of social science, is related to notions of democratic empowerment. Although defining "power" as solely in the hands of the oppressors (he has in mind the Nazis in Germany), Fay (1987) provides a ground for the understanding of the power embedded in social science research. Fay provides, for the purpose of illustration, an incomplete definition of power based upon the writings of Brecht: "Power is the ability to get people to behave in a certain way through the use or threat of harm. . . . Power is the exercise of force or the promise thereof." But this is insufficient. Such a view would forever render the oppressed unable to define themselves in an emancipatory way. The powerful have that power only partially owing to the willingness of the oppressed to allow them to excrcise power, Fay points out (pp. 119–120). "Power must arise out of the interactions of the powerful and the powerless, with both sides contributing something necessary for its existence. Power must be dyadic" (p. 120).

In Charles Sanders Peirce's 1877 article on pragmatism (later called "pragmaticism"), "The Fixation of Belief," we find the role of inquiry to be fundamental. Peirce found four barriers to inquiry: (1) the assertion that something is absolutely true; (2) the assertion that something can never be known; (3) the assertion of an ultimate end; and (4) the assertion that a law or truth has arrived at its perfect formulation. To discover the nature of thought, one must begin by identifying the kind of life condition in which the activity of thought (inquiry) arises along with the function that it serves human experience. The clue to this understanding is "doubt" as it is contrasted to belief. Producing belief is the sole action of thought and inquiry.

As creatures of habit, humans tend to believe until the believing is upset by doubt. Thus, pragmatic inquiry is the effort to secure belief in the face of "real and living doubt" for Peirce (Buchler, 1955, pp. 5–22).

John Dewey's theory of inquiry begins with a specific situation which is indeterminate. This indeterminacy moves us to discover what constitutes the problem. Here familiarity with similar problems helps us focus on the new difficulty. Certain relevant ideas are looked at as possible solutions to the problem. Next, we engage in reasoning to develop a hypothesis that may be the object of experimentation. The results of this experiment tell us whether to accept or reject the hypothesis. When we perform the experiment we seek to alter the conditions under which we started. The inquiry comes to a close when the difficulties out of which the problem arose are settled. The new situation is more unified and the blocks to action have been removed or erased.

While Peirce saw science as a special discipline, Dewey believed that scientific method was the method of reflective thinking. The pragmatist believed that truth was the goal and outcome of experimental research. At the heart of it, pragmatism is the method for making conduct rational. Pierce wrote: "Consider what effects, that might conceivably have practical bearings, we conceive the object of our conception to have. Then, our conception of these effects is the whole of our conception of the object" (Buchler, 1955, p. 31). Pierce's definition of pragmatism is applicable to things as well as concepts such as "empowerment" and "leadership."

When we take the pragmatic maxim and apply it to the problem of leadership in education, we find that one of the best measures of the effectiveness of schooling is the total impact schools have on living human beings. This criterion raises certain fundamental questions however. How can adults determine the course of experience for a child without at the same time determining the moral and intellectual frames of vision through which the child will view the world in which he/she will live (Childs, 1956, p. 208)? This question of setting the frame of reference or worldview of children introduces the matter of indoctrination. Can inquiry be free from indoctrination? This is to say: Is it possible to teach children to be reflective thinkers without teaching them certain factual matters that may be declared false now or in the future?

George Counts (1934) wrestled with this matter and declared that if schools were to truly reform society, indoctrination was necessary. Theodore Brameld introduced "defensible partiality" as his caveat to indoctrination: teachers were to declare which position they supported in a controversial issue, while encouraging the children to develop their own position and rational. The specific bearing of the whole question of objectivity in inquiry has become highlighted in the "quantitative" versus "qualitative" research debate in education. A debate has been going on among educational researchers for more than fifteen years in which three issues have emerged: (1) the epistemological issue in which differing notions of knowledge, meaning, explanation, accuracy, truth, and agreement have emerged; (2) the technological debate in which methodological superiority is played against appropriateness; and (3) the methodological debate over goals of inquiry, the audience to be served, and technique to be used.

Essentially, the assumptions driving this difference in approach are rooted in the role of values in inquiry. Where the researcher believes that value may be suspended and inquiry conducted on an objective value-free basis, he/she has been termed a "quantitative" researcher. On the other hand, where the inquirer posits the notion that values play a continuous role in research, we term him/her a "qualitative" researcher.

The problem may be seen as one of the viability of relativism of methods versus the absolutism or foundationalism view of method. A narrowly structuralist conception of educational inquiry adopts the view that there is "*the* scientific method" and all studies must be done in terms of that singular method. To some extent, John Dewey was arguing this point when he laid out his version of reflective thinking, although it is a gross oversimplification of his view. Where studies are conducted that disavow any of the tenets of this structuralist view, they are labeled "unscientific" and relativistic.

Naturalistic or qualitative research postures assume the fact of multiple methods of doing educational research, as well as the normative stance that such a pluralism of inquiries is valuable. Cherryholmes's "critical pragmatism" provides a philosophical justification for this notion. He writes: "If there is a foundation there is something to be relative against but if there is no foundation there is no structure against which other propositions can be 'objectively' judged" (1988, pp. 279–280).

The educational research paradigm as it touches educational administration and teaching is presently undergoing radical change. "Qualitative research" and "naturalistic inquiry" have emerged to confront earlier structuralism and naive positivism. The question before us here is: How may a reconceptualization of "empowerment," as developed in this essay, impact upon the research posture of inquirers in educational administration and teaching as it is driven by these new models of research?

Cherryholmes (1988) writes of the need to embrace a "critical pragmatism" in educational work. Rouse (1987) asserts: "The experimental and theoretical practices of the sciences are themselves forms of power" (p. 248). How may we come to the means for a critical assessment of the scientific enterprise where it is aimed at an epistemological rendering of educational practice? Crucial to this question is the degree to which educators are going to be empowered to deconstruct educational research that bears upon their practice. Heretofore, the effort has been one of doing research for its own sake, or providing popular policy-relevant findings of research for practitioners. The shift seen in the works today is to empower teachers and administrators so that they may do *critical* examinations of such research. In some sense what is called for is that "the users are the choosers." The thrust of Cherryholmes's work (1988), and particularly the work of Scholes (1985), has been to show that educators can develop critical stances towards their own pedagogy. The methods of hermeneutics and deconstruction, as well as the metaphor of the "text," are used effectively to provide a focal point for this analysis.

Whatever the center for the exchange, the empowerment relations inform only insofar as they arise out of inquiry in its primitive forms and research in academic terms. The claim being made here is that power is not free from epistemological considerations. A groundswell is taking place in which educational settings are being translated into "texts." It is argued, following Derrida and others, that our institutions are open to deconstruction. The role of philosophic thought is to reveal the intertextuality of such settings and to investigate metaphysical narratives as these seek foundational explanations. The position taken here, following that of Aristotle, is that what is required is an empowering *phronesis* (practical competence). Teachers, to be empowered, must have a professional character which rests not only upon praxis, but the capacity to engage in pedagogical acts with a practical judgmental faculty operative.

Foucault points out (1977), "there are no relations of power without resistances" (p. 142). Michael Apple (1982) asserts that there will be resistances by teachers to administrative hegemony. Where curricular materials are set in advance by others, teachers find ways of subverting them. Such resistances may become creative cultural forms of their own over time. Students, too, may find ways of creatively using the power systems for their own ends. The content, form, and lived culture generate beliefs by which students and teachers live and conduct their work. Each of these elements must be focused upon relative to the concept of power (pp. 152–157). And the text of education may become a focal point in which the meanings of human life are deconstructed and reconstituted through a critical pragmatism.

If "knowledge is power," then the search for knowledge is empowering. The restoration of inquiry in teaching is significant for the empowerment of educators. Teacher/researcher is one model that has been advocated. By allowing teachers to *do* research in their own classrooms, it is argued that educators will come to sense the tenuous nature of pedagogical knowledge. Others, like Pinar and Grumet (1976), argue that teaching involves "reconceptualization" of received knowledge. Teachers are placed at the center of educational reform through epistemological empowerment.

Inquiry and teaching cannot be divorced, only sublimated. It is proposed that the act of teaching rests upon the search for knowledge. Democratic empowerment adds the dimension of commensurability. Resistance to received points of view by teachers has been the first step in the reunification of inquiry and pedagogy: the empowerment of teachers.

CONCLUSIONS

There are three conclusions that may be drawn from the foregoing. First, the nature of "empowerment" has been vastly misrepresented by the literature of education and educational reform. Empowerment is fundamentally a transactional concept, it is argued in these pages. Educators as leaders are empowered where they engage in *resistance* and *release* stemming from a new sense of *hope*. Second, empowerment is related to leadership in the fact that leadership as pedagogy is seen as a shared matter in which educators engage, collegially, in "practical judgment," such that the norms, policies, and decisions are open-ended and flexible discourse/practices result. Finally, it is significant to see empowerment as related to democratic culture and inquiry. Leadership viewed in this normative democratic setting requires informed participants. Information is a product of inquiry. Inquiry serves as the ground floor upon which teacher empowerment and leadership rest.

In sum, educational leadership requires that educators engage in an empowering discourse/practice that is based on a *critical* and reflective inquiry (practical in nature).

9

The Artist-Leader and the
Problem of Design

Our efforts to develop a pragmatic and critical characterization of educational leadership must intersect with assumptions regarding what constitutes practice. Schools are settings in which leaderly activities take place. Leadership, therefore, entails redefined *praxis* as well as *phronesis.*

And beneath the practical acts of leading are to be found the assumptions as to such matters as experience, culture, and human nature—all of which have bearing upon the context and success of this leadership. These categories are in turn attached to scientific and aesthetic value interests, the origins of which have become blurred over time.

When we attempt to discover the nature of leadership as practice, our lenses are distorted by the historical commitment within the academic community toward a positivistic ideology. This legacy of Descartes, which focuses upon the relative autonomy of inquiry from its objects, its commitment to objectivism and foundationalism, has overshadowed any effort to specify the aesthetic nature of leadership.

In this chapter we shall explore artistic design and creation as it is played out upon the textures of normative human action. The school, taken as a culture, is taken to be a site for a new kind of artistic leadership, conceived of as communal and participatory design. Within the following pages, we shall look at leadership as critical and pragmatic design, fusing the rational with the artistic, against the technical and scientistic. Here, experience, culture, and human will be viewed in relation to the category of the artistic. It shall be argued that the new educational leader, as a leader of learning, should be a reasoning artistic practitioner. At stake in this normative recommendation is a reaction to the received notion that leading is a function of rational-technical organizational manipulation and an undervalued aesthetic.

Let us turn first to the historic origins of contemporary conceptions of school leadership as business management.

THE NEW SCHOOL EXECUTIVE

Modern educational administration texts (see Synder and Anderson, 1986) speak of "managing productive schools" and the "work culture" of schools. Borrowing heavily from the research on industrial and business management, it is assumed that schools are "workplaces" just like factories. Educational leaders are seen as managers of "workers" with the aim of enhancing "productivity." The so-called "work culture," although "loosely coupled" (following Weick, 1976) is nonetheless a species of business culture with Japanese models dominating current theorizing (Synder and Anderson, p. 36). Success flows from the proper leading of work-groups through cooperation and coordination.

Callahan (1962) traces the history of the replacement of the school administrator as teacher with that of the "professional school executive."

The combination of the development of specialized graduate work in school administration, and the growing influence of business on education with the subsequent conception of education as a business, led to the idea of school administration (and especially the superintendency) as a "profession" distinct from teaching. This idea had been advanced even before 1910, but it was hardly a defensible claim as long as administrators had no specialized training. In the years after 1911 the idea of a separate profession developed as a natural corollary of the adoption of business-industrial practices and, especially, of the adoption of the business organizational pattern to the schools. (Callahan, pp. 215–216)

With the trappings of the business model of efficiency and control (especially over "manpower" and money), the school executive was sharply distanced from the pedagogue. What might have happened if the model for school administrators had been the professional artist?

It may be argued that it was logical that school administrators would adopt "leadership" as a descriptive conception of their activities, owing to the penchant for businesses to garner strong leaders. However, schools were not run-for-profit businesses, and teachers were not "hands." The shift from teacher/leader to administrator/leader was a function of modernity. The bureaucratization of American life necessitated a shift in power/relations. Just as businesses moved to professional managerial styles, schools—under pressure from the community—sought to emulate the model of the bureaucracy.

One part of this modernism was fueled by the philosophical legacy of Descartes. Philosophers since Descartes had accepted a chasm separating actors and events. Just as mind dictates to body, authorities "cause" subservients to behave the way they do. Leadership came to mean management control over journeymen. Interestingly, it is noteworthy that managers who managed "things" were never considered leaders. The conquest of the frontier west was translated into the conquest of recalcitrant labor. Leader/manager/executive functioned to get followers to do their bidding, and that bidding was production translated into profits. Beneath this imposition, however, was the truism that leadership was short-lived if the consent of the followers was abrogated.

There are fundamental difficulties with this classic causal model, however. Philosophers had the tendency, following Descartes, to replace aesthetics with epistemology. Thus, art and life came to be separate. The logical and practical result was the separating of the "fine arts" from the "sciences." John Dewey was instrumental in trying to bridge the gap. In *Art as Experience* he focused upon life, not primarily "fine art." A life well lived could thus be considered a "work" of art. Ordinary experiences could be seen as artful. The rush to knowledge-based judgment had short-circuited this natural proclivity to live life with an artful skill.

Humans, upon casual inspection, seem to both provoke changes in experience as well as being changed by experience. Agentry is embedded within the matrix of experience and only reflection allows us to hypothesize an external foundational view of that relationship—which in turn sees it as causal. While business and industry have been used historically to provide models for school organizations, a turnaround has come in the work of Peter M. Senge. In *The Fifth Discipline: The Art and Practice of the Learning Organization* (1990), he speaks of the need to convert businesses into "learning organizations" (i.e., schools of sorts). He emphasizes that no organization can survive today that does not invest in learning. It would seem proper to expropriate this notion to the schools, where learning is already one of the primary goals. The school ought to be a "learning organization."

Senge writes:

> The new view of leadership in learning organizations centers on subtler and more important tasks. In a learning organization, leaders are designers, stewards, teachers. They are responsible for *building organizations* where people continually expand their capabilities to understand complexity, clarify vision, and improve shared mental models—that is, they are responsible for learning. (Senge, p. 340)

Senge tells us that the most neglected leadershship role is that of *designer*. When asked to imagine their organization as an ocean liner and themselves as occupying the leadership role, most executives describe themselves as "the captain," or "the navigator," or "the engineer." These characterizations of leadership, while popularly accepted, overlook a key role: designer of the ship.

There are some negative aspects to leadership deemed as design. Few designers are given credit or praise for their productions. Designers are not as highly visible, because they work behind the scenes. The results are often long in coming. Designers are not really in control, nor do they profit financially like high-profile CEOs. The positives are: deep satisfaction in empowering others and being a part of an organization they care about (Senge, p. 341).

The design work in educational leadership is that of creating overall policies, missions, goals, and the normative gestalt of the school. We have seen that such artifacts require an over-arching philosophic view, but it also requires that the school be tested in practice. Senge tells us that the leadership task is designing the learning processes whereby the people in the organization can deal productively with the critical issues that they face and develop mastery in the learning disciplines (Senge, p. 345).

The first step in coming to understand the notion of leadership as learning is to see the role *experience* plays in our choices and futures.

EXPERIENCE AND CULTURE

Perhaps no pragmatic philosopher before or since has captured the value of "experience" more appropriately than John Dewey. Here I wish to demonstrate that Dewey's notion of "experience," and his emphasis upon "experiment," provides a key in the arch of a pragmatic theory of educational leadership. Moreover, Dewey fuses the concern for scientific rigor and laboratory technique with the interest in artistic creativity.

T. M. Alexander (1987) tells us: "By understanding the term 'experience' one obtains the Northwest Passage to Dewey's philosophy; failure to understand it inevitably leads to shipwreck" (p. 57). Dewey wrote the following about "experience" in his 1922–23 course syllabus for "Types of Philosophic Thought."

The word "experience" is here taken nontechnically. Its nearest equivalents are such words as "life," "history," "culture" (in its anthropological use). It does not mean processes and modes of experiencing apart from what is experienced and lived. The philosophical value of the term is to provide a way of referring to the unity or totality between what is experienced and the way it is experienced, a totality which is broken up and referred to only in ready-made distinctions or by such words as "world," "things," "objects" on the one hand and "mind," "subject," "person," "consciousness" on the other. Similarly "history" denotes both events and our record or interpretation of them; while "events" include not only the acts and sufferings of human beings but all the cosmic and institutional conditions and forces which in any way whatsoever enter into and affect these human beings—in short, the wide universe as manifesting itself in the careers and fortunes of human beings. (Dewey, *Middle Works*, 13:351)

Both William James and John Dewey saw "experience" as a consciousness inhabiting a "field" which faded toward a "fringe" or "horizon" (Alexander, 1987, p. 73). It was the fundamental "impulsion," to use Dewey's term, to engage in the world with a heightened sense of meaning and value realization. This engagement was the aesthetic experience (Alexander, 1987, p. xvii). As we seek to make sense of our life-world, meaning for Dewey becomes a "transactional" event mediated by symbolic communication and requires community.

Ilya Prigogine and Isabelle Stengers, in *Order Out of Chaos* (1984), tell us that the scientist in his/her search for order in nature confronts chaos. That the universe is not entirely orderly is a truism. Therefore, what is needed is a deeper look at the chaos, under which is to be form and regularity of a profound sort. It may be implied that the teacher ought to be in the business of gathering in this order for students, demonstrating the regularities, and helping develop a method of dealing with the seeming chaos. While the term "chaos" may be strong, it can be argued that schools in which leadership operates are at least "sticky," in the sense that the problems confronted by leadership are not resolved easily.

Experience for John Dewey was the result of an interaction between objective conditions and organic energies. The educative experience, as a special type of experience, involved the use of experimentation to bring about a resolution of a problem. Dewey's famous "problem-solving" paradigm for the schools resulted from this insight. The teacher was to be a guide in helping students work through a problem to its solution. In the process of problem solving, students gained skill at instrumentalist thinking. Dewey saw intelligence being applied to an experience, to refine and direct it toward a good end. The product of such a process of intelligence is knowledge (Maxcy and Stanley, 1986).

From a philosophic standpoint, the experience was the elemental unit, the first category of existence. Experiences were had in very fundamental ways. Each of us interacts with the world at this elemental experience level. Moreover, each and every experience begins with a resident qualitative aspect. While an experience may profit from the addition of intelligence and yield knowledge, that experience begins with quality as an earmark. Influenced by Charles Sanders Peirce's notion of quality as Firstness, Dewey adopted the notion that value resides in every experience, but must be translated through intelligence via appraisal and evaluation. Our primary tendency as human creatures is to like, value, and in other ways warmly attend to some things and events rather than others. The reason for this primal reaction is that quality forms an essential ingredient within such experiences. It is perhaps proper to speak here of an experience being had.

The pragmatist begins with the commonsense world. Perceptual qualities are not subjective data used in inference to things, but rather are immediately experienced qualities of things. Some philosophers, such as Sir Russell Brain, talk of this commonsense world as made up of "sense data." But this is to assume that experience is waiting for human interactivity. This is not the case for Dewey. Dewey expressly states that the existential matrix of inquiry is the interaction of an organism (human or other) and the environment. At this primary level, natural occurrences involving humans and the environment occur. These experiencings are not "known," but rather "had." What transforms an experience into a knowing experience is the necessity of a problem and the role of logical thinking (intelligence) in resolving that problem. For Dewey things are had and used before they are known (Piatt, 1939, pp. 105–134).

Perception is a noncognitive occurrence for Dewey. When we perceive something, we have an immediate experience—of a qualitative sort—of the environment. We attend to things, but we do so more for what they suggest (in terms of future action) than for what they are in their own right. We engage in inference. For Dewey, inference is the "sign-significance" relation. This is to say that we may perceive a dark cloud. We take that cloud as a sign that it will rain. We derive from this a symbolic meaning in which we derive an implication. By using language (symbol) we are able to reconstitute a natural sign (cloud) into a significant sign (yielding "signification"). There are for Dewey three kinds of meaning:

1. Intrinsic Meaning: The meaning intrinsic to natural events as experienced immediately: had experiences.
2. Sign-Significance Meaning: The relation of inference ("significance"). Extrinsic or Instrumental Meaning.
3. Symbolic Meaning: This type of meaning is used in linguistic operations in developing the implications of experience. (Piatt, pp. 105–134)

In *Experience and Nature* (1929), John Dewey called for a philosophy of empirical naturalism, naturalistic empiricism, or naturalistic humanism. By these names, he wished to emphasize the importance of paying attention to experience and nature in connection. He found that too often traditional philosophies, in casting aspersions upon experiential objects and events, denied the power of common life to develop regulative methods and to furnish from within itself worthy goals, ideals, and criteria. In effect such philosophies thus claimed a private access to truth, Dewey believed.

The evidence that the world of empirical matters was at once uncertain, unpredictable, uncontrollable, and hazardous was a truism for the empirical naturalist. We have fear because the world is perilous and precarious. Fear of nature and her chaos provokes man into creating gods. The universe is chaotic. On the other hand, there are regularities and continuities in nature.

The change of the seasons, the tides, and other events lend a predictability and flow to life that bespeaks order not chaos (Dewey, pp. 42–45). The fallacy of philosophy has been to elevate the regular and recurring over the transient and chaotic. Aristotle, for example, became stuck upon the fixed or eternal. Our magical impulse has been to substitute superstition for the chaos of nature; science has sought to impute order beneath the chaos: both views seem excessive.

William James proposed: "The body is the storm center, the origin of co-ordinates, the constant place of stress in all that experience-train" (James, 1976, p. 86). It is possible to see similarities in the phenomenological views of Dewey and Husserl relative to "life-world" and "horizon." As William Garrison and Emanuel Shargel (1986) put it, "both philosophers are eager to redress certain imbalances resulting from what they see as the fundamental error of metaphysics—the loss of meaning for life (and learning) that has resulted from forgetting or ignoring the original meaning-giving foundation, that is the practical activities of everyday experience" (p. 260).

While the aesthetic experience was one kind of experience, for Dewey it revealed what all species of experience were all about (Alexander, 1987, p. 60). Hans-Georg Gadamer writes: "The aesthetic experience is not just one kind of experience among others, but represents the essence of experience itself" (Gadamer, 1985b, p. 63). In addition, the transactional nature of an art experience is echoed in Gadamer's hermeneutic: "The work of art would seem almost by definition to become an aesthetic experience, that means however, that it suddenly takes the person experiencing it out of the context of his life, by the power of the work of art, and yet relates him back to the whole of his existence" (p. 63). If life was art for Dewey, it would seem to be the same for Gadamer. "An aesthetic experience always contains the experience of an infinite whole. Precisely because it does not combine with others to make one open experiential flow, but immediately represents the whole, its significance is infinite" (p. 63). Moreover, the concept of experience then becomes foundational to the world of art. "For aesthetics the conclusion follows that so-called Erlebniskunst (the art of experience) appears as the true art" (p. 63).

Toward the close of his life, John Dewey sought to rework the concept of experience into that of "culture." A new book, *Culture and Nature*, was to replace *Experience and Nature*; however, only a few pages of notes survive. "Experience" no longer carried the meaning that Dewey wished:

The historical obstacles are now so conspicuous that I can at times but wonder how they came to be overlooked. There was a period in modern philosophy when the appeal to "existence" was a thoroughly wholesome appeal to liberate philosophy from desiccated abstractions. But I failed to appreciate the fact that subsequent developments inside and outside philosophy had corrupted and destroyed the wholesomeness of the appeal—that "experience" had become effectively identified with experiencing in the sense of the psychological, and the psychological had become established as that which is intrinsically psychical, mental, private. My insistence that "experience" also designates *what* is experienced was a mere ideological thundering in the Index for it ignored the ironical twist which made this use of "experience" strange and incomprehensible. (Dewey, *Later Works*, I: 362)

Dewey would shift to using "culture" as the procedure whereby nature is transformed to culture's own ends. Communication and language were to link experience and existence. This move may also be seen to be an effort by Dewey to avoid any historic metaphysical system in elaborating his philosophy (Sleeper, 1986, pp. 106–108). It may be argued that educational leadership/artistry requires this transformative questioner, and that culture/experience is the essential unit of meaning we must face.

DEMOCRATIC CULTURE AND ARTISTIC LEADERSHIP

At the heart of our explanation of practice is a primacy of experience. One way to speak of this experience/culture is to call it "political." This category of political experience/culture constrains and informs the educational research effort (Eisner, 1988). It is vital to see a creative leadership conception as a function of the group process (a collection of egos) and "not the exclusive possession of top management" (Raup et al., 1943, p. 245). The aesthetic, for Dewey, generated the democratic community by standing for the possible fulfillment of a shared life dedicated to the realization of meaning and value brought about through the creative process of intelligence (Alexander, 1987, p. 60).

Viewing the leader as a CEO (whether of a school system, individual school, or classroom) allowed management theorists to ask how the organizational culture enhanced or constrained leadership. "The functions of the executive . . . are those of control, management, supervision, administration, in formal organizations," wrote Chester I. Barnard (1938, p. 6). But this vision of a "corporate culture" failed to reveal the compositional and decompositional elements of managed leading. The "culture" concept was all wrong for the ecology of the school and leadership did not translate well. Research on business or corporate culture was nested in a complex of assumptions about what people were like and what they needed to do.

By "culture," Dewey had in mind the complex and varied ways in which people live together in the world; how we understand and use the resources of nature; and how we understand and appropriate each other. "The name 'culture' in its anthropological (not its Matthew Arnold) sense designates the vast range of things experienced in an indefinite variety of ways" (Dewey, *Later Works*, I:362). Culture included artifacts, activities, customs, beliefs, dispositions, morals, arts, knowledge, and worldviews. The term "culture" referenced all the uses to which these are put. Moreover, they carry with them the term "ideal," or "spiritual" (p. 362). Culture names "the material and ideal in their reciprocal inter-relationships" (p. 363). For Dewey, culture may be seen as the shared life of people as found in terms of meaning and value (Alexander, 1987, pp. 70–71).

Ann Liebermann et al. (1988) write:

We are only beginning to understand the nature and impact of these new roles [teacher/leader] in schools and the subtleties of fashioning new ways of working with the school community. From studying these teacher-leaders, we see that some sort of team, teacher center, or site committee—a structural change—appears necessary to the creation of collegial norms in schools. More cooperative work, increased interaction across department lines, and support groups for new teachers require new modes of collaboration to replace the existing isolated conditions in most schools. (Liebermann et al., p. 165)

Art played a significant role in Dewey's educational theory. He wrote glowingly about art in *Reconstruction in Philosophy* and *Human Nature and Conduct*. Art functioned to make people aware of ideals (Alexander, 1987, pp. 53–60). The artist/leader, like the sculptor/painter, produces a creation which others may (or may not) come to take pleasure in and value. For the artist/leader, followers are necessary for the equation of the aesthetic to occur. These followers take part in the images, perceptions, and visions developed by the artist/leader through the appreciation of the followers. Without the shared regard (artist/leader and followers) for the aesthetic product (institutional mission, goals, ends-in-view, etc.), the aesthetic component may be seriously thwarted or submerged. Followers follow when it is possible for them to either share in the rationale of the artistic product, or in other ways come to share in the feelings and emotions that gave rise to that image. "To be a good leader, one must find a way to be followed," write McPherson, Crowson, and Pitner (1986, p. 251). And to be a good leader/artist, one must discover avenues that elicit shared aesthetic valuing for the image or design.

LEADERSHIP AND DESIGN

The style of leading in American schools is traditional: the principal gives directions and attempts to manipulate teachers toward goals. Leaders are seen as strong-minded individualists who make the key decisions and instill moral imagination in their followers. The history of the westward movement in the United States covered the leader with a patina of the heroic. Principals are seen in a great fight (with illiteracy, inequality, etc.), meeting crisis after crisis in the schools. The myth of the charismatic leader still invests politics with the cult of personality, but in educational states-of-affairs it is out of date.

Beneath this view of leadership is the deeply held belief that teachers, pupils, and parents are powerless and without vision or knowledge of change. This deficit-filling notion of leadership has lasted because it has never been successfully challenged—until recently. Today school decentralization is occurring all over the country with the concomitant development of "team leadership." It is realized that schools are best run by cooperative efforts of administrators, teachers, staff, parents, and students; who hold a common vision and are deeply committed to success in improving what schools do for children and youth. But where does this common vision come from and how may it be developed in such a time of crisis? This is a question of *design*.

Perhaps the earliest successful attempt to apply the concept of design to organizations is to be found in the work of Herbert Simon: *The Sciences of the Artificial* (1971). Here, following upon his successful 1945 work aimed at creating a science of administration, Simon sought to develop a science of design. Donald Schon applauded Simon's work as it focused upon the importance of design, while criticizing a number of his generalizations. Simon wrote:

Everyone designs who devises courses of action aimed at changing existing situations to preferred ones. The intellectual activity that produces material artifacts is no different fundamentally from the one that prescribes remedies for a sick patient or the one that devises a new sales plan for a company or a social welfare policy for a state. Design, so construed, is the core of all professional training; it is the principal mark that distinguishes the professions from the sciences. (Simon, 1971, p. 129)

However, Simon, while highlighting the need for professional schools to develop a science of design, characterized that science as "a body of intellectually tough, analytic, partly formalizable, partly empirical, teachable doctrine" (Simon, p. 132). While the natural sciences were concerned with how things are, the science of design was to be focused on how things *ought to be*, with creating artifacts to attain goals (Simon, pp. 132–133). But this emphasis upon the should or ought did not dissuade Simon from maintaining that standard logical/statistical processes could be employed. He argued that if we look at design practice we find standards of logical rigor that meet the demand. He refers to the "optimization methods" found in decision theory and management. Here there is an "inner environment" in which we find a certain set of action alternatives, which Simon refers to as "command variables." The "outer environment" is represented by the set of parameters. The task is to locate the goals of adaptation of the inner to the outer environment. Simon tells us:

The optimization problem is to find an admissible set of values of the command variables, compatible with the constraints, that maximize the utility function for the given values of the environmental parameters. (Simon, p. 135)

Simon gives an example of this optimization handicap in the "diet problem." Here a list of foods is provided; the command variables are the amounts of the various foods to be included in the diet. The environmental parameters are the cost and nutritional value of the foods. The utility function is the cost of the diet, where certain constraints intrude (e.g., the diet be limited to 2,000 calories, certain minimum vitamins and minerals be included, and rutabaga not be eaten more than once per week). These constraints are the inner environment. The problem, then, is to pick foods that meet the nutritional needs and side conditions set with the lowest possible purchase total for the foodstuffs. Simon characterizes this diet problem as "a simple example of a class of problems that are readily handled, even when the number of variables is exceedingly large, by the mathematical formalism known as linear programming" (Simon, p. 136).

Simon goes to great length to demonstrate that the design process is a rational process and that evidence for its scientific designation are to be found in successful efforts in utility theory and statistical decision theory, linear programming, dynamic programming, geometric programming, queuing theory, and control theory. These provide sufficient means for determining the design of normative systems.

In addition, Simon is quick to point out that we never have a choice between satisfactory and optimal solutions, rather we engage in "satisficing" choices based on moderate searches (Simon, p. 139). Hence, while our design "science" may be rigorous, it is never complete and cannot rival the hard sciences in the area of precision. And in the design of complex systems, such as cities, buildings (or educational services), we must see the design process as a value as well as the outcome. Simon believes that where many members of a community participate in the design process there is a value (Simon, p. 151).

Designing an educational institution is different from designing a nuclear powerplant or a bridge. Simon talks of the goal of placing a man on the moon and the framing of the American Constitution. The NASA project he finds relatively simpler owing to the narrowness of the goal, the cooperative environment in which the goal was addressed, and the financial resources dedicated to the accomplishment of the goal. The Constitution is also seen as a triumph of "bounded rationality," owing to the fact that it had limited objectives: preservation of freedom in an orderly society. The framers did not propose remaking human beings.

Simon concludes that "the success of planning on such a [social] scale may call for modesty and restraint in setting the design objectives and drastic simplification of the real-world situation" (Simon, p. 163). Obstacles to the design of social institutions include the representation problem, or how to conceptualize the problem. Next, the quality of the design is "likely to depend heavily on the quality of the data available" (Simon, pp. 168–169). Finally, one must address the question "who is the client?" when designing a large social system. Simon emphasizes:

The members of an organization or a society for whom plans are made are not passive instruments, but are themselves designers who are seeking to use the system to further their own goals. Organization theory deals with this motivational question by examining organizations in terms of the balance between inducements that are provided to members to perform their organizational roles and the contributions that the members thereby provide to the achievement of organizational goals. (Simon, p. 177)

Then Simon notes that time and space provide considerations for the designer; and finally he points to the necessity to design without final goals in mind, designs subject to regular revision. In representing a curriculum for the teaching of social design, Simon suggests five topics: "Bounded rationality. . . . Data for planning. . . . Identifying the client. . . . Time and space horizons. . . . and Designing without final goals" (Simon, p. 190).

He argues:

The proper study of mankind has been said to be man. But I have argued that man—or at least the intellective component of man—may be relatively simple, that most of the complexity of his behavior may be drawn from man's environment, from man's search for good designs. . . . The proper study of mankind is the science of design, not only as the professional component of a technical education but as a core discipline for every liberally educated person. (Simon, p. 159)

While the work of Herbert Simon has been influential, the positivistic strain in his theories has prompted reaction.

Schon (1983), for one, has argued that most treatises on design deal with the design of objects such as buildings, machines, and so forth; however, there is a newer notion of design that bears our watching: design of organizations, policies, and theoretical constructs. This "stretched" notion of the design activity may include a full range of human-built artifacts (p. 110). Coincident with this new interest in expanding the arena of designing is the realization "that the most important areas of professional practice now lie beyond the conventional boundaries of professional competence" (Schon, 1987, p. 7). There is an "indeterminate zone of practice." Here uncertainty, uniqueness, and value conflict dominate. These messy areas are not subject to resolution through the conventional moves of "technical rationality." Technical problem solving requires a well-formed problem to work on, but the irony is that setting this problem is the most problematic. The practitioner is beset by the insight that he/she cannot handle the problem solely through application of theories or techniques given in his/her storehouse of professional knowledge. There is something confounding about the situation. This characterization of the current difficulty facing practitioners in education is disabling the professional, and those in the business of preparing professionals for their work have become keenly aware of the difficulty (Schon, 1983, pp. 6–7).

At the heart of the confusion surrounding the use of design in education is the effort to reduce design to simple problem solving. Schon (1990) tells us that we must also see designing as entailing the creative setting of the design problem itself. Schon levels a number of criticisms at the Simonistic theory of design. Schon finds that Simon's model of design as rational decision assumes that the design structure must be given in the presented problem. This is not the case. The model does not explain how we come to make and remake design structures in the process of designing; "well-formed problems and technical problem solving tend to occur in actual designing only in later phases, after a basic design structure has stabilized" (Schon, 1990, p. 111). Another difficulty that Schon highlights is the failure of the Simon model of design to account for the learning that occurs within and across episodes of design. We do not know how designers learn how to prepare for future projects. And Schon points out that Simon's rational decision model fails to account for the fact that design is a social process requiring conflict and dialogue (Schon, pp. 111–112).

Simon's rational decision model divides designing into two parts: the generation of alternatives (or what Schon calls "design proposals"); and selection of alternatives according to some set of decision rules. The diet problem is a good example of how design works within this frame. We are given information statements that are complete; the rules specifying the procedures for selection of the best alternative are laid out. The designer simply follows the logic within the microworld specified to accomplish the aim of controlling the diet for a specific purpose (Schon, 1990, pp. 113–114). However, this fully formed design structure is academic at best. We may apply the diet problem to any medication design and quickly realize that the actual results and side-effects are highly problematic. Our options are not all that clear and logical. Frequently we cannot determine all the choices or even recognize the best choice among alternatives. Nor are we fully confident that we have generated the best set of alternatives for choice. The components may interact as well in ways unpredictable on first inspection. The diet problem is complicated by the interaction of foods (Schon, 1990, p. 121).

Schon tells us that the Simon model as well as other design models often rest upon an assumed biological and social evolutionary metaphor of randomness and incrementalism. Schon cites Charles Lindblom (*The Intelligence of Democracy*, 1963) as arguing that policy makers and planners adhere to the view that one always begins with an existing design, but owing to limited knowledge and constraints of situation, they must initiate only minor changes to existing policies. Schon himself notes finding business firms in the 1950s and 1960s using a random process for generating many proposals coupled with a tight control over selection by the boss (Schon, 1990, pp. 117–118).

This "suggestion box" theory of design is touted to be attached to a democratic value (equity of input); in practice, workers propose solutions to specific ills in an organization, with the management selecting the best likely option according to their own criteria of acceptability. Leadership in organizations resting upon this conception of underlaborer voice separate design from discovery.

The rational decision model of design fails to acknowledge the role of society and/or culture in the design process. While arguing that design is a function of rational purposing, these theorists are also drawn to a notion of design as "super-organic" or "cosmic" in origin. Simon must specify a "bounded" universe for his design process to appear to work; however, such a limited field assumes that the rest of the universe is orderly and will not impinge upon the nested world to the detriment of order.

It is no more rational to assume, as Simon does, that one can single out an alternative and isolate it from others. In actual designing, proposals are often competing, complex, and interdependent (Schon, 1990, p. 120). In the final analysis, Simon's view suffers from an artificially constructed problematic state-of-affairs which favors simplicity, or additive complexity (Schon, 1990, p. 121).

Ultimately, conceiving of the design problem as a structure holding the options for solution masks a subtle conservative characterization of the process. We are encouraged, in designing, to follow traditional patterns and work within parameters of accepted choice (Schon, 1990, p. 122). The Simon model of random and programmed selection teaches us to design cautiously rather than boldly. It is better to believe, as Schon asserts, that design proposals are not just a function of the structured problem, but are created and selected through processes of learning that involve regard for figural complexity. The application of a design solution changes the original design structure that sets the conditions for judging the fit or lack of fit (Schon, 1990, p. 125).

In systematic synthesized searches for options, cases in which no choices are evident in the design structure, Simon adheres to a rational model: an alternative is advanced and then tested against criteria. The origin of alternatives, the search for options, Simon characterizes as pursuing paths. Paths are like avenues through mazes and the designer is a runner of mazes. But, as Schon points out, "systematic search does not account for cases in which running the maze changes the maze" (Schon, 1990, p. 128).

Schon points out that there seems to be no adequate theory of design option synthesis, despite Simon's "systematic" search approach. Schon proposes that we engage in the use of "generative metaphors." By this he has in mind "families of familiar ideas carried over (metapherein, in the Greek) to a new situation for which they serve as projective models" (Schon, 1990, p. 131). We are familiar with metaphorical meanings of "education," (e.g., "pitching hay into a wagon," "filling little pitchers," etc.). Generative metaphors, however, give us a new way of thinking about a situation that provides valued ways of seeing the system as transformed. Generative metaphors frame the problem and thus give us potential answers as well as means for examining these answers (Schon, 1990, pp. 131–132).

It is important to see the designer utilizing a repertoire of such metaphoric images, from which he/she may build problem-setting stories. They form alternative ways of seeing the design problem. In place of Simon's path through the maze, Schon sees the designer scanning a collection of metaphorical representations out of a set of prototypes from a kind of "design culture" or individual design style. The designer is here an artist engaged in creative development of representations of situations in need of settlement.

BETWEEN STRUCTURE AND STRICTURE

If we are to learn anything for leadership from this conversation between Simon and Schon on design, we must see that the design process must rest between the polar opposites of structured science and free anarchistic play. How shall our design process for education be characterized then?

We may draw both upon the structured analysis of the problem and the creative generation of options, as the design process reconstructs the original problem. The designer/leader moves between the given figural components and the unique reconfigurations using a set of tools such as randomness, incrementalism, and metaphor. To these I would add the useful devices of analogy, similitude, and (following Goodman, 1978) composition, decomposition, weighting, ordering, deletion, supplementation, and deformation. The issue here seems to be one of employing a variety of techniques to generate design versions. Simon is committed to certain logical and statistical procedures, Schon is not. Where we adhere to a single method for all problematic instances, or even a cluster of methods, we run the risk of making the articulation of the method the design itself. While linear equations and statistical programming may be "beautiful" in their own right, we must avoid the compulsion to turn these into "habits of the heart." How much is involved in constructing the initial problematic structure as we are involved in searching for optimal solutions? While the problem of locating options within and without the structured design problem is significant, we must not overlook prospects of converting their characterization into new versions. Nelson Goodman (1978) is helpful here. We may speak of educational design as "ways of worldmaking." Goodman tells us that there are many world versions, operating at the same time, in our universe. This rather radical relativism has been criticized (by foundationalists), but it is informative here. For designing need not be singular: there may be plural versions of educational designs. Each design being relatively logical, adequate, and fruitful with respect to its version. There is nothing preventing a Simonistic version alongside a Schonean scheme. Here holism as a rather loosely-related set of theories (D. C. Phillips, 1976, identifies several versions) provides some help. Design deals with bounded systems, or following Goodman, "worlds." But these worlds are also linked or networked with others. Unstructured collectivities vie for structured space through conjoint effort. Clubs, cliques, and societies—all kinds of human aggregates—compose and decompose over time. The responsibility of the leader/designer is to articulate these into meaningful collectivities around certain perceived aims or goals.

Leadership rests, as we have pointed out, upon the transactions between leader and led such that dialogue and conversation results in reasoned options for problematic solution. Design in this way is a social process. Moreover, the use of metaphor and analogy are helpful, along with systematic rational procedures, in moving us toward both a logic of discovery as well as a logic of proof.

When we look at the role of educational institutions in building leadership for schools, the problem of teaching leadership is primary. Despite the failure of professional schools, and here we may include educational schools in the business of "training" future administrators and school leaders, some professionals are competent and excellent practicing administrators and teachers. I shall argue, following Schon, that this is owing to the fact that these professionals have learned to turn practice into art. Schon writes that "inherent in the practice of the professionals we recognize as unusually competent is a core of artistry." Moreover,

Artistry is an exercise of intelligence, a kind of knowing though different in crucial respects from our standard model of professional knowledge. . . .

In the terrain of professional practice, applied science and research-based technique occupy a critically important though limited territory, bounded on several sides by artistry. There is an art of problem framing, an art of implementation, and an art of improvisation—all necessary to mediate the use in practice of applied science and technique. (Schon, 1987, p. 13)

The forms of future social institutions, like schools, cannot be dissociated from the aims and purposes for which the institutions stand. However, the means through which we come to know these purposes cannot be deduced solely from the design structure nor the design methods that are used in developing the future plans. When we look at the problems confronting urban planners, for example, it is clear that a diversity of methods have been utilized in designing new urban centers. Planners draw upon art, architecture, policy studies, sociopolitical analysis, anthropology, and so forth, to produce visions of the new. T. M. Alexander (1987) demonstrates that the skills and knowledge needed for the design of new urban centers are attached to the values and purposes of the people inhabiting them. He writes: "Every project must first be experienced, and then expressed, as a vision which can be seen in the inner eye (literally). It must have this quality so strongly that it can also be communicated to others, and felt by others, as a vision" (Alexander, 1987, p. 50). The technique of design, then, while involving formal skills, also requires the perspective of the artist as *inhabitant* of the very designs generated.

A pragmatic and critical theory of leadership rests upon the assumption that such a theory is also a theory of social welfare based upon a democratic form of life. The task of democracy is to help us rework and redefine the sociocultural to fit our democratic ideals. Educational leadership plays a crucial role in fostering social change. Giroux (1988) speaks of "teachers as intellectuals" engaged in a melioristic effort to better schools, students, and society at large. The educator as "transformative intellectual" is a metaphor that bears upon the question of how design comes to fit the role of administrator/teacher. Design is the creative effort to transform the substantive problem into a fruitful product that allows for greater aesthetic value and practical appreciation. This design process is inherently a process of fostering the growth and development of the community through continuous dialogue and discourse. Openness is an aspect of the aesthetic that must be carried into the design process in the schools. When these components of our critical pragmatic theory of leadership are implemented, we shall see a new democratic and critical leadership that will transform education and the schools into engines of hope.

Roland Barth (1988) talks of leadership as "craft knowledge" (p. 130). Raup et al. (1943) speak of the "artist leader" as one who has an aesthetic understanding. Leadership here requires not naked visionaries, but rather critically imaginative pragmatists. Armed with "practical judgment" as an aspect of their moral/ethical character, artist/leaders would use creative imagination. Taking aim at the "whole" of human situations is another mark of leading as artistic (p. 245).

Chester Barnard wrote:

The creative function as a whole is the essence of leadership. It is the highest test of executive responsibility because it requires for successful accomplishment the element of "conviction" that means identification of personal codes and organizational codes in the view of the leader. This is the coalescence that carries "conviction" to the personnel of organization, to that informal organization underlying all formal organization that senses nothing more quickly than insincerity. (Barnard, 1938, p. 281)

Beyond conviction, Barnard found "persuasion" the essential catalyst for leadership as an executive function (Barnard, 1952; 1986, p. 158). Moreover, people were to be persuaded by (1) example; (2) prestige; or (3) argument; or some combination of these ingredients of persuasion. While Barnard went on to say that with respect to lawyers the public found "something deeply offensive involved in persuasion," it may be argued that, among educators, persuasion is relatively understressed. A correction in the public's attitude toward persuasion, as it may aid in the legal profession, seems to be unrelated to the educator's craft (p. 158).

Leadership requires a high level of morals. Leadership, generally speaking, does not mean the increase of welfare, income, or prestige of the individual leader, but rather the sacrifice of selfish position, Barnard argued. What Barnard said of the importance of service upon the part of the lawyer/leader may be said for the educator/leader. What is needed, Barnard asserted, is the development of incentives for service, rather than for money, prestige, or personal glory. It is a matter of adopting a higher order of morality, Barnard believed (pp. 158–159).

Barnard cautioned that the increased complexity of the organizational system as well as technology has made it more frustrating to be a leader. Finally, Barnard stressed the necessity of quick decision making, and the concomitant release of employee stress, as a mark of good leadership. There is a loss of interest in the work when workers have to wait for extended periods for a decision to be made (pp. 159–160).

Each particular conception of "leadership" presupposes a notion of human nature and a view of culture—and thus, "leadership" is always an affair with ideas. But fundamental to this interrelation is the fundamental context out of which leadership as art must emerge. Here it is important to trace the ideas of Dewey, Husserl, Heidegger, and others as they spoke of the "life-world."

The problem this demand for the aesthetic sets for educational leadership is that it requires of leaders an artistic eye and human heart, yet leadership training programs typically exclude any talk of art or humanness. One solution to this absence is to move toward a discourse/practice that emphasizes design. The design process may aid leadership in the following ways:

1. We have stressed that any pragmatic view of leadership must have a conception of political life and that the best form of that life is a democracy. Design plays a key role in how democracies come to work on a day-to-day basis. Through the crafting of new schemes of interrelationship, the many points of conflict may come to resolution. New patterns of choice may arise through the joined efforts of the organizational team as they seek to confront chaos.

2. Education, in the sense of schooling, should play a role in the development of children and youth. Part of that development involves the nurturing

of leaderly skills on their part. Artistic design highlights the creative posture we must take in building these leadership capacities. By creative play and games, very young children may be taught to share in leadership/followership. As Alan Jones (1938) wrote: "Contrary to popular belief, intelligent leaders do not just happen; they result only from careful planning. It is, therefore, of the utmost importance that society adopt some definite plan by which such leaders may be assured" (p. 3).

3. Leadership, we have seen, requires a vision of the future state-of-affairs. I have criticized efforts to separate such vision from the methods of derivation of vision as well as the absence of any imbeddedness in the social/cultural context that gives vision its meaning. But beyond this there *is* a requirement that the leaders have some overall picture of what the organization ought to resemble. This concern for the figural whole is inimicable to art. Schon (1990) alludes to this grasp of the larger whole when he criticizes Herbert Simon's followers and their view of design as mere rational decision making. The interest in the entire design structure, whether it be in Turkish shawls or institutions, moves leadership from a piece-meal rational decision-making model to that of a holistic pragmatic theory grounded in art.

4. Perhaps nowhere is the necessity of design skill more logically related than in the characterization of the present condition of society as "postmodern." Here, the novel nature of contemporary socioculture calls for creative efforts to both understand and fashion the new. Post-modern art and architecture provide a viable approach to the understanding of art as it may be directed at the fashioning of school organization.

5. Finally, the power-empowerment issue in educational leadership calls for a clearer view of the whole. Design processes reveal that power emerges in the transaction between the artist and the canvas, paper, or computer screen. Design is the power to release the capacities of raw unstructured materials so that they may become arranged or structured into new patterns of meaning.

HUMAN NATURE

"Leadership becomes, like politics, the art of getting what one (either a politician or a leader) wants and making people like it" (Titus, 1950, p. 51). The tendency in views like the foregoing has been to overlook the individual in favor of the study of the organization. Chester I. Barnard wrote in 1938:

I have found it impossible to go far in the study of organizations or of the behavior of people in relation to them without being confronted with a few questions which can be simply stated. For example, "What is an individual?" "What do we mean by a person?" "To what extent do people have power of choice or free will?" . . . Even if we avoid answering such questions definitely, we cannot evade them. We answer them implicitly in whatever we say about human behavior." (p. 8)

Green (1968) writes: "For it is undeniable that, whenever education is consciously undertaken, it will be strongly influenced by such amorphous but widely held sometimes hidden but nonetheless operative beliefs concerning the nature of man—what it means to be an individual, a member of society, a part of a certain history" (pp. 5–6).

Thus, educational leadership qua theory is built upon the notion of what constitutes the nature of human nature. Dewey tells us ([1922] 1957) that the essential problem has been: how alterable is human nature? The historic record has been that early reformers such as Locke and Helvetius believed that human nature was completely plastic. Through the mechanism of experience, humans could build upon a human nature that was both empty and passive. On the other hand, more conservative social philosophers asserted that native instincts lent support for the view that human nature was unalterable. Conditions would change, but human nature remained the same. Oddly enough, both the radical social reformer and the abject conservative based their view on factors that weaken their case: The radical reformer rested his case for the ease and speed of social change on human habits and the impact of social institutions on shaping raw nature; the conservative builds his view on a psychology of instincts. Dewey argued that custom and habit have inertia, while instincts are modifiable through use and education (Dewey, [1922] 1957, pp. 101–103).

"Actual social change is never so great as is apparent change," Dewey wrote. It is difficult to change the habits of belief and practice. Habits of thought outlive habits of action. Therefore, the moral effects of social reform movements often do not surface until years after the political events that named them (Dewey, [1922] 1957, pp. 103–104). We must also see that human beings have certain "natural" penchants, one of which is toward action. Dewey demonstrates that we seek activities that are agreeable to us. The interest in building bridges, painting landscapes, and creating investment portfolios all fit within the interest of humans in making some gesture of an organized and sustained sort toward their environs. On the other hand, the social conditions temper and shape these impulses, cautioning against some and rewarding others (Dewey, [1922] 1957, p. 116).

The bearings of this pragmatic view of human nature as at once malleable and yet possessing certain impulses and proclivities allows us to construct our theory of leadership along more realistic lines. Leadership aimed at institutional change finds a conception of human nature as at once changeable by virtue of experience and culture, while also possessing tendencies of intractability owing to commitments to habitual social practices. Effective leadership is a teaching leadership that seeks to draw upon the aspects of human characterizations that are subject to change while reducing dependence upon outdated or impracticable habits of practice. Social change, in this view, is a function of criticism of both the *reproduction* of the ill-suited and under-justified social customs and habits of the institutional culture, and of *resistance* to the archaic conceptualization of human instincts and capacities which reduce human potential and devalue democratic values of equity, freedom, and intelligence. Finally, social change is a consequence of seeing human nature as properly action-directed and melioristic: a human nature built upon a philosophy of *hope*. Paulo Freire tells us that any analysis of the oppressive conditions that beset us must reveal a fundamental conception of human nature at their root. For Freire, humans not only exist *in* the world, they must exist *with* the world. The problem is that humans must also be able to gain some perspective on their condition, and to do so they must come to objectify themselves, question their status, and in other ways determine the reason for being. This is done through the medium of reflection (I and not-I). Through a dialectical relation between human objectification of the world and action upon that world, we achieve *consciousness* (Bugbee, 1973, pp. 47–50).

In terms of leadership, we may see Freire's characterization of human nature to be revealing of the means whereby individuals in social organizations, like schools, may come to see their relationship to bureaucratic leadership. By seeing human beings related to their worlds by virtue of praxis or reflected-upon action, Freire helps us realize that humanizing leadership requires consciousness of the conditions that subordinate individuals to group goals and techniques; it responds to this oppression through cultural acts indicating freedom. Thus, emancipation of authoritative and bureaucratic notions of leadership will stem from the consciousness and subsequent critique of these disabling conditions. When we link these attitudes to the natural capacity to create, through design, life-worlds which enhance the nature of human nature, we have a vested commitment to a kind of leadership that is both continuous and emancipatory.

A NORMATIVE MODEL OF LEADERSHIP AS DESIGNING

Experiments in school reorganization (e.g., "site-based management" and "decentralization") will have impacts upon school leadership in the United States. However, unless a planned program for leading is developed, there is a likelihood that such efforts will lead to confusion and disorientation. A normative vision of educational leadership entails both technical grasp of the facts and evidence of the case (disciplined inquiry skills, statistical methods, empirical techniques, etc.); it also requires a set of enabling criteria that inform the nature of this new leadership. It is the "surround" of conditions that brings into bold relief the artistic nature of leading. Attending to the scope and sequence of instruction implies a grasp of the grand design of pedagogy. It is possible to paint the kind of society and community that will emerge from such crafting. Thomas Popkewitz (1984) argues strongly for educational research to focus upon the larger social values that justify and support inquiry. Research in education is time-bound and culture-bound: methods of inquiry reveal assumptions about the human being, the structure of the brain, the role of schools in preparing workers, and so forth. We cannot divorce these social interests from the techniques of data collection, factor analysis, or regression equation.

The aim of leadership is to be the nurturing of social organization such that all those involved in teaching/learning may come to see one another as possessing *human dignity*. Drawing upon the work of Israel Scheffler on the education of policy makers (1985), it is proposed here that leadership entails respect for followers. Such regard assumes that followers are to be taken to have the potential to share their intelligence and to exercise the *power* of free choice in decision making. And finally, we wish to argue that the aim of leadership entails the belief (willingness to act upon the notion) that each follower possesses the *potential* to lead and must be nurtured to that end. The ultimate criterion of leadership is to enable followers to lead themselves (Scheffler, pp. 102–103).

While the question of what "leadership" *is* has failed to produce answers, the query as to how we may *evaluate* leaders has not. Viewed from a pragmatic perspective, we may argue that leadership is the concrete results of what leaders in fact do. We may thus appraise or evaluate leadership on the grounds of what results from the leader's thinking and action (American Institute of Management Incorporated, 1959, pp. 6–7). We have argued that leading is a creative act and that it results in an aesthetic achievement (not necessary a plastic artifact, for we may have a performance that is a leadership consequent).

When speaking of leadership as art, it is not intended that the moral function be abrogated. Rather, leaders/artists must be allowed to engage in both *play* and *art*. Dewey, in *Human Nature and Conduct* ([1922] 1957), suggests that play and art have an "indispensable moral function" (p. 150). By this Dewey meant that art and play release human impulses in quite different ways than ordinary activities. This careless rapture has a moral dimension as it performs a function for human nature: that is, by "softening rigidities, relaxing strains, allaying bitterness, dispelling moroseness, and breaking down the narrowness consequent upon specialized tasks" art frees up life's meanings (pp. 151–152). "Art releases energy and focuses and tranquilizes it" (p. 152). Imagination is brought to bear through activity upon and shapes material. It releases impulses that are often bottled up or thwarted, forced into disguise (pp. 152–154).

When viewed from an organizational perspective, art and play as connected with the liberation of capacity and impulse provide a means for institutional renewal. Creative craftsmanship that is connected with the aesthetic need for release replaces revolution and upheaval. A school management philosophy must either accommodate itself to the continuous reconstruction of itself through aesthetic leadership, or run the risk of either repression on the one hand or vicious revolts on the other. Here the psychological conditions fuel creative artwork and connect with human nature and the nature of school culture. School climates that thwart creative leadership deny art—the art of life in which career and work are in harmony with human purposes and goals. For the teacher as well as the administrator, "making a living, economically speaking, will be at one with making a life that is worth living" (Dewey, [1948] 1960, p. 211).

Where Dewey argues against metaphysical explanations, he replaces idealistic and Hegelian conceptions of experience with an empirically based notion of experience. It is important to see his use of *communication* as the means whereby existants are appropriated for human use. Language and communication are central to the processes of transforming the undeveloped existence into the types of human experiences that lead to growth and change (Sleeper, 1986, pp. 6–9).

Administration in general, and educational administration in particular, is *art*—because life is art, or should be practiced as art. Interestingly, the social sciences have come to dominate how we think about administration and leadership, and they are not particularly sensitive to aesthetic methods. Elliot Eisner (1988) tells us that "the politics of method ultimately has to do with the politics of experience. Method influences how we think and what we are permitted to feel" (p. 19). In *Truth and Method*, Hans-Georg Gadamer traces the history and meaning of "experience" in the mid-nineteenth century. Dilthey's work revealed a view of experience that is not passive (and hence only open to analytic depiction), but rather intentional and purposive (what Simmel called "an element in the life process itself") (Ward, 1984, pp. 30–31).

In this chapter, we have argued for a critical emancipatory view of knowledge in which leadership is seen neither as a function of positivistic science nor as folkloristic art. A leadership of rational design that accepts the assumptions that human beings are in the business of crafting futures and that organizations, to be free and democratic, require the pedagogical function of leading to support a practice of resistance as well as hope. There is a necessity to refocus our attention in educational leadership upon the field of play as well as the language that inscribes it.

The world of day-to-day practice of educational leading may be seen to draw upon knowledge arising from inquiry (research) and expertise in design (art). However, Yeakey and Johnston (1986) point out that neither positivist science nor art have been particularly helpful in solving the practical problems of real world administration.

Efforts to construct a "qualitative" research posture in educational research has received widespread applause from researchers and practitioners alike. By removing the "positivist" elements in educational inquiry, it is argued, a more accurate depiction of the school and teaching will emerge. The literature in support of this philosophical position is so large it is impractical to cite it. In simple form, the argument runs something like this: Since so-called scientific research has failed to provide a predictable picture of educational practice, and since all inquiry is based upon assumptions and values, it is the case that research should admit to its biases and imprecision and researchers direct their attention to the multiple paradigms and explanations.

It is possible to speak of "creative leadership" in the sense of leading identified with a value or complex of values. This type of leadership is different from the typical representative leadership that is associated with a role or position. Here the leader attempts to innovate, rather than logically extend extant matters. These innovations are traceable to particular paradigms, frameworks, or schemes and are warranted by good arguments rather than data.

The designing leader is more prone to move from "qualitative" assumptions to "quantitative" test. The "positivistic leader," as bald empiricist, is more likely to work from numeric data to value assertion. The so-called "Theory Movement" in educational administration research took on itself the collection of massive data in the hopes of generating theories. The data collection became interminable and the theories never came (T. B. Greenfield, 1975).

CONCLUSIONS

This chapter has sought to demonstrate the necessity of design as an element of an aesthetic interest in the operation of leadership in the schools. It has been argued that a critical and pragmatic theory of leadership as art rests upon the tripartite concepts of experience, culture, and human nature. Historically, positivistic conceptions of business-like school leadership have undervalued the artistic in favor of the linear and procedural technical rationality of management. We have explored two competing notions of design, finding between them a space into which leadership qua design may function for educational settings.

10

Conclusions

The present effort has been one of developing a normative social philosophic position in which educational leadership becomes a means for the transformation of American schools. At the heart of the issue of educational leadership is the operative notion of leadership *as teaching*. As we have seen, educational leadership is a unique form of leadership (as distinct from military leadership or religious leadership) owing to the fact that educational leaders engage in discourse/practice that is instructional. Just as philosophy of education is a special form of philosophy, differing in intention and content from philosophy at large, I wish to argue that educational leadership is distinct from the other brands of leading.

Education is defined as "educare" or to lead out, and it is the case that this definition has historically been linked to Socratic dialogue and the method of critical reflection. In the present circumstance of an advanced information culture, there is a need to reconstruct this earlier definition of education as along the lines of true leadership. By leadership, we have in mind the capacity to interact with self or others in terms of moving a discourse/practice toward an end based upon criteria that are at once rational and moral/ethical. Leading is not so much telling others what is true or false, but rather helping them come to know for themselves the merits or demerits of a case.

The method used to develop the kind of self-understanding prerequisite for this reconstructed notion of "leadership" is at once critical and pragmatic. The understanding of "leadership" in educational settings requires the method of critical social science, again seen not as inquiry aimed at knowledge solely, but knowledge for transformative action. It is argued in the pages that precede that educational leadership as inquiry is necessarily emancipatory where it seeks to know so as to inform others. Leadership in this sense is normative, or recommendational, of future states-of-affairs.

Throughout this text we have stressed the view of leadership as "transactional." Leaders and followers are interdependent. Yet leadership as imposition and following as compliance is the incomplete characterization that has informed the research on leadership in the social sciences literature. At any point in a discourse/practice of leading, it is possible to locate the quanta of leadership on either side of the equation. Leading is in the hands of the follower insofar as he/she accedes or seeks to resist the power of the leader. Empowerment, rather than the benign parts-ing out of elements of strength, usually via decisions and decision making, is seen as emerging from the realization (self-understanding) of the unempowered that they may release the potential for practical judgment. Empowerment, in this definition, is a transactional concept like leadership, in the sense that power is always a process term. The trick is to come to the understanding that power is tensional and supports leadership discourse/practice.

Throughout this text, we have been interested in seeing educational settings as "texts" in their own right. Schools write their own practice through such vehicles as decisions, policies, and norms regulating practice. The text of the school is a discourse, and as speech acts, school speech is capable of being unpacked, deconstructed, and in other ways analyzed. "Styles" of textual writing are evident in the various school cultures. There are as many different leadership/empowerment styles as human beings involved in such transactions. The important point is to see the potential and capacity for leading and self-empowering that teachers may possess in the face of historic efforts to define educational power relations as structurally functional distillates of bureaucracy.

We have seen how twentieth-century Western civilization has sought via a Cartesian characterization of knowledge and inquiry to locate truth in the capacity to dichotomize discourse/practice into such polar opposites as "leader/lead," "powerful/powerless," "authority/freedom," and "true/false." It is asserted here that such dualisms, rather than describing states-of-affairs, capture the characteristics of the ideological view informing the method of inquiry. Administrative/pedagogical leadership, in this light, is seen as relations and not opposites. The discourse/practice of leadership needs to be seen in this ebb and flow of action/thought.

Research into the early learning of leadership ideologies has displayed the fact that kindergarten is not too early to teach people the mythologies of leadership. That some people have "natural leadership" while others are "followers" stems not so much from genetic facts or "sociobiological" evidence as from the prejudices of the teachers inducting children into the mainstream culture. The opportunities for aiding each child in developing the capacity of leadership has been stilted and twisted by the demand for "excellence," and via the method of competition. Older equalitarian ideals were seen as leveling influences, while newer competitive modes are "necessary if we are to compete with the Japanese." There is an inconsistency in American schooling where these two ideals clash. Policy is a prime arena in which to see leadership living or dying. In the policy operation, the unleashing of power and leadership has been carefully monitored. The institutionalization of roles and the concentration on the ends of policy over the reasons (ethical and otherwise) for maintaining a particular course of action have blind-sided the efforts to educate new teacher/leaders in curriculum and other kinds of decision making.

We have been particularly interested in recent efforts to introduce "moral imagination" as a guide to administrative leadership and the development and implementation of policy. This effort, it has been argued, has been interested in drawing upon an older "charismatic" leader model to warrant an authoritarian (and at times Machiavellian) view of leadership and power. The critical pedagogues have shown that the emphasis on ends and the failure to raise questions of rational justification have in the end produced a technical/rational school culture. The obverse would be a moral/ethical model that confronted and sought to reconstruct this narrow vision. Unfortunately, the liberation of future educational conditions is insured to misfire where "moral imagination" becomes the singular image of an authoritarian educator.

In this light, we have argued throughout this text for a democratic context for leadership. It has been asserted that only in the medium of democracy can the fully operative leadership concept emerge. Leaderships are always truncated and narrow when power is invested in the few. Leading that ebbs and flows between participants in discourses/practices, in terms of the decisions at hand, allows for the pedagogical authority that Benne and others have talked about.

Modernism, it has been further argued, has failed. Postmodernity has potential to improve upon the incomplete and imprecise conceptions of leadership and power operative in western cultures. While post-modern is not clearly defined, and while there may well emerge a post-postmodernity, it is nonetheless essential that the circumspect nature of technical/rational, charismatically driven moral models of educational leadership be reconstructed with new and superior modes. The preparation of educational leaders is not to be seen as the sole function of "leadership academies," "leadership workshops," or other bureaucratic structuralist mechanisms for perpetuating the unsound educational control of the past. We are arguing for new groundings for educational leadership resting in the expertise, collegiality, and democratic tendencies of human beings in social groups.

Empowerment is seen as the catalyst for such leadership, where power is no longer dichotomized and reduced to force and distance. While it is tempting to wrest control and direction from principals and superintendents and to move it to teacher-driven models of governance, we wish to argue that such moves overlook the interesting *process* nature of leadership. We find such radical gestures to be either bad faith (in which case the empowered seek to control the empowered-to-be) or naive and disabling.

In the final analysis, leadership is an auto-machine, in which we are at once the driver and the vehicle: only be seeing power as our own self-understanding and emancipation of interest can we see the enlargement of justice, equality, and the good life for all in society.

In this chapter I wish to just touch upon what bearings this viewpoint may have for educational governance and teaching. I shall be interested in pointing to the requirements that must be met for leadership to occur in education.

THE GENERIC REQUIREMENTS OF LEADERSHIP IN EDUCATION

We have charted a kind of reflective image of leadership as it relates to complicated organizations like schools; however, it will be necessary to reveal the map of that terrain. Sokoloff points to the need for a more generic set of requirements for leadership beyond mere mapping, where the metaphorical calls for leading and the informal nature of leadership role and context are acknowledged (1984, pp. 339–341). Given Sokoloff's view of leadership, educational administrators, teachers, and supervisors may be leaders and never deal with policy (except perhaps to implement it unthinkingly) or critical decision making at all. There are ways in which "leadership can be exercised through collecting and interpreting data" for school officials, he argues.

By moving the focus away from leading and normative issues, leading and ethics, leading and goal setting, he denudes leadership into a kind of subservience role. Leaders are taken to be working in the background engaging in "underlaborer" tasks: leaders become "philosophers" in the worst sense of modernist carriers of water for kings. By focusing on formal leadership and moving informal leading into the spotlight of formal organizations such as schools, I wish to argue we democratize leadership and through empowerment via self-initiating structuring create a kind of problem-solving leader who will make a difference in schools and communities throughout societies. Purely analytic philosophic moves will never bring this into being, solely because analysis "leaves everything the same." Rather, we need a reconstruction and reconceptualization of leadership as enlightened, critical, and pragmatic action— a notion of leadership that looks to everyone who participates in teaching/learning for the kinds of thought and effort that will result in a reformed education. This is our hope.

Bibliography

Alexander, C. (1983). "Ometz: A New Conception of Leadership Development for the Conservative Movement." *The Melton Journal*, 4 (Winter), pp. 25–26.

Alexander, C., H. Neis, A. Anninou, and I. King (1987). *A New Theory of Urban Design*. New York: Oxford University Press.

Alexander, T. M. (1987). *John Dewey's Theory of Art, Experience and Nature: The Horizons of Feeling*. Albany, N.Y.: SUNY Press.

American Institute of Management Incorporated (1959). *Executive Evaluation*. New York: American Institute of Management Incorporated.

Apple, M. (1982). *Education and Power*. Boston: Ark.

Archambault, R. D., ed. (1966). *Dewey on Education: Appraisals*. New York: Random House.

Aronowitz, S., and H. A. Giroux (1985). *Education Under Siege: The Conservative, Liberal and Radical Debate Over Schooling*. New York: Bergin and Garvey.

Austin, G. (1979). "Exemplary Schools and the Search for Effectiveness." *Educational Leadership*, 37, no. 1, pp. 10–14.

Bachrach, P., and M. S. Baratz (1962). "The Two Faces of Power." *American Political Science Review*, 56, no. 4, pp. 947–952.

Bailey, F. G. (1988). *Humbuggery and Manipulation: The Art of Leadership*. Ithaca, N.Y.: Cornell University Press.

Ballinger, S. (1965). "The Nature and Function of Educational Policy." Occasional Paper No. 65–101 (May). Indiana University, Center for the Study of Educational Policy.

Barnard, C. I. (1938). *Functions of the Executive*. Cambridge: Harvard University Press.

———. (1952). *Organization and Management: Selected Papers*. Cambridge, Mass.: Harvard University Press.

———. (1986). *Philosophy for Managers: Selected Papers of Chester I. Barnard*, ed. by W. B. Wolf and H. Iino. Tokyo: Bunshido.

Barrow, R. (1976a). "Competence and the Head." In R. S. Peters, ed., *The Role of the Head*, pp. 63–91. London: Routledge and Kegan Paul.

———. (1976b). *Plato and Education*. London: Routledge and Kegan Paul.

———. (1981a). "Philosophic Competence and Discriminatory Power: A Reply to Alan Smithson." *Journal of Philosophy of Education*, 15, no. 2, pp. 229–231.

———. (1981b). *The Philosophy of Schooling*. New York: John Wiley.

———. (1983). "Does the Question 'What Is Education?' Make Sense?" *Educational Theory*, 33, nos. 3 and 4 (Summer/Fall), pp. 191–196.

———. (1984). *Giving Teaching Back to Teachers*. London: Althouse.

Barth, R. (1988). "School: A Community of Leaders." In Ann Liebermann, ed., *Building a Professional Culture in Schools*, pp. 129–147. New York: Teachers College Press.

Barzun, J. (1983). *A Stroll with William James*. New York: Harper and Row.

Bass, B. M. (1981). *Stogdill's Handbook of Leadership*. New York: Free Press.

Bates, R. (1990). "Leadership and the Rationalization of Society." Paper read before the American Educational Research Association. Boston, April.

Benne, K. D. (1970). "Authority in Education." *Harvard Educational Review*, 40, no. 3, pp. 385–410.

———. (1990). *The Task of Post-Contemporary Education*. New York: Teacher's College Press.

Bennett, W. J. (1987). "Educators in America: The Three R's." Speech before the National Press Club, Washington, D.C., March 27, 1985. Cited in A. Gutmann, *Democratic Education*. Princeton, N.J.: Princeton University Press.

Bennis, W., and B. Nanus (1985). *Leaders: The Strategies for Taking Charge*. New York: Harper and Row.

Bernstein, R. J., ed. (1960). *On Experience, Nature and Freedom: Representative Selections John Dewey*. Indianapolis: Bobbs-Merrill.

———. (1961). "John Dewey's Metaphysics of Experience." *Journal of Philosophy*, 58, no. 1, pp. 5–8.

———. (1983). *Beyond Objectivism and Relativism*. Philadelphia: University of Pennsylvania Press.

Beyer, L. E. (1988). *Knowing and Acting: Inquiry, Ideology and Educational Studies*. London: The Falmer Press.

Beyer, L. E., W. Feinberg, J. Pagano, and J. A. Whitson (1989). *Preparing Teachers as Professionals: The Role of Educational Studies and Other Disciplines*. New York: Teacher's College Press.

Bidwell, C. E. (1972). "Schooling and Socialization for Moral Commitment." *Interchange*, 3, no. 4, pp. 1–27.

Blanchard, K. H., W. Oncken, Jr., and H. Burrows (1989). *The One Minute Manager Meets the Monkey*. New York: Morrow.

Bloom, A. (1987). *The Closing of the American Mind*. New York: Simon and Schuster.

Blum, L. (1980). *Friendship, Altruism, and Morality*. Boston: Routledge and Kegan Paul.

Blumberg, A. (1988). *School Administration as a Craft: Foundations of Practice*. Boston: Allyn and Bacon.

Blumberg, A., and W. Greenfield (1980). *The Effective Principal: Perspectives on School Leadership*. Boston: Allyn and Bacon.

Bode, C., ed. (1947). *The Portable Theoreau*. New York: Viking.

Borger, J. B., C. Lo, Sung-Sam, and H. J. Walberg (1985). "Effective Schools: A Quantitative Synthesis of Constructs." Paper delivered at the annual meeting of the American Educational Research Association, Chicago, April.

Bossert, S. (1979). *Tasks and Social Relationships in Classrooms*. Cambridge: Cambridge University Press.

Bower, E. (1988). "Getting Tough." *Time*, 131, no. 9, pp. 52–53.

Bowers, C. A. (1987). *Elements of a Post-Liberal Theory of Education*. New York: Teacher's College Press.

Brain, Sir R. (1959). *The Nature of Experience*. London: Oxford University Press.

Brent, A. (1983). "Response to Maxcy." Unpublished paper read before the Philosophy of Education Society of Great Britain, Strawberry Hill, England.

Brown, M. (1933). *Leadership Among High School Pupils: A Study of Pupils Selected by Fellow Pupils to Positions of Leadership in a Certain High School*. New York: Bureau of Publications, Teachers College, Columbia University.

Bryman, A. (1986). *Leadership and Organizations*. London: Routledge and Kegan Paul.

Buchler, J., ed. (1955). *Philosophical Writings of Peirce*. New York: Dover.

Bugbee, J. (1973). "On the Quality of the Moral Partisanship of the Pedagogy of Paulo Freire." Unpublished doctoral dissertation. Bloomington, Indiana: Indiana University.

Burbules, N. C. (1986). "A Theory of Power in Education." *Educational Theory*, 36, no. 2, pp. 95–114.

———. (1989). "Issues and Trends in the Philosophy of Education." *Educational Administration Quarterly*, 25, no. 3 (August), pp. 229–252.

Burlingame, M. (1987). "Images of Leadership in Effective Schools Literature." In W. Greenfield, ed., *Institutional Leadership: Concepts, Issues and Controversies*. Boston: Allyn and Bacon.

Burns, J. M. (1978). *Leadership*. New York: Harper and Row.

Cahoone, L. E. (1988). *The Dilemma of Modernity: Philosophy, Culture, and Anti-culture*. Albany, N.Y.: State University of New York Press.

Callahan, R. (1962). *Education and the Cult of Efficiency*. Chicago: University of Chicago Press.

Campbell, A. (1977). "Are Instructional Leaders Still Needed?" *Educational Leadership*, 35, no. 1, pp. 11–14.

Campbell, C. M.,. and G. R. Koopman (1952). "The Need for Dynamic Leadership in a Free Society." In Clyde M. Campbell, ed., *Practical Applications of Democratic Administration*, pp. 3–27. New York: Harper and Brothers.

Campbell, R. F., T. F. Fleming, L. J. Newell, and J. W. Bennion (1987). *A History of Thought and Practice in Educational Administration*. New York: Teacher's College Press.

Carnegie Foundation for Advancement of Teaching (1988). "Change Trendlines: The Rise and Fall of Education as a Major." *Change*, 20, no. 4, pp. 27–32.

Cherryholmes, C. (1988). *Power and Criticism*. New York: Teacher's College Press.

Childs, J. L. (1931). *Education and the Philosophy of Experimentalism*. New York: The Century Company.

———. (1956). *American Pragmatism and Education*. New York: Holt.

Clark, D., L. Lotto, and T. Astuto (1984). "Effective Schools and School Improvement: A Comparative Analysis of Two Lines of Inquiry." *Educational Administration Quarterly*, 20, no. 3, pp. 41–68.

Clayton, A. S. (n.d.). "Professionalism and Problems of Power." Unpublished paper. Bloomington, Ind.: Indiana University.

Clifford, G. J., and J. W. Guthrie (1988). *Ed School*. Chicago: University of Chicago Press.

Cohen, M. (1982). "Effective Schools: Accumulating Research Findings." *American Education*, 148, no. 1, pp. 13–16.

Counts, G. S. (1934). *The Social Foundations of Education*. New York: Charles Scribner's Sons.

Cremin, L. A. (1961). *The Transformation of the School*. New York: Vintage.

Dahl, R. A. (1957). "The Concept of Power." *Behavioral Science*, 2, no. 3, pp. 201–205.

De Bevoise, W. (1984). "Synthesis of Research on the Principal as Instructional Leader." *Educational Leadership*, 41, no. 5 (February), pp. 15–20.

Deleuze, G., and F. Guattari. (1980, 1987). *A Thousand Plateaus: Capitalism and Schizophrenia*, B. Massumi, trans. Minneapolis: University of Minnesota Press.

De Pree, M. (1987). *Leadership as an Art*. East Lansing, Michigan: Michigan State University Press.

Dewey, J. ([1916] 1961). *Democracy and Education*. New York: Macmillan.

———. ([1922] 1957). *Human Nature and Conduct*. New York: Modern Library.

———. (1927). *The Public and Its Problems*. New York: Henry Holt.

———. ([1929] 1958). *Experience and Nature*. New York: G. P. Putnam's Sons.

———. (1930). *Individualism Old and New*. New York: Minton.

———. ([1934] 1980). *Art as Experience*. New York: G. P. Putnam.

———. (1935). "Toward Administrative Statesmanship." *The Social Frontier*, 1, no. 6, pp. 9–10.

———. (1937). "Democracy and Educational Administration." *School and Society*, 45, no. 162, pp. 457–462.

———. (1939). *Freedom and Culture*. New York: G. P. Putnam's Sons.

———. ([1948] 1960). *Reconstruction in Philosophy*. Boston: Beacon Press.

———. (1963). "Theory of Valuation." In P. W. Taylor, ed., *The Moral Judgment: Readings in Contemporary Meta-Ethics*, pp. 163–187. Englewood Cliffs, N.J.: Prentice-Hall.

———. (1967–1972). *The Early Works (1882–1898)*. Vols. 1–5. Carbondale, Ill.: Southern Illinois University Press.

———. (1976–1981). *The Middle Works (1899–1924)*. Vols. 1–15. Carbondale, Ill.: Southern Illinois University Press.

———. (1981–   ). *The Later Works (1925–1953)*. Vols. 1–16. Carbondale, Ill.: Southern Illinois University Press.

Dewey, J., and A. F. Bentley (1949). *Knowing and the Known*. Boston: Beacon Press.

Dooley, P. K. (1974). *The Philosophy of William James*. Chicago: Nelson-Hall.

Drory, A., and U. M. Gluskinos (1980). "Machiavellianism and Leadership." *Journal of Applied Psychology*, 56, no. 1, pp. 81–86.

Dubin, R. (1968). *Human Relations in Administration*. 2nd ed. Englewood Cliffs, N.J.: Prentice-Hall.

Dumm, T. L. (1988). "The Trial of Postmodernism. II. The Politics of Post-modern Aesthetics. Habermas Contra Foucault." *Political Theory*, 16, no. 2, pp. 209–228.

Edmonds, R. (1982). "Programs for School Improvement." *Educational Leadership*, 40, no. 3, pp. 4–11.

Eisner, E. W. (1979). *The Educational Imagination: On the Design and Evaluation of School Programs*. New York: Macmillan.

———. (1988). "The Primacy of Experience and the Politics of Method." *Educational Researcher*, 17, no. 5, (June/July), pp. 15–20.

Etzioni, A. (1961). *A Comparative Analysis of Organizations*. New York: Free Press.

Fay, B. (1987). *Critical Social Science*. Ithaca, N.Y.: Cornell University Press.

Feyerabend, P. (1978). *Science in a Free Society*. London: Verso.

Fiedler, F. E. (1967). *A Theory of Leadership Effectiveness*. New York: McGraw-Hill.

Foster, H., ed. (1983). *The Anti-Aesthetic: Essays on Postmodern Culture.* Port Townsend, Washington: Bay Press.

Foster, W. P. (1980). "Administration and the Crisis in Legitimacy: A Review of Habermasian Thought." *Harvard Educational Review,* 50, no. 4, pp. 496–505.

———. (1982). "A Critical Appraisal of the Leadership Construct." Paper read before the American Educational Studies Association, Nashville, Tennessee, November.

———. (1986). *Paradigms and Promises: New Approaches to Educational Administration.* Buffalo, N.Y.: Prometheus Books.

———. (1989). "School Leaders as Transformative Intellectuals: Toward a Critical Theory." Unpublished paper presented at the American Educational Research Association annual meeting, San Francisco, April.

Foucault, M. (1977). *Power and Knowledge: Selected Interviews and Other Writings, 1972–1977.* Edited by C. Gordon. New York: Pantheon Books.

———. (1980). *The History of Sexuality, Volume I: An Introduction.* New York: Vintage.

Gadamer, H. G. (1975a). "Hermeneutics and Social Science." *Cultural Hermeneutics,* 2, no. 4, pp. 307–316.

———. ([1975b] 1985). *Truth and Method.* New York: Crossroad.

Garcia, J. (1989). "Power to the Teachers." *The Dallas Morning News,* March 5, 1A; 24A.

Garrison, J. W., and E. I. Shargel (1986). "Dewey's *Experience and Nature* and Husserl's *Crisis*: A Surprising Convergence of Themes." In N. C. Burbeles, ed., *Philosophy of Education 1986,* pp. 255–264. Normal, Ill.: Philosophy of Education Society.

Geiger, G. R. ([1958] 1964). *John Dewey in Perspective.* New York: McGraw-Hill.

Gerth, H. H.,. and C. W. Mills, trans. (1946, 1958). *From Max Weber: Essays in Sociology.* New York: Oxford University Press.

Gilligan. C. (1982). *In a Different Voice.* Cambridge, Massachusetts: Harvard University Press.

Giroux, H. A. (1981). *Ideology, Culture, and the Process of Schooling.* Philadelphia: Temple University Press.

———. (1983). *Theory and Resistance in Education: A Pedagogy for the Opposition.* New York: Bergin and Garvey.

———. (1986). "Authority, Intellectuals, and the Politics of Practical Learning." *Teachers College Record,* 88, no. 1 (Fall), pp. 22–40.

———. (1988). *Teachers as Intellectuals: Toward a Critical Pedagogy of Learning.* New York: Bergin and Garvey.

Goodlad, J. (1984). *A Place Called School.* New York: McGraw-Hill.

Goodman, N. (1978). *Ways of Worldmaking.* Indianapolis: Hackett.

Gouinlock, J. (1972). *John Dewey's Philosophy of Value.* New York: Humanities Press.

Gouldner, A. (1950). *Studies in Leadership.* New York: Free Press.

Grady, M. L., W. W. Wayson, and P. A. Zirkel (1989). *A Review of Effective Schools Research as it Relates to Effective Principals.* UCEA Monograph Series. Tempe, Arizona: The University Council for Educational Administration.

Graham, H. D. (1984). *The Uncertain Triumph: Federal Education Policy in the Kennedy and Johnson Years.* Chapel Hill: The University of North Carolina Press.

Green, T. F. (1968). *Work, Leisure, and the American Schools.* New York: Random House.

———. (1985). "The Formation of Conscience in an Age of Technology." *American Journal of Education,* 94, no. 1, pp. 1–32.

Greene, M. (1970). "Imagination." In Ralph A. Smith, ed., *Aesthetic Concepts and Education,* pp. 305–327. Urbana: University of Illinois Press.

Greenfield, T. B. (1975). "Theory About Organizations: A New Perspective and its Implications for the Schools." In M. Hughes, ed., *Administering Education: International Challenge*, pp. 71–99. London: Athlone.

———. (1984). "Leaders and Schools: Willfulness and Nonnatural Order in Organizations." In T. J. Sergiovanni and J. E. Corbally, eds., *Leadership and Organizational Culture*, pp. 142–169. Urbana: University of Illinois Press.

———. (1986). "The Decline and Fall of Science in Educational Administration." *Interchange*, 17, no. 2 (Summer), pp. 57–80.

Greenfield, W. (1986). "Moral Imagination, Interpersonal Competence, and the Work of School Administrators." Paper read before the American Educational Research Association, San Francisco, April.

———. (1987a). "Moral Imagination and Value Leadership in Schools." Paper read before the American Educational Research Association, Washington, D.C., April.

———. (1987b). "Moral Imagination and Interpersonal Competence: Antecedents to Instructional Leadership." In W. D. Greenfield, ed., *Instructional Leadership*, pp. 56–73. Boston: Allyn and Bacon.

Griffith, F., ed. (1979). *Administrative Theory in Education*. Midland, Michigan: Pendell.

Grumet, M. (1987). "The Politics of Personal Knowledge." *Curriculum Inquiry*, 17, no. 3, pp. 319–329.

Guertzkow, H., ed. (1951). *Groups, Leadership and Men*. Pittsburgh: Carnegie Press.

Gutmann, A. (1987). *Democratic Education*. Princeton, N.J.: Princeton University Press.

Habermas, J. (1987). *The Philosophical Discourse of Modernity*. Cambridge, Mass.: MIT Press.

Haller, E. J., and K. A. Strike (1986). *An Introduction to Educational Administration: Social, Legal, and Ethical Persrpectives*. New York: Longman.

Halpin, A. W., and D. B. Croft (1963). *The Organizational Climate of Schools*. Chicago: University of Chicago Press.

Hannah, W. (1980). "Towards Administrative Philosophies." *Journal of Educational Administration*, 18, no. 1, pp. 114–131.

Harman, G. (1984). "Conceptual and Theoretical Issues." In J. R. Hough, ed., *Educational Policy: An International Survey*, pp. 13–27. London: Croom Helm.

Harris, B. H. (1976). "Supervisor Competence and Strategies for Improving Instruction." *Educational Leadership*, 33, no. 5, pp. 332–335.

Haskell, T. J., ed. (1984). *The Authority of Experts*. Bloomington: Indiana University Press.

Hemphill, J. K., and Coons, A. E. (1957). "Development of the Leader Behavior Questionnaire." In R. M. Stoghill and A. E. Coons, eds., *Leader Behavior: Its Description and Measurement*. Columbus: Ohio State University Bureau of Business Research.

Heslep, R. D. (1987). "Conceptual Sources of Controversy Over Educational Policy." *Educational Theory*, 37, no. 4, (Fall), pp. 423–432.

Hindress, B. (1977). *Philosophy and Methodology in the Social Sciences*. Atlantic Highlands, N.J.: Humanities Press.

Hodgkinson, C. (1978). *Towards a Philosophy of Administration*. Oxford: Blackwell.

———. (1983). *The Philosophy of Leadership*. New York: St. Martin's Press.

Hollander, E. P. (1978). *Leadership Dynamical: A Practical Guide to Effective Relationships*. New York: Free Press.

Holmes Group (1986). *Tomorrow's Teachers*. East Lansing, Mich.: The Holmes Group.

Howe, K., and M. Eisenhart. (1990). "Standards for Qualitative (and Quantitative) Research: A Prolegomenon." *Educational Researcher*, 19, no. 4 (May), pp. 2–9.

Hoy, W. K., and C. G. Miskel (1982). *Educational Administration: Theory, Research, and Practice*. 2nd edition. New York: Random House.

Hoy, W. K., and J. Ferguson (1985). "A Theoretical Framework and Exploration of Organizational Effectiveness of Schools." *Educational Administration Quarterly*, 21, no. 2, pp. 117–134.

Hullfish, H. G., and P. G. Smith (1961). *Reflective Thinking*. New York: Dodd, Mead and Co.

Hunt, J. G., B. R. Baliga, H. P. Dachler, and C. A. Schriesheim, eds. (1987). *Emerging Leadership Vistas*. Lexington, Mass.: Lexington Books.

James, W. (1956). *The Will to Believe and Other Essays in Popular Philosophy and Human Immortality*. New York: Dover.

———. (1976). *Essays in Radical Empiricism*, F. Burkhardt and F. Bowers, eds. Cambridge, Mass.: Harvard University Press.

John, D. (1980). *Leadership in Schools*. London: Heinemann.

Jones, A. B. (1938). *The Education of Youth for Leadership*. New York: McGraw-Hill.

Kaplan, A. (1964). *The Conduct of Inquiry*. San Francisco: Chandler.

Kerr, D. (1976). *Educational Policy: Analysis, Structure and Justification*. New York: David McKay.

Kestenbaum, V. (1977). *The Phenomenological Sense of John Dewey*. Atlantic Highlands, New Jersey: Humanities Press.

Kirk, R. (1978). *Decadence and Renewal in the Higher Education*. Southbend, Indiana: Gateway.

Koopman, G. R., A. Miel, and P. J. Misner. (1943). *Democracy in School Administration*. New York: D. Appleton-Century Company.

Korman, A. K. (1968). "The Prediction of Managerial Performance: A Review." *Personnel Psychology*, 21, no. 3, pp. 295–322.

Lakomski, G. (1987). "Values and Decision Making in Educational Administration." *Educational Administration Quarterly*, 23, no. 3, pp. 70–82.

Larson, M. S. (1984). "The Production of Expertise and the Constitution of Expert Power." In T. L. Haskell, ed., *The Authority of Experts*, pp. 28–80. Bloomington: Indiana University Press.

Lasch, C. (1984). *The Minimal Self*. New York: W. W. Norton and Co.

Levine, D. U., and L. W. Lezotte (1990). *Unusually Effective Schools*. Madison, Wisconsin: National Center for Effective Schools Research and Development.

Liebermann, A., E. R. Saxl, and M. B. Miles (1988). "Teacher Leadership: Ideology and Practice." In Ann Liebermann, ed., *Building a Professional Culture in Schools*, pp. 148–166. New York: Teacher's College Press.

Lipham, J. (1964). "Leadership and Administration." In *National Society for the Study of Education Yearbook 1963*. Pt. 2, pp. 119–141. Chicago: University of Chicago Press.

———. (1981). *Effective Principal, Effective School*. Reston, Virginia: National Association of Secondary School Principals.

Lukes, S. (1974). *Power: A Radical View*. London: Macmillan.

McCall, M. W. and M. M. Lombardo, eds. (1978). *Leadership: Where Else Can We Go?* Durham: Duke University Press.

MacIntyre, A. (1981). *After Virtue*. Notre Dame, Indiana: Notre Dame University Press.

McLaren, P. (1988). "Foreword: Critical Theory and the Meaning of Hope." In H. A. Giroux, *Teachers as Intellectuals: Toward a Pedagogy of Learning*. New York: Bergin and Garvey.

———. (1989). *Life in Schools*. New York: Longman.

McPherson, R. B., R. L. Crowson, and N. J. Pitner (1986). *Managing Uncertainty.* Columbus, Ohio.: Charles E. Merrill.

Maeroff, G. I. (1988). *The Empowerment of Teachers: Overcoming the Crisis in Confidence.* New York: Teachers College Press.

Magee, B. (1979). *Men of Ideas.* New York: Viking Press.

Maxcy, S. J.(1979). "The Teacherage in American Rural Education." *Journal of General Education,* 30, no. 4 (Winter), pp. 267–274.

——— . (1983). "Conceptions of Leadership and the Conduct of Educational Administration." In *The Philosophy of Education Society of Great Britain: Papers of the Annual Conference,* pp. 40–56. Twickenham, England: St. Mary's College.

——— . (1984). "Leadership, Administration and the Educational Policy Operation." In E. Robertson, ed., *Philosophy of Education 1984,* pp. 329–338. Normal, Ill.: Philosophy of Education Society.

——— . (1985). "Administrative Leadership, Democracy and the Qualities of Philosophic Mind." Paper delivered at the annual meeting of the American Educational Research Association, Chicago, April.

Maxcy, S. J., and W. B. Stanley (1986). "The Conception of Problem and the Role of Inquiry in Social Education." *Theory and Research in Social Education,* 14, no. 4 (Fall), pp. 295–306.

Merton, R. K. (1969). "The Social Nature of Leadership." *American Journal of Nursing,* 69, no. 12, pp. 2614–2618.

Metcalf, H. C., and L. Urwick, eds. (1942). *Dynamic Administration: The Collected Papers of Mary Parker Follett.* New York: Harper and Brothers.

Mintzberg, H. (1973). *The Nature of Managerial Work.* New York: Harper and Row.

——— . (1982). "If You Are Not Serving Bill and Barbara, You're Not Serving Leadership." In J. Hunt, U. Sekarian, and C. Schriesheim, eds. *Leadership: Beyond Establishment Views,* pp. 239–259. Carbondale, Ill.: Southern Illinois University Press.

Misumi, J. (1985). *The Behavioral Science of Leadership.* Ann Arbor, Michigan: University of Michigan Press.

Morris, V., et al. (1984). *Principals in Action: The Reality of Managing Schools.* Columbus, Ohio: Charles E. Merrill.

Neville, R. C. (1989). "Value, Courage, and Leadership." *Review of Metaphysics,* 43, no. 1, pp. 3–26.

Noddings, N. (1984). *Caring: A Feminine Approach to Ethics and Moral Education.* Berkeley: University of California Press.

Norris, C. (1987). *Derrida.* Cambridge: University of Massachusetts Press.

Nyberg, D. (1981). *Power Over Power.* Ithaca, New York: Cornell University Press.

Nyberg, D., and P. Farber (1986). "Authority in Education." *Teachers College Record,* 88, no. 1, pp. 3–14.

Odden, A., B. Anderson, and E. Farrar (1986). *Causal Linkages of Local School Variables Associated with Successful Implementation of State Education Improvement Programs.* Denver: Education Commission of the States.

Olafson, F. A. (1979). *The Dialectic of Action: A Philosophical Interpretation of History and the Humanities.* Chicago: University of Chicago Press.

Pateman, C. (1970). *Participation and Democratic Theory.* London: Cambridge University Press.

Peters, R. S. (1959). *Authority, Responsibility and Education.* London: George Allen and Unwin.

———. (1973). *The Philosophy of Education*. London: Oxford University Press.

———. (1976). "Introduction: The Contemporary Problem." In R. S. Peters, ed., *The Role of the Head*, pp. 1–8. London: Routledge and Kegan Paul.

Peters, T. J. (1988). *Thriving on Chaos*. New York: Alfred A. Knopf.

Peters, T. J., and R. H. Waterman, Jr. (1982). *In Search of Excellence: Lessons from America's Best-run Companies*. New York: Harper and Row.

Pfeffer, J. (1978). "The Ambiguity of Leadership." In M. W. McCall, Jr. and M. M. Lombardo, eds., *Leadership: Where Else Can We Go?* pp. 13–34. Durham, N.C.: Duke University Press.

Phillips, D. C. (1976). *Holistic Thought in Social Science*. Stanford, Calif.: Stanford University Press.

———. (1987). *Philosophy, Science and Social Inquiry*. Oxford: Pergamon.

Piatt, M. (1939). "Dewey's Logical Theory." In Paul A. Schilpp, *The Philosophy of John Dewey*, pp. 105–134. Evanston, Ill.: Northwestern University Press.

Pinar, W. and M. Grumet (1976). *Toward a Poor Curriculum*. Dubuque, Iowa: Kendall/Hunt.

Pitner, N. J. (1983). "Principal Influence on Teacher Behavior: Substitutes for Leadership." Paper read before the American Educational Research Association, Montreal, Canada.

Podsakoff, P. M., W. D. Todor, R. A. Glover, and V. L. Huber (1984). "Situational Moderators of Leader Reward and Punishment Behaviors: Fact or Fiction?" *Organizational Behavior and Human Performance*, 34, no. 1, pp. 21–63.

Pondy, L. R. (1978). "Leadership Is a Language Game." In M. McCall, Jr., and M. M. Lombardo, eds., *Leadership: Where Else Can We Go?* pp. 87–99. Durham, N.C.: Duke University Press.

Popkewitz, T. S. (1984). *Paradigm and Ideology in Educational Research*. London: Falmer Press.

Pratte, R. (1988). "Civic Conscience and Religious Conscience: A Fundamental but not Fundamentalist Distinction." In B. Arnstine and D. Arnstine, eds., *Philosophy of Education 1987*, pp. 213–223. Normal, Ill.: The Philosophy of Education Society.

Prigogine, I., and I. Stengers (1984). *Order Out of Chaos*. New York: Bantam Books.

Pullium, J. (1987). "Futures Philosophy for Educational Excellence." In S. J. Maxcy and D. O. Maxcy, eds., *The Future of the Self*, pp. 3–8. Fayetteville, Ark.: University of Arkansas College of Education.

Quine, W. O. (1976). *The Ways of Paradox and Other Essays*. Revised and enlarged edition. Cambridge, Mass.: Harvard University Press.

Rappaport, J. (1985). "The Power of Empowerment Language." *Social Policy*, 16, no. 2, pp. 15–21.

Rauch, C. F., and O. Behling (1984). "Functionalism: Basis for an Alternate Approach to the Study of Leadership." In J. G. Hunt, D. M. Hosking, C. A. Schriesheim, and R. Stewart, eds., *Leaders and Managers*, pp. 45–62. New York: Pergamon.

Raup, R. B., G. Axtelle, K. Benne, and B. O. Smith (1943, 1950). *The Improvement of Practical Intelligence*. New York: Harper and Brothers.

Ravitch, D. (1983). *The Troubled Crusade: American Education 1945–1980*. New York: Basic Books.

Reddin, W. J. (1970). *Managerial Effectiveness*. New York: McGraw-Hill.

Ringer, R. J. (1977). *Looking Out for Number One*. Beverly Hills, Calif.: Los Angeles Book Co.

Rorty, R. (1979). *Philosophy and the Mirror of Nature*. Princeton, N.J.: Princeton University Press.

———. (1982). *Consequences of Pragmatism*. Minneapolis: University of Minnesota Press.

Rosenthal, S. B. (1986). *Speculative Pragmatism*. La Salle, Ill.: Open Court.

Rouse, J. (1987). *Knowledge and Power*. Ithaca, N.Y.: Cornell University Press.

Rowan, B., S. T. Bossert, and D. C. Dwyer. (1983). "Research on Effective Schools: A Cautionary Note." *Educational Researcher*, 12, no. 4, pp. 24–31.

Rugg, H. (1963). *Imagination*. New York: Harper and Row.

Sartre, J. (1962). *Imagination*, F. Williams, trans. Ann Arbor, Michigan: Michigan State University Press.

Sashkin, M., and R. Fulmer (1987). "Toward an Organizational Leadership Theory." In J. G. Hunt et al., eds., *New Leadership Studies*, pp. 13–53. Boston: Lexington.

Scheffler, I. (1960). *The Language of Education*. Springfield, Ill.: Charles C. Thomas.

———. (1973). *Reason and Teaching*. Indianapolis: Bobbs-Merrill.

———. (1985). *Of Human Potential*. Boston: Routledge and Kegan Paul.

Scholes, R. (1985). *Textual Power*. New Haven: Yale University Press.

Schon, D. A. (1983). *The Reflective Practitioner*. New York: Basic Books.

———. (1987). *Educating the Reflective Practitioner*. San Francisco: Jossey-Bass.

———. (1990)."The Design Process." In V. A. Howard, ed., *Varieties of Thinking*, pp. 110–141. New York: Routledge.

Schultz, F. (1974). *Social-Philosophical Foundations of Education*. Dubuque, Iowa: Kendall-Hunt.

Schultz, W. (1977). *Leaders of Schools: FIRO Theory Applied to Administrators*. La Jolla, Calif.: University Associates.

Schutz, A. (1974). *The Phenomenology of the Social World*, G. Walsh and F. Lehnert, trans. Evanston, Ill.: Northwestern University Press.

Scott, W. G., and D. K. Hart (1979). *Organizational America*. Boston: Houghton Mifflin.

Selman, M. (1988). "Ideology and What? A Response to Harvey Siegel." *Educational Theory*. 38, no. 2 (Spring), pp. 261–265.

Selznick, P. (1957). *Leadership in Administration*. New York: Harper and Row.

Senge, P. M. (1990). *The Fifth Discipline: The Art and Practice of the Learning Organization*. New York: Doubleday.

Sergiovanni, T. J. (1979). "Is Leadership the Next Great Training Robbery?" *Educational Leadership*, 36, no. 6, pp. 388–394.

———. (1982). "Ten Principles of Quality Leadership." *Educational Leadership*, 39, no. 5, pp. 330–336.

———. (1984). "Leadership and Excellence in Schooling." *Educational Leadership*, 41, no. 5, pp. 4–13.

Sergiovanni, T., and F. D. Carver (1980). *The New School Executive: A Theory of Administration*. New York: Harper and Row.

Sergiovanni, T., M. Burlingame, F. D. Combs, and P. Thurston (1980). *Educational Governance and Administration*. Englewood Cliffs, N.J.: Prentice Hall.

Sergiovanni, T., and J. E. Corbally, eds. (1983). *Administrative Leadership and Organizational Culture*. Urbana: University of Illinois Press.

Sergiovanni, T., and J. H. Moore, eds. (1989). *Schooling for Tomorrow: Directing Reforms to Issues that Count*. Boston: Allyn and Bacon.

Sergiovanni, T., and R. J. Staratt (1979). *Supervision: Human Perspectives*. 2nd edition. New York: McGraw-Hill.

Sheridan, A. (1980). *Foucault: The Will to Truth*. London: Tavistock.

Siegel, H. (1988). *Educating Reason*. New York: Routledge.

Silver, P. (1983). *Educational Administration: Theoretical Perspectives on Practice and Research.* New York: Harper and Row.

Simon, H. (1971). *The Sciences of the Artificial.* Cambridge, MA: MIT Press.

Simpson, D. J., and M. B. Jackson (1984). *The Teacher as Philosopher.* Toronto: Metheun.

Sizer, T. (1985). *Horace's Compromise: The Dilemma of the American High School.* Boston: Houghton Mifflin.

Sleeper, R. W. (1986). *The Necessity of Pragmatism.* New Haven: Yale University Press.

Smith, J., and J. Blase. (1987). "Educational Leadership as a Moral Concept." Unpublished paper. Athens: University of Georgia.

Smith, P.G. (1956). *Philosophic Mindedness in Educational Administration.* Columbus: Ohio State University Press.

———. (1964). "Democracy in Relation to Education: Excerpts for *Philosophy of Education: Introductory Studies.*" *School and Society*, 92, no. 26 (December), pp. 414–418.

———. (1965). *Philosophy of Education.* New York: Harper.

Smithson, A. (1983). "Philosophic Competence, Educational Policy and the Technocratic Threat to Democracy." *Journal of Philosophy of Education*, 17, no. 2, pp. 275–284.

Smyth, W. J. (1986). "Peer Clinical Supervision as 'Empowerment' versus 'Delivery of Service.' " Paper presented at the annual meeting of the American Educational Research Association, San Francisco, April.

Sokoloff, H. (1984). "Response to Professor Maxcy." In E. Robertson, ed., *Philosophy of Education 1984*, pp. 339–341. Normal, Ill.: Philosophy of Education Society.

Stoghill, R. M. (1950). "Leadership, Membership and Organization." *Psychological Bulletin*, 47, pp. 1–14.

Stone, C. D. (1987). *Earth and Other Ethics.* New York: Harper and Row.

Strauss, D. (1988). *A Longitudinal Examination of the Structure, Membership and Benefits of the Louisiana Association of Principals.* Unpublished doctoral dissertation. Baton Rouge: Louisiana State University.

Synder, K. J., and R. H. Anderson. (1986). *Managing Productive Schools: Toward an Ecology.* Orlando, Fla.: Academic Press.

Tarrant, J. M. (1984). "J. Wilson and B. Cowell on the Democratic Myth." *Journal of Philosophy of Education*, 18, no. 1, pp. 123–127.

Task Force on Teaching as a Profession (1986). *A Nation Prepared: Teachers for the 21st Century.* New York: Carnegie Forum on Education and the Economy.

Taylor, R. (1989). "The Potential of Small-Group Mathematics Instruction in Grades Four Through Six." *The Elementary School Journal*, 89, no. 5, pp. 634–642.

Thorsen, T. L., ed. (1963). *Plato: Totalitarian or Democrat?* Englewood Cliffs, N.J.: Prentice-Hall.

Titus, C. H. (1950). *The Processes of Leadership: Human Relations in the Making.* Dubuque, Iowa: Wm. C. Brown.

Toulmin, S. (1968). *The Uses of Argument.* Cambridge: Cambridge University Press.

Toulmin, S., R. Rieke, and A. Janik (1984). *An Introduction to Reasoning.* 2nd edition. New York: Macmillan.

Trawick-Smith, J. (1988). "Let's Say You're the Baby, OK?: Play Leadership and Following Behavior of Young Children." *Young Children*, (July), pp. 51–59.

Tyack, D., and E. Hansot (1982a). "Hard Times, Hard Choices: The Case for Coherence in Public School Leadership." *Phi Delta KAPPAN*, 63, no. 8, pp. 511–515.

———. (1982b). *Managers of Virtue.* New York: Basic Books.

Urwick, L. F. (1957). *Leadership in the Twentieth Century.* London: Sir Isaac Pitman and Sons.

Walker, J., and C. Evers (1984). "Towards a Materialist Pragmatist Philosophy of Education." *Education Research and Perspectives*, 11, no. 1 (June), pp. 23–33.

Ward, J. F. (1984). *Language, Form, and Inquiry: Arthur F. Bentley's Philosophy of Social Science.* Amherst: University of Massachusetts Press.

Warnock, M. (1976). *Imagination.* Los Angeles: University of California Press.

Wayson, W. W. (1988). *Up From Excellence.* Bloomington, Ind.: Phi Delta Kappa.

Weber, M. (1947). *The Theory of Social and Economic Organization.* New York: Oxford University Press.

Weick, K. E. (1976). "Educational Organizations as Loosely Coupled Systems." *Administrative Science Quarterly*, 21, no. 1, pp. 1–19.

White, P. (1983). *Beyond Domination.* London: Routledge and Kegan Paul.

Willower, D. J. (1987). "Inquiry into Educational Administration: The Last Twenty-five Years." *Journal of Educational Administration*, 25, no. 1 (Winter), pp. 12–26.

Willower, D.J., and J. W. Licata (1975). "Environmental Robustness and School Structure." *Planning and Changing*, 6, no. 2, pp. 120–127.

Wilson, J. (1961). *Reason and Morals.* Cambridge: Cambridge University Press.

———. (1971). "Politics and Expertise." *Philosophy*, 96, no. 75, pp. 34–37.

Wilson, J., and B. Cowell (1983). "The Democratic Myth." *Journal of Philosophy of Education*, 17, no. 1, pp. 111–117.

Wimpleberg, R. K. (1987). "Managerial Images and School Effectiveness." *Administrator's Notebook*, 32, no. 4, pp. 1–4.

Wimpleberg, R. K., C. Teddlie, and S. Stringfield (1989). "Sensitivity to Context: The Past and Future of Effective Schools Research." *Educational Administration Quarterly*, 25, no. 1, pp. 82–107.

Wirt, F. M., and M. W. Kirst (1989). *Schools in Conflict.* 2nd edition. Berkeley, Calif.: McCutchan.

Witte, J. F., and D. J. Walsh. (1990). "A Systematic Test of the Effective Schools Model." *Educational Evaluation and Policy Analysis*, 12, no. 2 (Summer), pp. 188–212.

Wolff, K. H. (1976). *Surrender and Catch.* Dordrecht, Holland: D. Reidel.

Wynne, E. A. (1980). *Looking at Schools: Good, Bad, and Indifferent.* Lexington, Mass.: D.C. Heath.

Yeakey, C., and G. Johnston (1986). "Of Philosophy, Epistemology, and Administrative Thought." In C. Yeakey and G. Johnston, eds., *Research and Thought in Administrative Theory*, pp. 163–180. Lanham, Md.: University Press of America.

Yukl, G. (1981). *Leadership in Organizations.* Englewood Cliffs, N.J.: Prentice-Hall.

Zeigler, E. F. (1968). "The Employment of Philosophical Analysis to Supplement Administrative Theory and Research." *The Journal of Educational Administration*, 6, no. 2, pp. 132–151.

Zeitlin, I. (1968). *Ideology and the Development of Sociological Thought.* Englewood Cliffs, N.J.: Prenctice-Hall.

Zolla, E. (1978). *The Uses of Imagination and the Decline of the West.* Ipswich, England: Golgonooza Press.

Index

ABOUT THE AUTHOR

SPENCER J. MAXCY is Professor of Education at Louisiana State University. He has also taught in secondary schools in Chicago, Blue Island, and Oak Lawn, Illinois. His published works include *Practical Thinking for Educators* and *Educational Philosophy for the Future*, together with articles and contributed chapters on a variety of subjects in education.

YORK COLLEGE OF PENNSYLVANIA 17403

0 2003 0048921 4

LB 2805 .M295 1991
Maxcy, Spencer J.
Educational leadership